D0331820

# THOSE DAMN YANKEES

# THOSE DAMN YANKEES

## THE SECRET LIFE OF AMERICA'S GREATEST FRANCHISE

### DEAN CHADWIN

VERSO

New York • London

First published by Verso 1999
© Dean Chadwin 1999
Paperback edition first published by Verso 2000
All rights reserved

VERSO
UK: 6 Meard Street, London W1V 3HR
USA: 180 Varick Street, New York, NY 10014-4606

Verso is the imprint of New Left Books

Design by POLLEN
Composed in Monotype Bell and Adobe Grotesk
Printed by R.R.Donnelley

ISBN 1 85984 283 6

British Library Cataloguing in Publication Data
A catalogue record for this book is available
from the British Library

Library of Congress Cataloging-in-Publication Data
A catalog record for this book is available
from the Library of Congress

# Contents

For my grandfathers Lou Chadwin and Ben Deutsch,
the catcher and the outfielder

# Acknowledgments

Although there is just one name on the cover of this book, a much larger team of players was involved. A number of interview subjects were exceedingly generous with their time. Thanks go to Bill Deane, Dave Kaplan at the Yogi Berra Museum, the legal department at the New York City Parks Department, Phil Mushnick, John Pastier, Edward Pavia, Mark Rosentraub, Greg Schwalenberg and Michael Gibbons at the Babe Ruth Birthplace and Museum, Scott Wild, and Timothy Wiles and the research librarians at the National Baseball Hall of Fame Library. Marvin Miller, Buster Olney and Jeff Pearlman generously shared their experiences for the paperback edition of this book. The following libraries were useful in the research on this project: National Baseball Hall of Fame Library, New York Public Library, and Sterling Memorial Library of Yale University.

If you're lucky enough to be a baseball fan, the game becomes part of your lifetime of conversation. My discussions with so many friends have shaped the way I think about the game and the nature of this book. Thanks to Justin Badine, Dan Becker, Tom Boyle, Spence Burkholz, Dave Davis, Paul Feinberg, Doug Gansler, Jean Gottlieb, Peter Killough, Chris Knopf, Rich Krevolin, Rob Krevolin, Jay Leu, Gary Levene, Rodd Macklin, Amy Minett, Mike Nadol, Bill Reeves, Mike Saltzman, Steve Tucker, and David Warren.

This book would have been unimaginable without the generous support of my grandparents, Benjamin and Vera Deutsch, and my parents, Adrienne and Mark Chadwin. Everyone at Verso was wonderfully supportive under tremendous time pressure. Colin Robinson, my editor at Verso, put his heart, soul, and, most importantly, mind into a book about baseball despite being raised on Liverpool soccer. His efforts cannot be overstated. Philomena Mariani copyedited the manuscript and offered many useful suggestions. Mike Davis, Nancy Jacobs Miller, and Peter Vogel each gave me helpful comments after reading sections of the book. Rebecca Chadwin and Kennan Ferguson not only read pieces of the manuscript, but they also offered emotional support during the most difficult parts of the work. Mike Marqusee read the entire manuscript and provided particularly astute insights. Again, thanks to one and all.

Prologue

# WEAPON OF MASS DISTRACTION

1998 was baseball's best season ever. The critics were unanimous. The national pastime's summer of love reigned from sea to shining sea, clearing away any premillennial tension. A white man, a dentist's son from the Southern California suburbs, and a black man, a shoeshine boy from another baseball cradle, the Dominican Republic, hit home runs out of ballparks faster than the game's accountants could keep up. They were breaking Ruth's record. Anything was possible in baseball (and in America). Baseball, our permissible national distraction, was back, better than ever. America was still great.

If America's grandeur persisted despite global economic distress and the political turmoil inside the Beltway, then surely her Mecca of postindustrial capitalism, New York City, must be responsible. New Yorkers of all types bragged endlessly about their city and how much it had improved under the current mayor. Attempts at dissent, whether comic or serious, were challenged through intimidation and litigation. Organizers of street protests were regularly denied rightful permits and had to go to court to secure their marching papers. The city's lawyers even sued *New York* magazine to stop an ad campaign that poked fun at the mayor's tendency to take credit for everything. Humorless accord was all that was required in RudyLand, thank you very much.

An era of assent in the nation's first city was a perfect backdrop for the seemingly apolitical ascent of America's first game. How fortuitous, then, that the town's foremost team had a season of historic proportions during baseball's epic campaign. En route to a championship, the 1998 Yankees broke the American League record for most wins. That AL mark for victories had been owned by the 1954 Indians, and that team's ace, Bob Feller, challenged the Yankees' superiority by reminding everyone that they played eight extra games in the expanded schedule and won just three. Feller's churlish dissent was quickly dismissed as sour grapes, especially because those Indians lost to another New York team, the Giants of Mays and Irvin. But a closer look revealed serious cracks in the narrative of baseball's rebirth.

The major leagues drew over 70 million fans, an increase of 8 million over the prior season. The Yankees participated in this apparent growth, smashing the team mark for home attendance. Nevertheless, the boom was an illusion. A couple of new teams and a pair of home-run hitters were responsible for baseball's entire renaissance at the box office. The expansion Devil Rays and Diamondbacks alone accounted for 6 million new fans. The other 2 million were a direct result of the exploits of Mark McGwire and Sammy Sosa. In 1997, the Cardinals (McGwire's team) were watched by nearly 4.8 million fans in home and road games; in 1998, the Year of the Homer, they drew almost 6 million, an increase of over a million fans. In 1997, the Cubs (Sosa's team) were seen by 4.5 million fans; in 1998, the Cubs drew 5.5 million, a gain of a million fans.

If this stasis seems hard to believe, look at the Yankees' road attendance in 1997 and 1998. The Yankees led the American League both years. Their fans scattered across the country, as well as opposition fans who want to see their locals beat anything from New York, make the Yankees a consistently excellent draw. The '98 Yankees were a much better team than the '97 squad and therefore could expect to attract tremendous crowds. It didn't happen. Despite their historic season, the Yankees drew only about 500 more fans per game on the road during the 1998 season.

Baseball is not on the brink of financial collapse, nor does it need to grow. Owners are making tens of millions, players are making millions, and the worst teams are drawing more fans to the park than the Yankee dynasty did four decades ago. The problem was not the reality, but the hype that interest in baseball was at an all-time high.

Perhaps all the fuss correlated to growth in the TV audience. Every televised game during the McGwire/Sosa home-run race seemed to set a new audience record. As the end of the wealthiest cable deal in the history of baseball approached, the Yankees' local TV audience exploded, too. However, when baseball reached the 1998 postseason, the time when television earns back the huge rights fees it has paid for the national pastime, McGwire was gone, Sosa soon followed, and the Yankees appeared invincible. An expected lack of competition diminished fan interest. Ratings dipped to an all-time low.

While the billions generated by baseball annually continue to grow, that revenue stream depends in no small amount on real competition. Yankee success sends pain to Kansas City, Pittsburgh, Minnesota, Oakland, and a dozen other cities with weak major-league franchises.

The Yankees are not America's team now. None exists in baseball. As the pint-sized TV ratings for the World Series sweep over the Padres proved, Yankee fans alone can never provide a healthy national audience for the game. When the Yankees are this good, Yankee haters know the score and avert their eyes, just as they did forty years ago during the game's last era of New York City domination.

*                    *                    *

That the narrative for the Yankee season centered on the game itself was an upset, especially after a quarter-ton expansion joint crashed through a seat in the loge section along the third-base line only hours before the fourth home game of the season. So many off-field matters threatened to break through: contract disputes, rumors about the sale of the team, a PR war over the final days of Yankee Stadium, and a romance between Derek Jeter and Mariah Carey (with echoes of Joltin' Joe and Marilyn Monroe amidst reports of DiMaggio's failing health). No development loomed larger than the events surrounding the approaching expiration of the Yankees' lease with the city, landlord of Yankee Stadium. Steinbrenner's people and the Boss himself engaged in a campaign of speculation and misinformation designed to flesh out the best offers. The Boss sought to move the club to Manhattan, or maybe it was New Jersey, or perhaps he just wanted to create the appearance that all his options were open to jack up the franchise's value in the midst of negotiations to sell. Meanwhile, the mayor supported Steinbrenner's explorations, warned the governor of New Jersey to keep her hands off his teams, and battled his rival, Peter Vallone, the head of the city council and author of a ballot referendum that would allow the voters to forbid the use of public funds to facilitate the Boss' move from the Bronx to Manhattan along the Hudson.

City taxpayers did not want to hand hundreds of millions to a billionaire, and Vallone's initiative unleashed a rare wave of populist sentiment in New York City. The stadium brawl threatened to over-whelm talk of the Yankee season and discussion of any other matters of public interest. New York One, an all-news channel that was Time-Warner's local analogue to big brother CNN, had panels that touched on the Yankee Stadium imbroglio nearly every night. The host of "On The Line," the closest thing WNYC, the city's preemi-nent public radio station, has to local public-affairs programming, decided to ban discussion of the stadium battle when it threatened to swamp the open-phone-lines segment of the show for a spell during the summer of '98. Sports talk radio paused to look over the mess with a quick glance, as if staring at a car accident, and then resumed its religiously depoliticized programming.

The people were outraged and finally had something to talk about, but no one, it seemed, wanted to listen. Those both above and below the fray proved reluctant to engage the issues of public financ-ing for stadiums and the value of pro sports in civic life. What made a serious discussion even more difficult was the season the Yankees were having on the field. By May, it was clear that the 1998 Yankees were a special team, a balanced combination of pitching, hitting, and defense rarely seen, a team blessed with speed, strength, patience, agility, intelligence, and confidence. Few wanted to bury themselves in esoteric explorations of balance sheets and prior franchise moves when they could instead talk about last night's game.

As stunning as the Yankees' objective performance was, even more compelling was the season's persistent appeal to the Ghosts of Yankee Stadium. The team's brilliance called to mind the great teams in the Yankee tradition: the '27 club dominated by Ruth and a young Gehrig, the '39 team led by Gehrig and a young DiMaggio, squads in the late forties and early fifties that won five straight titles with a bal-anced combination of power, pitching, and defense, and the '61 edi-tion which featured the home-run duel by Maris and Mantle that highlighted the sluggingest Bomber team ever.

The Babe was everywhere, evoked by the idolization by staff ace David Wells, the home-run race of McGwire and Sosa, and the towering home runs crushed by a wiser, older Darryl Strawberry. August 16, 1998, was the fiftieth anniversary of Ruth's death, and the Bambino reclaimed his past glory, with documentaries on HBO and ESPN, cover stories in numerous magazines, and an outpouring of affection that included a pilgrimage by hundreds of young fans to Ruth's gravesite. The game at Yankee Stadium that day began with a moment of silence to allow fans to pay their respects to the game's greatest player, and ended with an even more fitting tribute. Bernie Williams, a brilliant switch-hitter batting lefthanded like the Babe, crushed a Ruthian blast into the top deck of the right-field stands, the Yankees' first game-winning blast in the bottom of the ninth inning all season.

If the Babe's wondrous teammate, Lou Gehrig, always seemed to reside comfortably in the Sultan of Swat's immense shadow, 1998 was no different, but his ghost poked around a few times, too. When Cal Ripken finally ended his impossible streak of reliability (fewer than fifty players have played as many games in their career as the Oriole ironman played consecutively), Larruping Lou's accomplishments were rediscovered. When Darryl Strawberry and Catfish Hunter both suffered life-threatening illnesses, Gehrig's difficult early death lingered poignantly in the background.

More hopefully, the ghosts of Gehrig and his still-living teammate DiMaggio seemed to have found a new body to haunt. Gehrig was 24 years old when the 1927 Yankees destroyed all opposition, DiMaggio also 24 when the 1939 Yankees smashed their rivals, and now Derek Jeter, at 24 already the best shortstop in the franchise's storied history and, like his ancestors, unsurpassed in his grace on the field and off, was a central figure on the great 1998 team. That squad's button-down approach echoed the efficient '39 Yankees of Gehrig and DiMaggio much more than the two sybaritic eras dominated by Ruth and Mantle or the brawling Bronx Zoo days of Billy Martin and Reggie Jackson.

Mickey Mantle, too, was represented by the amazing fan response to Mark McGwire and his towering home runs. Memories of the friendship between Mantle and his roommate Maris during their pursuit of the Babe's record were evoked by the fraternal joy shared by McGwire and Sosa. Even lesser figures in Yankee lore had their day in the sun. Jim Bouton, the one-time Yankee pitcher who broke baseball's code of silence when he authored *Ball Four,* a hilarious and incisive look at the travails of an outsider in a seductive but difficult subculture, returned to the fold. Although he'd won World Series games for the Yankees and became a local sportscaster after his retirement, the book made Bouton persona non grata around Yankee Stadium. In 1998, Steinbrenner invited Bouton to Old Timers' Day after the ex-pitcher's son wrote a moving editorial in the *Times'* sports page on Father's Day. Don Larsen, author of what had been the sole perfect game at Yankee Stadium (and which remains the only performance of its kind in World Series history), was reclaimed when David Wells delivered his three hours of immortality in late May. The warm glow became brighter after it was discovered that Wells had attended the same high school in San Diego four decades after Larsen. It was a rich enough tapestry to overwhelm more practical concerns about the unresolved stadium issue. It was the most sentimental of seasons.

And no ballclub has been more loved or more hated than the New York Yankees. The arrogance of the Bronx Bombers and their supporters insures that fans from Baltimore to Boston and Los Angeles to Miami share a common joy in Yankee humiliation. Yet the team is so beloved in the five boroughs that Giuliani, a Yankee fan despite growing up in Brooklyn in an era when every decent kid fell under the spell of the Dodgers of Robinson, Reese, and Snider, wore his team cap and jacket to many appearances during his 1997 reelection campaign, sartorial proof that he was a regular guy.

\*          \*          \*

American passions may have been diminished by endless hours of television, but the desire for sports (a mass entertainment fortunate to have a symbiotic relationship with the picture box unlike art, literature, or theater) grows larger and stronger annually. During months of media fascination with a presidential scandal, the only other stories that penetrated the national radar screen for more than an instant involved a gifted hoopster stepping off the stage and two ballplayers swatting home runs at a record rate. Players' salaries, television rights contracts, and franchise values continue to soar at an astronomical pace. Fans at home with a cable hookup can be immersed in the world of sports twenty-four hours a day.

In their desire to win this audience, the media giants have engaged in their most serious conflict. Five years ago, the News Corporation's unprecedented bid for rights to half of the NFL Sunday afternoon contract disrupted the informal agreement of the Big Three networks to control prime sports programming in America. It also announced the seriousness of Rupert Murdoch's effort to establish a strong fourth network. While Fox grew, the loss of football caused ratings to erode at CBS. News Corporation next secured rights to the national TV contracts for baseball and hockey while building a massive empire of regional sports cable stations to compete with Disney-owned sports cable giant ESPN. The Fox Sports Network entered the 1999 season owning more than 90 percent of the cable contracts for baseball, basketball, and hockey. Its control of regional cable sports had grown so complete that Disney, who owned hockey's Mighty Ducks and baseball's Angels, decided to sell the cable rights to Murdoch rather than go ahead with a rival sports network in Los Angeles, the nation's second largest market. To top things off, the billionaire, who had reportedly never been to a baseball game before he owned the TV product, purchased the Los Angeles Dodgers and their privately owned stadium for the then-whopping sum of $311 million in early 1998.

Murdoch was not alone. While Disney had lost control of the local cable programming market to News Corporation, ESPN and ABC, its subsidiaries, spent over a billion dollars to win the bidding war in 1998 for NFL prime-time programming over the next five years. While maintaining a huge stake in college basketball and football, CBS bought their way back into the professional pigskin sweepstakes with a $500 million bid for the half of the Sunday afternoon contract that had been owned by NBC. NBC responded by spending billions to secure the broadcast rights to the National Basketball Association (NBA) and the Olympics for the next decade. Time-Warner, through its multiple cable arms, owned and presented the Atlanta Braves, aired NBA games, controlled a sizable chunk of boxing, and offered Ted Turner's answer to the Olympics, the Goodwill Games.

It's not just the present game, either. Designed to appeal to sports nostalgists, the Classic Sports Network, a cable channel that airs only old games and sports-related talk shows from decades ago, established a small niche in the declining audience of men watching television. Disney spent hundreds of millions to buy the sporting equivalent of the History Channel before the network was even out of its diapers, and can now offer America the opportunity to watch the 1980 Little League World Series over and over again. Sports junkies were being provided access (if they could afford a cable bill or a satellite dish) to televised product as never before.

*               *               *

The best example of the increasing devotion of American sports fans can be found in the right-field bleachers at Yankee Stadium. The Bleacher Creatures, Yankee zealots who assemble in Section 39 of the cheap seats for each game to chant, drink, and swear, may be the closest thing this country has to the hooligans that have terrorized soccer. These extremists represent baseball's pinnacle of organized chanting and uncivil activity. Baseball, like soccer, is a game with long stretches of seeming inactivity between moments of high drama. Both games reward patience and sophistication in connoisseurs; however, for diehards, the challenge is to find ways of alleviating the restlessness between scores. Organized vocal support, often in song, common at so many soccer games is unfamiliar to most baseball fans (except in Japan, where the cheering in the stands is often better coordinated than the play on the field). American spectators generally choose to pass the time stuffing themselves with concessions or engaging in long conversations with their neighbors about the game and life. The Bleacher Creatures started small, but their ranks quickly expanded into a loud and sometimes violent thicket hundreds strong.

As fan behavior deteriorated at the House that Ruth Built, the Town that Rudy Ruled witnessed a push for better manners. Minor crimes like jaywalking and littering were attacked with ever-greater ferocity. For a twenty-four-hour period, the mayor considered arresting those devious enough to dispose of their gum improperly. Thanks, however, to a blind spot larger than the old Stadium's left-field power alley, the ever-scolding mayor never aimed his citywide campaign for increased civility at Yankee fans, no matter how noxious their words or actions. Giuliani bathed in the reflected glow of every Yankee triumph and could not possibly attack anything associated with his beloved team.

We are assured that baseball teaches us important lessons about the proper interplay between an individual and a group, vital for citizens seeking community in a democracy as large as ours. A key myth created about the 1998 Yankee team was that it had no stars. The New York media chanted this untruth like a mantra, ignoring the presence of brilliant players like Jeter, Williams, O'Neill, Cone, Pettitte, and Wells, not to mention the top pitchers from Australia, Cuba, Japan, and Panama, on the roster. In fact, the Yankees were a team made up, to an unprecedented degree, entirely of stars.

If you believed the lie, then this Yankee squad, with "the best record ever," was an exemplar of all that's good in sports. 125 wins. 24 titles. The greatest team in history. A lesson for us all.

If only We the People could be more like They the Yankees.

Where baseball beat writers secured the hubris to preach to their readers is uncertain, but the righteous tone underlying the accolades for the Yankee season springs from the opening stanzas of American history. John Winthrop galvanized the first wave of Puritans before they'd even come ashore when he asserted that their community would be "a city upon a hill," a model for the Christian world to emulate. By paraphrasing Matthew 5:14 (Ye are the light of the world. A city that is set on an hill cannot be hid.), Winthrop insured the nation's very foundations rested on faith in American exceptionalism. These beliefs have created both a framework for dissent directed at our ability to embody those ideals and a rhetoric for triumphalism presented most effectively by right-wing icon Ronald Reagan. Never are we more likely to lecture to the rest of the world than in the afterglow of victory.

The frenzied response to the 1998 Yankees reflects an unspoken sense that those guys were "a team on a hill." Quintessentially American, the iconic ballclub embodies the immense raw materials we possess and attract. Our ability to mold those resources—men of great talent from around the globe—into brilliance must be a moral guide. The instructions to be taken from on-field conquests are never translated by baseball's proponents, but symbols abound.

And, on a "team without any stars," what better emblem of team-work than Joe Torre. Torre was elevated by the media to a new position: Nicest Guy Who Finished First. Torre's countenance called to mind that of Richard Nixon, another battle-scarred veteran who reached his ultimate goal late in life. During games, Torre's calm demeanor in the dugout seemed directly at odds with the uneasiness displayed by his doppelganger Nixon even after he claimed the White House. Perhaps Torre's resemblance to Nixon explained both

Steinbrenner's diminished restlessness (the Boss loved Tricky Dick and frequently hosted the ex-president in his luxury suite) and the free pass issued by a notoriously hostile local press (maybe Nixon ... *oops, Torre* ... had suffered enough).

The breathless coverage was exemplified by a piece that ran during the 1998 World Series in the usually tough-minded *New York Observer*. Headlined "The Last Superhero: Pride of the Yanks Is a Guy Named Joe—A Nation Turns Its Eyes from White House Sleaze to a New York Throwback—Torre Tames Steinbrenner Beast," the cover story included a huge cartoon of Torre as Superman with the Yankee NY across his chest and read as follows:

> It is equally easy to appreciate his style, so out of sync with the age of tawdry self-absorption and of spinelessness posing as empathy. He has achieved without kicking and screaming, without back-page controversies, and, most of all, without calling attention to himself. ... Mr. Torre has performed the remarkable achievement of putting a new finish on a legacy that had been tarnished by one man's tackiness, that man being George Steinbrenner ... Joe Torre is our antidote to the frauds, liars and self-promoters who have defined the decade.

Teenage girls panting for Derek Jeter aren't so lovestruck. Prior to helming the Yankees, Joe Torre had a clear record of failure. He had mismanaged the Mets, Braves, and Cardinals, departing before each team became consistent winners. Looking back, Torre claimed that the owners of those teams never gave him the horses, but the record of those who followed him denied that logic. New York's Davey Johnson, Atlanta's Bobby Cox, and St. Louis' Tony LaRussa each took Torre's former teams to the playoffs. What will make Gentleman Joe the longest-running manager in the Steinbrenner era is a simple fact beyond his control: Billy Martin's death. Without Plan B a phone call away, Steinbrenner's threats to fire Torre (the

Boss tried to replace Torre less than a month after he hired him) have proved empty.

Torre is the right man for this type of team. He is neither a fiery motivator nor a great teacher nor a brilliant strategist. The key elements in Torre's managing style are patience and loyalty, perfect for an expensive roster loaded with talented, fully developed veterans. His most important task has been serving as a buffer between the egomaniacal Steinbrenner and the players.

The 1998 Yankees essentially managed themselves. The two greatest strengths of this brilliant squad were the hitters' ability to reach base and the consistency and depth of the starting pitching. The prior management bequeathed these two gifts to Torre. He did not teach Paul O'Neill, Chuck Knoblauch, and Tino Martinez how to work the count, nor did he show David Wells, David Cone, El Duque, and Andy Pettitte how to beat hitters. Torre "achieved without calling attention to himself" because he didn't do much. Nevertheless, the buzz among baseball insiders is that Torre, a great player in his own day, is closing in on selection to the Hall of Fame. He will stay with the Yankees and endure Steinbrenner's abuse silently so that he can pursue the third title that may secure his enshrinement in Cooperstown.

Torre's elevation began when the Yankees won the 1996 World Series during his brother's life-or-death struggle while awaiting an organ transplant, and culminated with the publication of his memoirs. That book, *Chasing the Dream*, did not come close to recouping its half-million dollar advance, a fact the *Observer*, despite its obsessive interest in the publishing industry, failed to note. Even a favorably reviewed narrative bursting with moral uplift (dedication rewarded, a good man struggling against adversity, and a family pulling together to cope with tragedy) could not inspire buyers.

After the 1998 World Series, another publisher offered the Yankee manager a high six-figure advance for his contribution to the newest con game exploited by celebrity coaches: books that present sports as a metaphor for life, and especially for corporate management. Hesitant to annoy owners who hire them and players who can get them fired, coaches are reluctant to say anything in public about behind-the-scenes battles. Books that tell those stories—from John Feinstein's tales of Bobby Knight's excesses to Sam Smith's exposé of Jordan's Bulls and Jim Bouton's peek behind the major-league curtain—sell well. Coaches with seven-figure salaries are understandably reluctant to trade one big score for a lifetime of employment. Instead of offering editors and thus readers access to the stories they would not otherwise hear, the coaches have found a way to repackage their barren offerings as self-help books for businessmen looking to be comforted by the wisdom of those who manage ballplayers. Torre is merely the latest New York sports figure who has been sanctified (Pat Riley, Rick Pitino, Phil Jackson) and then moved to cash in with another of the endless supply of books offering a variation on the "Life Lessons I Learned Coaching Ball" theme. From there, it's an easy step onto the five-figure per appearance guest lecture circuit.

\*          \*          \*

If you think the 1998 Yankees were something to behold, you should have seen the 1869 Cincinnati Red Stockings. 125–50 is an impressive record, but the sport's first professional team went unbeaten, suffering only one tie in sixty contests. The team featured nine exports on its ten-man roster, the most prominent being George and Harry Wright, who had played shortstop and outfield for New York's great Knickerbocker squads. The brothers Wright each earned over a thousand dollars to play for a team that one writer claimed "would never have been heard from outside its own locality" had it used local talent.

However, the definition of homegrown talent has expanded to include players with an organizational connection. In the thirties, Cardinal boss Branch Rickey popularized the farm system (major-league control over hundreds of ballplayers on affiliated minor-league teams) as a way for major-league teams to nurture rising young players. The '98 Yankees weren't exactly bursting at the seams with players from New York City; no one on the roster had grown up in the five boroughs. By the broader definition, the Yankees could claim that a quarter of the roster featured "native" talent. Bernie Williams, Andy Pettitte, Derek Jeter, Mariano Rivera, Jorge Posada, and Ramiro Mendoza each had made the long journey through the low minors to the Stadium in the Bronx to take their place alongside Ron Guidry, Don Mattingly, Mickey Mantle, and other Yankee legends developed in-house.

The 1998 Yankees, like all their successful ancestors, were built primarily through poaching. Whether by trade or through free agency, the vast majority of Steinbrenner's pinstriped warriors had no minor-league indoctrination in the Yankee way. The team that had stolen the Babe from Boston now used its deep farm system (courtesy of organizational patience facilitated by Steinbrenner's suspension during the early nineties) and an even deeper bank account to pick up a handful of key players every offseason. The '95 season brought David Cone and John Wetteland. The following year Tino Martinez, Tim Raines, Joe Girardi, Dwight Gooden, and Jeff Nelson arrived. The next season saw the addition of David Wells, Hideki Irabu, Chad Curtis, and Mike Stanton. While some years the Yanks merely tread water to keep up with free-agent departures, 1998 was a lot better than that. Securing an All-Star second baseman (Chuck Knoblauch), a solid third baseman (Scott Brosius), a veteran run producer (Chili Davis), and Cuba's top pitcher (Orlando Hernandez) made the Yankees a team without a visible weakness.

When the team without a flaw faced a schedule filled with lousy opponents, the results were obscene. Fifty times during the 1998 season the Yankees hosted teams with a losing record. They won forty-six of those games while losing just four, an impossible .920 winning percentage. Over the course of those contests, the Yanks' amazing pitching gave up two runs or fewer half the time. They also scored eight or more runs one out of every three of those games. Playing at home, the Yankees swept six games apiece from the expansion Devil Rays and the mediocre Tigers, as well as taking five games from the impoverished Royals. They outscored those teams by five runs a game at the Stadium. Somehow the Bombers were even better in close games against bad teams, going an amazing twenty-four and two when the outcome was decided by three runs or less. The odds against a lousy team coming to the Stadium and ambushing their hosts were better than eleven to one.

The fans marveled at the professionalism implied by the consistency of their team's performance, but this was victory without honor. The Yankees surely played hard every day, and, with the prices the Boss charged for tickets, the fans had every reason to expect this kind of effort. However, the players liked winning so much that they seemed to relish playing the cupcakes on their schedule even more than their tougher rivals.

The teams that appeared on dozens of "Guaranteed Yankee Win" Nights were owned by the same partners with whom the Boss refused to share his spoils. Their feeble presence sated his TV audience's desire for a simulacrum of the Cnristians and the Lions, but the experience could only confirm their place in baseball's static class structure. The financial spoils shared after three days of devastation were not even enough to go out and buy a backup shortstop in the present market. Rarely had so many been sacrificed for the pleasures of so few.

There was a patch of games in the middle of the season when the Yanks seemed to pound a lightweight into the dust every night. Between June 1 and August 12, the Yankees played thirty home games. They hosted one game against the Indians, two against the Braves, and another twenty-seven against the dregs of the league. The Yankees won twenty-six of the twenty-seven mismatches by a combined score of 171–66. The stretch was so ridiculous it even baf-

fled the owner who made the enormous gap between baseball's lords
and serfs inevitable. "I can't explain it," Steinbrenner said. "In my 25
years in the game and 40 years in athletics, I have never seen anything like this. If I can compare them to a team, it would be the Big
Red Machine. They rolled over everybody."

The Boss, of course, was not referring to Stalin's iron grip on
Eastern Europe after World War II, or even that unbeaten first edition of the Cincinnati Reds. The Big Red Machine, a terrific offensive
team that won consecutive titles in the mid-seventies (sweeping
Steinbrenner's Yankees in his virgin World Series appearance in
1976), was the pride of Cincinnati until its front office and owners
proved unable to adapt to the first salary explosion. Richer teams tore
apart the great squad like tigers devouring a helpless gazelle.

Rest assured, the Yankees will not suffer that fate. Baseball's median
payroll was roughly $46 million during the 1998 season. Among the
teams that spent less than the league average, only the San Francisco
Giants had a winning record. None of the paupers made the playoffs. If
you counted the money the Boss spent to pay salaries of players traded
to impoverished clubs, as well as those no longer in uniform,
Steinbrenner probably topped the $80 million mark and outspent Peter
Angelos, his rival owner in Baltimore, who spent $74 million. After a
truly horrific season, Baltimore was the only team to spend significantly
above the median and end below .500. Their miserable performance still
left them ahead of more than a dozen of baseball's beggars.

Unless the sport's financial structure is altered profoundly, the
Bronx Bombers will always be predators, snatching players like
Brosius and Knoblauch from teams that could no longer afford their
services and outbidding all comers for free agents they covet like
Orlando Hernandez and Bernie Williams. Greed is good, at least if
you want to win baseball games.

\*                        \*                        \*

Atlanta, Cleveland, and the Yankees established dynasties in the years after the 1994 World Series was cancelled because of a labor dispute. Not only have the elite trio made the playoffs each year, they are the only teams to average six wins out of every ten regular season games during that period. This hegemony afield reflects their wealth. Only the Cubs, with their superstation revenues, could match the mad media money secured by the Braves and Yankees. While the Indians pull in a healthy amount from their local media deal, their stadium revenue (based on full season sellouts in the middle of winter) is the source of their power. The opening of Jacobs Field and the concurrent rise of Indian fortunes have appealed to Cleveland sports fans stung by the loss of their beloved Browns. In anticipation of the new stadium, the Indians built a better young ballclub to try to stir up interest. Increased ticket sales generated more revenue, which was spent to improve the roster, which attracted more fans, and so forth. For a lucky few, baseball's gravity-defying upward spiral is nearly as powerful as the downbound express.

In 1998, the Big Three owned the second, third, and fourth highest payrolls in baseball. Baltimore's mediocre 1998 season certainly offers proof that rich teams can screw it up. The lackluster final decade of O'Malley's well-to-do Doagers and the relentless ineptitude of the dollar-drunk Cubs (until the 1998 season) demonstrate that money can't buy a pennant if an organization makes lousy decisions.

That said, the teams that don't spend are not even in the game. If you are a fan of the Royals, Twins, Tigers, Athletics, Phillies, Expos, Brewers, and Pirates, you might as well expect to be miserable. These eight teams have compiled one winning season out of thirty-two chances in the four years since the last strike. Their franchises drew about 1.3 million fans apiece for the 1998 season, and their payrolls included eight of the bottom twelve for the 1998 season.

Things are only getting worse. At season's end, the Montreal Expos figured out that they had paid their entire team $8.3 million.

Mike Piazza, Bernie Williams, Randy Johnson, Kevin Brown, and Albert Belle will each make more than $10 million next season. The latest estimates suggest franchise revenues in 1998 ranged from $35 million (the Expos) to around $175 million (the Yankees, Indians, Braves, and Orioles were in this class). The Expos are one of a dozen teams without hope. "It's impossible," Montreal president Claude Brochu confided. "The Expos have by far the lowest payroll and by far the lowest revenues, so we are just between a rock and a hard place. It's very, very difficult."

During the Year of the Homer, dissonant voices were not welcome. The chorus celebrating the perfect season, the joys of teamwork, and the reclamation of dominance by New York City drowned out those who maintained any critical distance. In Gotham, it was, according to tastemakers and civic leaders, the best of times. Crime, according to all reports, had been abolished. Consumption, except at sex shops or from street vendors, emerged as the highest form of civic responsibility. Brilliant new restaurants opened faster than critics could herald them. Real estate prices soared so high that they engendered acceptance instead of outrage. And Disney, having engineered the successful celluloid transformation of street prostitution into a Doris Day movie starring Julia Roberts, spearheaded the makeover of Times Square, formerly seen as Main Street for sodomites, into America's favorite open-air shopping mall. Any persistent problems—overcrowded mass transit, suffocating traffic, overzealous policemen, underfunded public schools, decaying infrastructure—remained far off camera.

If you were concerned about the stadium issue, or any of the other serious matters surrounding the Yankees, by season's end, you were little more than a crank. Your credentials as an American, and certainly as a New Yorker, were in question. After all, it had been a helluva season.

*Baseball has played a prominent role in the American Imaginary—the process by which "America" strives to see itself coherently. Of course, without its own tongue or its own Volk, the nation has always relied on icons, and on the designation of a national character, for instance, to assert cohesion, to imagine a community, as Benedict Anderson would put it ... baseball renders America visible to itself.*

—Bill Brown

*... The resonance of the game throughout the country this season speaks to something larger than the Yankees, larger even than the amazing collection of broken records left in its wake ...*

*Indeed, the whole season seems to have been filmed through a Frank Capra lens ...*

*Baseball, after all, broke the color barrier long before the government got into the act. And it may not be too much to hope that it may lead us back to a national civility: It is worth noting that San Diego fans stood to applaud the Yankee achievement Wednesday night even in the face of a crushing loss.*

—*Wall Street Journal*, October 23, 1998

*Friday's parade saluting the Yankees' World Series victory was one of the city's great celebrations.*

*... We should also know that sports allow people the opportunity to learn, as author Albert Murray has pointed out, how to win with grace and lose with dignity, two of the biggest lessons we'll ever get in this life.*

*... We also love our sports because the games themselves, no matter how irritating the players and the owners might be, remain pure ... Part of the purity is in the objective aspect of what is assessed. That doesn't mean there aren't bad calls made by those put in charge of the game. But there are plenty of real facts. A ball hit into the stands is a home run; one hit into the wall below the seats is not an "interpretation" of a home run.*

—Stanley Crouch, *New York Daily News*, October 25, 1998

# 1

# CROWD PLEASERS

## SAVING A NATION

Major-league baseball drew 70 million fans to ballparks during 1998. A cumulative audience a dozen times larger than that caught games on the radio or television. The desire to consume the national pastime has not waned in the face of nasty disputes between labor and management, escalating ticket prices and salaries, and decreasing fan contact with the players.

Observers from George Will to Ken Burns tout the game's moral qualities. According to the Bill Bennett school of national pastime celebrants, when we watch baseball, we don't see physically gifted young men testing their skills against similarly talented opponents. Instead, if we're blessed with a certain kind of insight, we see lessons about the rewards of dedication and good character unfold on the diamond. In his 1990 bestseller *Men at Work*, Will wrote, "For an athlete to fulfill his or her potential, particularly in a sport as demanding as baseball, a remarkable degree of mental and moral discipline is required."

The strain to correlate athletic excellence with moral superiority suggests an unexamined faith in Puritan beliefs powerful enough to bury concrete reality. Lou Gehrig, Joe DiMaggio, Jackie Robinson, and Cal Ripken may be ballplayers *and* paragons of virtue, but the counterexamples to Will's mythology within Yankee history alone are many. Hal Chase, a brilliant gloveman when he wasn't corrupting his teammates, threw games. In his offseason job as a policeman, Jake Powell, an outfielder on the great teams led by Gehrig and DiMaggio, relished cracking black skulls. Babe Ruth, baseball's finest player, had appetites so large that his own teammates considered him an animal. Mickey Mantle, the greatest switch-hitter ever, was an alcoholic who ran around on his first wife. Billy Martin was a mean, racist drunk who held grudges and battled authority his whole life; he remains the team's greatest manager since Casey Stengel. If nobody on the 1998 Yankees cheated on their wives or girlfriends while they were on the road, it would have been the first time in franchise history.

Nice guys may not always finish last, as Leo Durocher, the original dark prince of managing, asserted. However, the converse propounded by baseball's ethics police, that first-place finishers are all nice guys, is no more accurate. In any case, the vast majority of baseball fans are not drawn by the moments when the game's narrative resembles that of a cheap movie-of-the-week. Those Capraesque elements may heighten the drama or comfort those closet Puritans who fear their devotion to the game is decadent and wasteful, but they are hardly essential. Nevertheless, the endless pull of the mythology that surrounds the game ensures someone will soon publish *The Book of Baseball Virtues*. With any luck, Steinbrenner will be the author.

When Mayor Giuliani urged schoolchildren to skip school to attend the Yankee victory parade, he asserted that he learned more from baseball than he ever did in a classroom. Giuliani did not specify whether the national pastime taught him to bristle at criticism, bully opponents, trash the First Amendment, coddle self-centered billionaires, or all of the above. Stanley Crouch and Albert Murray notwithstanding, baseball evidently did not teach the mayor how to win with grace and lose with dignity. However, the game certainly helped him nurture the special kind of intelligence that believes tens of thousands of schoolkids ditched classes to go to the Yankee parade in search of moral guidance. What else could explain Giuliani making public financing of four baseball stadia (plans include hundreds of millions for a new park for the Mets to match the Yankees and tens of millions for minor-league parks in Brooklyn and Staten Island) a higher priority than repairing abysmal public school buildings throughout the city? Save the kids, build a pro team a ballpark.

The prudes overstate baseball's moral quality and healing powers because they misread the game's history. Baseball was not expected to lift us up; it was designed to satisfy our base physical nature. Baseball's early popularizers did not intend the game to be an analogue to its older cousin, England's cricket. One of cricket's central functions in English culture was delineating highminded forms of leisure for the elite. Baseball's appeal was meant to be wider. Albert Spalding, player, sporting goods manufacturer, and owner, proclaimed:

> Baseball is a democratic game ... Base Ball is the American Game par excellence, because its playing demands Brain and Brawn, and American manhood supplies these ingredients in quantity sufficient to spread over the entire continent. ...

Cricket could never satisfy the red-hot blood of Young and
Old America.

During baseball's early days before and after the Civil War, the
game's players included recent immigrants from Ireland and
Germany who took to the game even more fiercely than the descen-
dants of England. Primarily Catholics, many of these young men
toiled at physical labor for six days a week. The more successful
WASPs could play baseball during the week if they wished. These
established Americans freely gave up their entire Sabbaths to the
church, while the new arrivals pushed for Sunday baseball. For those
men, who loved a game that allowed them to display their prowess, it
was Sunday afternoons or nothing.

As baseball's popularity grew among young men, the increase in
the quality of play drew thousands of spectators. New York City
hosted many of the best clubs in the game's early days, and, when
players and managers realized spectators would pay to watch games,
Union Grounds sprouted in Brooklyn right after the Civil War. The
game's original stadium was enclosed to allow admission to be
extracted from thousands of Brooklynites. The Brooklyn Atlantics,
Union Grounds' home team, were the initial passion of a borough
that would remain baseball-mad for a century.

The dimensions of that appeal come through in an account of an
early game at Union Grounds, the championship match between the
Philadelphia Athletics and the Brooklyn Atlantics. The following
story appeared in the September 12, 1868, *New York Clipper*:

> ... The spacious ballfield was filled with admirers of the
> national game, and it was estimated that at least 15,000
> persons were present. Every seat within the enclosure
> was filled by one o'clock and those who came later had to
> take their chances for good positions. As usual at all the
> grand matches on this ground, several thousands

managed to witness the game without dispersing the required admittance fee.

And it was curious to note the devices resorted to by the outsiders to get a look at the contest. Owners of trucks and other vehicles . . . stationed their establishments close to the high fence surrounding the ground and let out standing room only to those who preferred this method of looking on. Others secured the prominent peekholes in the fence while others, after the game was underway and the attention of the officers was centered in the exciting contest, boldly took up their positions on the fence and held them til the close.

Crowds came early, and late arrivals initiated a continuing tradition of sneaking into the park. The intense desire to see big games has existed for well over a century. That emotional current always involved the excitement of witnessing a defining event as it happens, and sports adds the thrill of the unknown, the narrative to be written. Neither of which necessarily involves any moral uplift. The uncertain narrative which fosters interest also creates the opportunity to bet on that which hasn't happened (and, presumably, isn't fixed). That particular base appeal goes back to the earliest games, as demonstrated in the *Clipper*:

. . . The result of the game is another illustration of the uncertainties of baseball. Before the commencement of the game and up to the sixth innings, the Atlantics were looked upon as sure winners. The betting was 100 to 40, and, even at these long odds, the Philadelphians were very shy. Considerable was invested on the game, however, one way and another . . . 15 was laid against 100 that the Athletics would win by the odds of two to one, and these long-headed chaps were winners to a large amount.

The long line of betting on baseball that runs from today's online point spreads back through Pete Rose's banishment to the fixing of the 1919 World Series traces its way to the game's earliest days. Union Grounds set aside a special seating section for gamblers, enabling them to bet easily throughout the game. While football, pro and college, has replaced baseball as America's national sports lottery, at least a part of the game's current appeal involves a gambler's high. Unlike the crowds in 1868, most of today's action revolves around fantasy-league owners who bet on their ability to select more productive players than their fellow Mittys. The millions who spend months playing these games have found a cheap way to access the real American Dream. Why imagine you can *play* like Mike Piazza when you can instead fantasize about *owning* him?

The *Wall Street Journal* is, of course, the daily diary of that national fantasy of ownership, but even the masters of the universe indulge themselves occasionally with a politically loaded, wildly inaccurate glance at more frivolous pursuits. The editorial singing the praises of baseball as national moral elevator swings and misses twice. That many San Diegans were gracious in defeat is unrelated to baseball and instead reflects the cultural chasm between the two coasts. New Yorkers are not good losers. The last time New York lost a World Series, Steinbrenner demonstrated his limited notions of sportsmanship. The Boss embarrassed himself, his team, their opponent, and the game itself when he apologized to Yankee fans for the defeat instead of accepting it with dignity.

More significantly, the idea that baseball broke the color barrier "long before the government got into the act" is laughable. The reality of whites and blacks laying down their lives during World War II in the U.S. military (the government's largest employer) created the historical context for this progress. One of the arguments used in that era, "if he's good enough for the navy, he's good enough for the majors," illustrates this nexus. Some of the earliest protests of the incipient civil rights movement demanded the removal of baseball's color line. Beyond this cultural suasion, legal efforts to mandate integration were under way almost two years before Jackie Robinson donned a Brooklyn Dodger uniform. On July 1, 1945, the Ives/Quinn law forbidding discrimination in employment came into effect in New York. Soon thereafter, Mayor LaGuardia established a commission to explore baseball's color issue. The panel existed to pressure the game's owners to change their misguided stance. Two days after the panel's first meeting, Branch Rickey met with Jackie Robinson for the first time. The *Wall Street Journal* editorial deliberately glosses over this reality in an attempt to reify baseball's role as past and future exemplar of American moral exceptionalism. In the middle of the American Century, baseball's lords were hardly moral leaders and included some of Jim Crow's fiercest defenders.

## TRIPLE PLAY

*Baseball isn't statistics; it's Joe DiMaggio rounding second base.*
—Jimmy Breslin

What draws fans to the game is rarely the riveting stimulation of having a financial interest at stake. It's not the illicit charge of sneaking into a ballpark, either. Neither is it the game's sanctimonious appeal nor its latent powers to heal a distressed nation. Baseball's true charm derives from statistics, stories, and performances. Basketball, football, and every other popular American spectator sport draw their appeal from the last two elements. Each has its legends and personal histories as well as the dance created when the game is played. Baseball alone works another magic on its devotees, hooking them with the music of numbers.

The quantitative appeal of baseball developed after Henry Chadwick, central in establishing more uniform rules for the sport in the 1860s, invented the batting average and the box score. Chadwick created the game's first key statistic and a condensed repository for vital data during an era categorized by Stephen Jay Gould as a period when "another trend, equally irresistible, swept through the human sciences—the allure of numbers, the faith that rigorous measurement could guarantee irrefutable precision." This period fostered numerous pseudosciences based on rigorous measurements. For example, craniometry, which asserted that differences in brain size correlated to difference in intelligence, flourished. White male craniometrists discovered that white males had the largest brains . . . Eureka! Craniometry has been thoroughly discredited; batting averages have retained their authority.

More significantly, the box scores that contain those averages, along with a wealth of other information, have become ubiquitous and serve as an important gateway, especially for young boys, to a budding interest in numbers. The gender difference in performance in mathematics is likely reinforced by baseball. By the age of four, I was scanning the box scores and calculating updated batting averages and ERAs in my head. This would be one piece of evidence to my parents that I should be placed in gifted math programs. Even though I was more proficient at other sports, I got hooked on baseball as a fan because I was a numbers junkie.

No other sport has this kind of appeal. Everyone knows the Babe hit 714 home runs during his career and 60 in his best year. They also know that DiMaggio hit safely in 56 straight games and that Gehrig played in 2,130 consecutive contests. No similarly magic numbers attach to elite performers in other major sports like Michael Jordan, Jerry Rice, or Wayne Gretzky.

I can randomly select Americans who don't even care about sports, ask them who owns the single-season record for home runs, and they'll know. Not only will they know McGwire's name, they'll know how many he hit and who finished second. They'll also know whose record McGwire broke and who held the record before the taciturn right fielder from Fargo.

If Chadwick was baseball's statistical pioneer, present-day author Bill James is responsible for the renaissance of the national pastime's numerologists. James, a revolutionary thinker, refused to accept the myths the game had developed over a century. Managers that make safe decisions are said to have gone "by the book," although no written testament, new or old, exists. Frustrated with conventional wisdom about baseball that went unchallenged in the dominant discourse by baseball insiders and a pliant media, James used statistical analysis as a tool to expose poor decision making or players with unrecognized value. The term he coined to describe his work, "sabermetrician," was a tribute to the Society of American Baseball Researchers (SABR), an organization of formal and informal historians devoted to detailed analysis of the national pastime.

SABR's members are among the sport's superfans. Instead of barhopping like neighboring diehards in the stands, they haunt libraries between games. SABR's membership is overwhelmingly Caucasian and male, with a high percentage Catholic, too. The impact of SABR, whose members have authored hundreds of books, is so diffuse that it is difficult to characterize. The articles in SABR's *Baseball Research Journal* often reexamine, if not reclaim, long-lost baseball history, however, many of its members' publications have been an effort to create a new sense of order (perhaps an innately Catholic enterprise) out of quantitative analysis. While James has spent his career seeking untested myths to smash, some of his peers seem stuck in rigid examinations of minute questions that deny the human narrative suggested by the numbers. Almost every week a member of SABR publishes his precise ranking of the greatest players of all time based on a new formula he invented that is more accurate than any seen before. Statistical analyses of the debate over the merits of Joe DiMaggio and Ted Williams seem about as likely to resolve that dispute as a calculator estimating how many angels there are on the head of a pin.

Many of James's baseball books have become bestsellers. Unfortunately, the mass media absorbed James's success as testimony to an unquenchable American thirst for data. Newspapers, sports weeklies, game telecasts, and even highlight shows have evolved into a delivery system for a blizzard of numerical junk. If you need to know how David Cone pitches on Tuesdays in May when the temperature dips below fifty degrees, there is undoubtedly a quant out there willing to sate your interest. This authoritative presentation of hundreds of pieces of data in the daily sports pages, journalism's zone of male escape, suggests a nation of clandestine accountants.

Baseball's obsession with magic numbers like "most home runs in a season" reflects an American yearning for simple quantitative explanations. The evening news compresses the complex reality of the economy into a ritualized recital of the wanderings of the Dow Jones Industrial Average. Certain cable channels keep the Dow on screen perpetually so millions of spectator-speculators never miss a moment of the national keno game. No matter that the chasm between Main Street and Wall Street remains huge and the Dow offers an incredibly imprecise window even on the limited landscape of equity investment. We want our Dow, and we want it now.

Numerology reaches its apex in the never-ending national survey. The powerfully mediated belief that polls offer an accurate snapshot of what we the people want (whether for breakfast or for president) persists in the face of present-day errors. None of the predictions by pollsters before the 1998 midterm elections were even close, the litany of postelection excuses was unconvincing, yet no media giant chose to cast aside their resident Nostradamus. Numbers generated by the wizards offer an illusion of concrete evidence too powerful to abandon.

Concurrently, America's statisticity has certified structural social advantages. Our key myth of America as a land of equal opportunity, a classless meritocracy with the possibility of upward mobility, underlies sport's unconscious appeal. The level playing field native to our spectator sports resides in our collective imagination waiting to be confirmed by quantitative tests that measure the citizenry. In a nation where economic outcome is determined less by breeding than by educational background (although, of course, legacy greatly impacts school choice), IQs, SAT scores, and the like determine our place in the national education lottery from preschool to grad school. That scores can be improved through costly preparation shows tests measure not aptitude alone but also temporal and economic resources. Nevertheless, these biased social filters retain great authority and an aura of objectivity because they can be reduced to numbers.

It can hardly be news that boys marshaling statistical evidence in arguments about whether Tony Gwynn (with his higher batting average) is a better hitter than Mark McGwire (with his many home runs) are quick to reduce intelligence to a single measure. What's shocking is that adults are rewarded for doing the same thing. The most noxious recent example of the deep roots of American faith in numerology had to be the overwhelming influence of *The Bell Curve*. Because authors Murray and Herrnstein cloaked their racist assumptions and necessarily racist findings (to wit, IQs accurately measure intelligence, whites have higher IQs and thus are smarter than blacks, IQs are immutable and, therefore, public money used to educate those in the inner cities is being wasted) in a quantitative framework, they avoided much criticism. The pair were accepted in the mainstream as scientists objectively revealing the flaws in misguided if kindhearted public policy. The authors' expansive use of mathematics to legitimize their argument intimidated many of those under attack. While the vast majority of *The Bell Curve*'s readers did not understand how the authors massaged their data, the intended audience surely appreciated the brute force of the numbers. The figures were not just evidence—they were the truth itself. The gospel of American numerology would be far less dominant without the reassuring drumbeat of baseball's box scores.

Baseball's numerological appeal should not be seen as distinct from the game's other sources of allure. What makes 56, the number of games Joe DiMaggio hit in consecutively, instantly recognizable for fans has nothing to do with qualities inherent to the number itself, such as its divisibility by seven. The number's familiarity emanates from the prodigious lore surrounding the Yankee Clipper, the images of Joltin' Joe's on-field exploits in the memories of those who saw him play and those who discover him anew on videotape, and the story of the streak itself: the close calls, the national interest, the media frenzy, and the pressure DiMaggio felt. Barely subterranean, 56 reemerges every time a current hitter gets a streak into the mid-twenties.

The game's narrative appeal works on connoisseurs and diehards alike. It's not enough for a good fan to watch Orlando Hernandez pitch and marvel at his wondrous delivery with its visual echoes of former Latin American aces Luis Tiant and Juan Marichal. The spectator must also know the legend of Hernandez's path to America (escape from Cuba by raft in shark-infested waters), his nickname (El Duque), his famous relative (half-brother Livan was 1997 World Series MVP for the Florida Marlins and became a local hero in anti-Castro Miami), his pain (the family, including young children, he left behind), his joy (in a city with countless temptations, El Duque openly embraced his new wealth and fame), his uncertain age (pegged at somewhere between twenty-eight and thirty-four, this very lack of quantitative certitude—*where were the guy's career stats?*—suggested a condescension toward foreign irrationality, a Cuba so backward that it couldn't even maintain accurate birth records or box scores), and his lucky break (David Cone was bitten by his mother's dog, allowing the Yankees a glimpse of El Duque in the majors). In the end, El Duque's narrative perfectly fit the archetypal American journey from rags to riches. After New York celebrated the World Series victory with a parade for all the Yankees, two New Jersey cities directly across the river from Manhattan in Hudson County (home to more Cuban Americans than anywhere in the U.S. besides Miami) threw their own party for El Duque, icon for thousands of recent immigrants.

Much of El Duque's story was compressed, ignored, or reworked to better reflect myths with broad cultural currency. If El Duque's constructed narrative shows a little wear under closer examination, not so his artistry afield. No Yankee pitcher has ever been this much fun to watch. The sharp turn, the impossibly high kick (rumor has it he can wrap his leg behind his head), shocking, too, in its speed, and, then, the loose arm flying through a half-dozen release points from eight o'clock to midnight. All this emanating from the taut body of an uncommonly handsome man with an otherworldly sense of composure. The Duke is surely not one of us, baseball's fans, nor even one of them, his average major-league peers. He is an icon of male grace and dignity like Joe DiMaggio, Ken Griffey, Jr., or similarly blessed teammate Derek Jeter. He is baseball royalty.

Some may prefer David Wells's scruffy, soft-bellied, open-shirt-ed, Everyman mess. In a thicket of unattainable idols like McGwire, Sosa, and Clemens, Wells's presence allows us to imagine we could still play in the big leagues. Until Boomer starts his pitching motion, he is Pigpen, an ugly cacophony of images and sounds trailing behind him. Then, in an instant, the whole coalesces into a model of precision and beauty unimaginable from the pieces present at any other time the big guy is breathing. Even as the game's players become more distant thanks to steroid-pumped bodies and carefully tailored public utterances, Wells remains one of us.

If the quantitative and narrative appeals of the game serve to certify our depth as spectators, to confirm our adulthood, then the performative appeal reconnects us with a childlike state of wonder. What's more breathtaking than watching Derek Jeter glide three steps to his right and climb a few rungs up an invisible ladder while twisting to fire a ball to a glove sixty yards distant at eighty miles an hour? Or more wondrous than seeing Darryl Strawberry flick his long arms at a low fastball and turn it around even faster than it arrived on a tremendous arc into the upper deck? Witnesses reduced to simple awe, we respond with wild celebration.

When the game reaches its apex, as it did in the bottom of the seventh inning of game one of the 1998 World Series, these three trains—statistics, narrative, performance—run simultaneously. During a brilliant playoff run, the Yankees nevertheless produced two possible goats to blame if things turned sour. Chuck Knoblauch became Public Enemy Number One in New York City when he suffered a brain cramp while covering first base after a bunt during the top of the twelfth inning of the second game of the Cleveland series. The first-base umpire called the Indian batter running inside the baseline safe after he was hit by Tino Martinez's throw. Instead of picking up the ball and making sure the runners didn't advance, Knoblauch argued the call for ten seconds, long enough for a runner to score. During his next at-bat in the bottom of the same inning, 50,000 Yankee fans greeted him with a chorus of boos. After the game, Knoblauch refused to admit he'd done anything wrong. The New York tabloids destroyed him, and the second baseman held a press conference a day later to admit his mistake and quiet the media feeding frenzy. Even after the Yankees beat the Indians (with Knoblauch playing well for the rest of the series), he remained under the microscope.

Knoblauch, a leadoff hitter whose compact, wide frame suggests performance-enhancing drugs, had set a personal record for home runs during 1998 while getting on base far less than his new team expected. Torre complained uncharacteristically about Knoblauch's affection for his newfound uppercut swing, and Knoblauch was seen as a disappointment during a flawless season. During game one of the World Series, the Yankees trailed by three runs entering the bottom of the seventh inning. Concerned fans wondered if their team could recover from another playoff home loss. Suddenly the Yankees had two men on base, and Padre manager Bruce Bochy pulled his ace Kevin Brown, with Knoblauch at the plate. Brown's replacement, Donnie Wall, missed high with two fastballs to the second baseman. Wall's next pitch, a half-foot lower, encountered Knoblauch's most pronounced low-to-high stroke, a swing that would have enraged Torre earlier in the year.

The ball soared into the New York night as Padre left fielder Greg Vaughn drifted back to the wall, waiting to time his jump to steal the ball out of the first row of seats. The ball hung in the air long enough to allow fans to wonder whether Knoblauch had wiped the slate clean. As the ball continued to hover, some even recalled the twelve-year-old who'd reached out from the first row of the opposite corner to turn a warning-track out into a crucial home run two years ago during the Orioles' series. Security and a new railing in the right-field stands prevented similar shenanigans over there, but in the left-field corner, no restraints had been put in place. Steinbrenner would not give up any advantage, no matter how unfair, unless forced into it. Would another fan win one for the Yankees? As the ball finally descended, Vaughn leapt and propelled his massive frame almost into the first row. The ball landed a half-dozen feet beyond his reach, the stadium erupted, and the dugout emptied to embrace a teammate whose sentence had been commuted.

Four batters after the three-run home run, brother goat Tino Martinez stepped up to the plate with the bases loaded and two out. First baseman Martinez was never punished like his infield partner for a lousy throw on the controversial play. But he was subjected to intense scrutiny after his abysmal batting performance in the playoffs continued a trend of poor postseason play for the Yankees. Reporters openly questioned Torre's loyalty in keeping Tino in the lineup, and team insiders spread rumors that the team would try to acquire slugging Red Sox first baseman Mo Vaughn in the offseason even though Martinez was under contract.

Tino's burdens were complicated by the presence of a new Padre hurler on the mound, Mark Langston, his old foe in the Angel-Mariner rivalry. With a two-and-two count, Martinez watched a low fastball cut the plate in two. Strikeout looking, game tied into the top of the eighth, right? No, home-plate umpire Rich Garcia, who'd had a big strike zone all night, squeezed Langston and called the pitch a ball. Angry at Tino's reprieve and afraid of walking in the go-ahead run, Langston served up a batting-pitch fastball in the heart of the plate. Tino unleashed his short, quick swing and sent the ball into the top deck of the right-field stands before you could blink. A different moment than Knoblauch's, without an instant's reflection, it cemented the U-turn in the contest's narrative. Tino too had been released, and the party was on. Fifty-seven thousand stood as one. The Stadium has never been louder. Seven innings in, the 1998 World Series was effectively over.

Baseball's three-fold appeal is made possible by its temporal fluidity. The dead spaces between pitches allow broadcasters to spew numbers and fans time to reflect on the common stories about the actors in the on-field drama. Sometimes, even when the ball is in play, the pace of the action shifts from real time to that of a novel, slow enough to allow the sweet interplay of memory with the present motion. Lifelong fans recognize in those moments a quality they don't find in other sports. Events infused with immense complexity yet instantly readable, like Knoblauch's moon shot, reward their interest.

## THE YANKEE NATION

*The Yankees became the quintessential representatives of the big city, of urban America with its sophistication, cosmopolitanism, and ethnic and religious heterogeneity . . .*

—Benjamin Rader

*The efficiently triumphant Yankee machine is a great institution, but, as they say, who can fall in love with U.S. Steel?*

—Gay Talese

*I represent both the overdog and the underdog in society.*

— Reggie Jackson

*All literary men are Red Sox fans. To be a Yankee fan in literary society is to endanger your life.*

— John Cheever

*Hating the Yankees is as American as pizza pie, unwed mothers and cheating on your income tax.*

—Mike Royko

After the Yanks finished off the Orioles on Independence Day to complete the best half-season in the history of the most successful franchise in American sports, a casually dressed gentleman in his seventies approached as I awaited the first train back to Manhattan at the far end of the platform. He'd been sitting near me in the bleachers and was muttering to himself about the game or the team or something. When he saw me, his eyes registered a brief glimmer of recognition. I doubt he remembered me. What he sought was visual confirmation of the Cap Day souvenir, indicating a receptive audience.

"They're not hitting, they're not hitting, they're not hitting," he said, with the agitation of a lifelong pessimist, "I don't know about this team."

"The pitching's been great, and that counts, too," I responded. "They're 61–20, right?"

"Yeah, yeah, but the hitting. They're not hitting. They can't keep winning if they're not hitting. They've got no Ruth, no Gehrig, no DiMaggio, no Mantle."

What makes every Yankee fan hard to love is their continued whining in the face of unparalleled success. Over the weekend, the Yanks had looked less than dominant in registering three low-scoring one-run victories over the sinking Orioles, but they had won and were continuing on a pace unmatched by any team in the history of the game. The euphoria on the platform reflected an era of good feeling in Yankeeland. What memories could this disgruntled fan have of Yankee baseball that were dishonored by the present squad?

His T-shirt and jeans were a false costume, a betrayal of his old-school values. No matter that the Yankees led the league in offense (runs scored per game) and that Tim Raines, possibly a future Hall of Famer thanks to his bat and speed, was no better than the twelfth best everyday player when every Yankee was healthy. This was an offensive machine equal to any squad in franchise history, a team without a weakness, but these weren't his Bronx Bombers. For this working-class Irish American, rooting for the Yankees offered an easy route to assimilation in white America, and those teams of his youth could never be surpassed.

"How long have you been going to games?"

"Went to my first game back in '35. I'll tell you something, when I gave the guy seven dollars for a bleacher seat today and all he gave me was a ticket, I asked for the rest of my change. It used to cost fifty-five cents a game, and I'll tell you the players were a lot better back then, too."

I started to ask him why he kept coming to the games: did he love the uniform or the game itself that much or did he just like to remind himself how much better it was in the old days? Before I could get a few words out, he continued.

"Back then, I made a quarter an hour. And I worked hard, too. Today, everyone's spoiled. It's not just the players who get too much money. That minimum wage is a lot of money, and the workers don't do anything for five dollars an hour, either."

"Living on ten thousand dollars a year's not easy in this city today."

"Yeah, yeah, but we made it on a lot less back then. Back then, this used to be a nice neighborhood, too, not like it is now, the right kind of people used to live back here then."

Before he could further explain his theories on race and the decline of the Bronx, the man wandered away in search of someone else to complain to about the Yankee bats. His musings about the Bronx and neuroses about the team would find a welcome home in the owners' box. Whether in the owners' box or the bleachers, the Yankees are a team for bullies and poor losers who never met an underdog they liked.

Yankee fans are not interested in sportsmanship or in facing an opponent with a sporting chance. They are a hegemonic nation interested only in the claims of monarchy, a tribe set on domination. When the national pastime has experienced eras of competitive balance indicative of health at every outpost, Yankee fans suffered miserably. They are the worst New York has to offer: loud, aggressive, unruly, unthinking, cocky, self-absorbed, dictatorial, ungenerous celebrants of triumphalism.

They are a million Rudy Giulianis, a throng of Roy Cohns, a stadium full of petty tyrants. They are the kids who went to the right schools (or send their kids to those expensive schools now). The difference between Yankee fans and other baseball fans in New York

City of a certain age is as simple as this: A pair of Italian-American kids living in the outer boroughs after World War II loved baseball. One was a Yankee fan, the other rooted for the Dodgers. They grew up to become two of the city's most famous bosses: Rudy Giuliani and Joe Torre. You guess which one was the Yankee fan.

This identification with a team, its uniform, and history involves baseball's most direct appeal to the gut. The tribalism displayed by a community of fans has an almost immeasurable force. It creates instant civic rivalries where none previously existed. Before the 1998 World Series, New Yorkers hardly gave San Diego and its residents a second thought. When the Padres conquered the Braves to become the Yankee opponent, the tabloids, radio stations, and TV stations sent their most overheated reporters out to San Diego to try to create a rivalry to match the one between Athens and Sparta. For ten days, the New York media reveled in finding new ways to insult San Diegans as lazy, sun-baked residents of a city with nice weather and nothing to do. This vicarious combat between cities that were hardly at war suggests that diehard fans need an enemy to root against as much as they need a team to love. Sport is often seen as a ritual that serves as a healthy release of chauvinistic tension, but it seems at least as likely that these passions can be inflamed by spectator sports. As soon as the Series ended, all hostility disappeared, too.

In his book, *Me and DiMaggio: A Baseball Fan Goes in Search of His Gods*, longtime *New York Times'* book critic Christopher Lehmann-Haupt can't decide if he's a gaping fan or a curious reporter. He's scared into silence the first time he steps onto the field during spring training, but he later pursues a rumored tale of his hero's corruption. This investigation is so halfhearted and clumsy that he causes his beloved DiMaggio pain but never really nails the story. The confessional book has one redeeming feature. Lehmann-Haupt is honest enough to admit that the Yankees don't interest him unless they are winners:

Why did I root for them, my beloved Yankees? . . . They were cold and arrogant, contemptuous of human frailty. They were rich—they bought their championships. They were invincible—they always won . . . They were one of the last teams to field a black player.

. . . I knew all this, and still I could defend myself . . . And now that I was old enough to understand more about myself, I'd come up with some deeper answers. I was the oldest of three brothers, and the Yankees were a team for oldest brothers. If you were the oldest you were expected to win; you couldn't afford ever not to win, otherwise you'd lose the authority thrust on you by the primacy of your birth. You had to win and go on winning just to stay in place, and the Yanks were as close to a perpetual-motion winning machine as it was possible to identify with . . . As for the New York Mets—I could only see them as a team for youngest brothers and for children. I loved the Yankees. The Yankees were for winners.

. . . Besides—as I liked to bait my many friends who hated the Yankees—it was no picnic rooting for them. . . . It was easy to root for underdogs and losers. It took character to be a Yankee fan.

Baseball is not about fathers playing catch with sons, implies Lehmann-Haupt, but rather about older brothers maintaining order and asserting the hard-earned claims of empire. These emotions reflect that segment of the Yankee Nation (primarily sitting in the box seats and the luxury suites) that loves Steinbrenner precisely because he owns a winning team. In their eyes, the ends—return of a dynasty to the Bronx—justify any means.

Any baseball fan over forty who roots for the Yankees has danced the Lehmann-Haupt shuffle, a linguistic jig for apologists about the difficult demands of dynasty. These locals turned their backs on the Brooklyn Dodgers in favor of a franchise that replaced the wild bunch led by the Babe with a roster full of hard-throwing, power-hitting tin men in search of a personality. Tribal membership is often an accident of birth, and those Yankee fans raised in pinstripes can be excused for their inability to escape the brainwashing.

## WELCOME TO THE BLEACHERS

*We were being severely tested, by the Indians, by Justice, by the rain, by the overcrowding, by everything.*
—**Filip Bondy**, *New York Daily News*

*They can't get any rougher on us unless they show up with Uzis.*
—Dave Justice

The Bleacher Creatures should have felt pure ecstasy as they watched the parade honoring the object of their devotion. Their team, the 1998 New York Yankees, had dominated the regular season and destroyed their postseason opponents. Now hundreds of thousands of their comrades in the Yankee Nation gathered in the streets of Lower Manhattan to watch Joe Torre, Derek Jeter, David Wells, Mariano Rivera, and company receive an honor reserved for astronauts, aviators, and soldiers.

To make the triumph even sweeter, the Creatures, through volume and collective personality, had accomplished a rare feat in American sports: they had forced professional athletes and a media interested only in those players to pay their respects. In the top of the first inning at every game, the Creatures would direct their rhythmic chant (*clap-clap, clap-clap-clap, BER NIE WILL IAMS*) at each Yankee fielder until he acknowledged the salute with a gesture of his own. Even the team's airmen, radio announcers John Sterling and Michael Kay, were included in the playful ritual.

The print media quickly discovered the populist allure of this knot of Yankee fans. The Creatures had their own Boswell, the *Daily News'* Filip Bondy, a sportswriter who consciously used the royal "we" to challenge enemy players and affirm his everyman appeal. After the Yankees announced a ticket policy for the 1998 postseason that featured reserved seats in the bleachers and a ridiculously low number of tickets for the general public, the dailies, even the *Times*, covered the Creatures' strenuous efforts to secure their place in the stands with a righteous tone reserved for martyrs and freedom fighters. Most found tickets somewhere in the bleachers and then massed in the right-field corner. Back in place, the throng of stockbrokers and service-industry workers resumed their vituperative support of the home team.

The Creatures regained the spotlight after an incident during the American League Championship Series. While David Wells warmed up before the fifth game in Cleveland, a few Indian fans taunted the Yankee ace by making nasty comments about his mother. When Wells settled down after a shaky first inning to beat the Indians, he sarcastically waved to the crowd at the end of the game and then aired his grievances (*"those fucking idiots . . . Cleveland's fans are the worst"*) during postgame interviews. It was never clear whether the knuckleheads who heckled the pitcher knew Wells's mom had died a few years earlier, but much of New York had heard the pitcher's life story after he authored that perfect game in May. Locals who knew that Wells wore a tattoo of his mom over his heart assumed the outside world was clued in, too. The offended Yankee faithful prepared an especially warm greeting for the enemy's next visit to the Bronx.

If they needed any more inspiration for their revenge, Indian designated hitter David Justice provided it, saying, ". . . [at Yankee Stadium] I've heard about my mother, everything about my history, too . . . I hate that it happened to [Wells], but Yankee fans, come on now, everyone knows how rough they can be." Justice seemed most bitter about the abuse he had endured after his marriage to actress Halle Berry disintegrated. Chants of BEAT YOUR WIFE rained down on him from the bleachers during that difficult period.

With the character of Yankee fans (and, by proxy, New Yorkers) being questioned, the Bleacher Creatures, the most extreme loyalists in the Yankee Nation, were scrutinized by some, praised by others. Security guards in the bleachers warned the Creatures they would be thrown out if they directed profanities toward any opponent's mother. Stories noted the Creatures' intimidation of all visitors, whether opposing players, rival fans, or "bleacher virgins," to their Bronx Zoo, characterizing the fans as a witty if crude source of power for the team itself. Some reports went further, calling the Creatures brave exponents of the First Amendment.

Despite the varied points of view, the stories shared a disturbing lack of specificity. When Al D'Amato called his rival Chuck Schumer a "putzhead" during their Senate campaign, the media served as a useful echo chamber. When it came to the actions of the Yankee faithful, however, there was a reign of silence. No journalist seemed willing to report the taunts being hurled at visitors. By presenting a sanitized version of the Creatures, the media cultivated their image as lovable loyalists, perhaps a tad more boisterous than the average Yankee fan, but in the end, as cute and cuddly as the Beanie Babies handed out before David Wells's perfect game.

The truth is more complicated. The vast majority of the Creatures' verbal abuse involved variations on a single theme: gay sex. Enemy right fielders patrolling the swath of green in front of the bleachers are serenaded with a chorus of insults about how much cock they sucked, how big the cock was that they sucked, and how much harder they sucked when they were paid to do it. Garden-variety homophobia, always a dependable source of abuse in the hypermasculine culture of team sports, now seems to be the sole terra firma for insults that can terrorize your enemy without disturbing your friend.

The apex of the Creatures' expression of their disgust with homosexuality comes nightly after the fifth inning. At this moment, the grounds crew drags the infield to reduce the number of bad hops. From this mundane work a joyous tradition has emerged. As the groundskeepers stride across the diamond, the stadium's sound system blasts the song "YMCA" by the Village People. The crowd has transformed a late seventies club song into the backbeat for a quick aerobic workout. The frenzy peaks during the chorus when the greensmen drop their tools and lead tens of thousands waving their arms in a group spell: $Y\,M\,C\,A$. The youngest fans in the park, who all dance along, love this ritual the most. The one-time gay anthem now inspires the most Rockwellian images of a young family's day at the ballpark. Out in the right-field bleachers, the experience was another matter entirely. The Creatures have changed the words of the song (which innocuously guided young men in trouble to regain their balance with a stay at the Y) so that they directly assault homosexuals. Here is the Creatures' version of the chorus:

*Gay man*
*Get up off of your knees*
*I said, gay man*
*What a mass of disease*
*I said, gay man*
*Don't touch me please*
*Because you have got a disease*

*I have to ask you*
*Why are you gay?*
*I saw you sucking some*
*D I C K*
*They have every size*
*For your mouth to enjoy*
*You can hang out with all the boys*

As they sing, the Creatures single out an individual or group in the stands and direct the song, with index fingers extended, at their target. If the scapegoat chooses to respond, the situation quickly escalates into a confrontation that teeters on the edge of physical violence.

Not all of the Creatures' vitriol involves reflexive homophobia. If the on-field target possesses a narrative weakness (for example, a history of drug abuse or marital problems) or vulnerable physical attributes, then the slander is more personal. As the Yankees finished off the Indians in the Bronx in the aftermath of the imbroglio featuring Wells and Justice, the crowd taunted the vanquished visitors with a chorus of NINE TEEN FOUR TEE EIGHT, the last year Cleveland won the World Series. When the hefty Tony Gwynn monitored right field at Yankee Stadium for the first time during the 1998 World Series, the Creatures serenaded the future Hall of Famer with a surgical suggestion, LI PO SUC TION. The line between positive municipal feelings and dangerous nativism may be difficult to draw, but it's clear that the Creatures, while lively and loyal, should not have become an unquestioned badge of honor for the city.

Why did the local media choose to edit out all these details, all this unpleasantness? First, in the shadow of the Yankees' overwhelming season, serious journalism (rare enough in the world of sports) transmuted into a one-note chorus of civic pride. The coverage was prolific but thoroughly uncritical. For example, Rupert Murdoch's *New York Post* featured on its cover over consecutive days a young Yankee fan living in Georgia whose claim to fame was that his school would not let him wear Yankee gear to the school's Atlanta Braves' day. This story ran during the month the witch hunt against Clinton became most delirious, the period between the publication of the Starr report and the House vote in favor of opening an impeachment inquiry. In the midst of a scandal that left the *Post*'s Republican command beside themselves with joy, even the slightest Yankee story rated the front cover. The story about the "conscientious objector" in Atlanta played into self-serving archetypes: Yankee fans as brave and rebellious innocents. Unstated, of course, was the righteousness of their faith.

Second, the world of sports, especially male team sports, is exceptionally hostile to homosexuality. Yankee Stadium is just a half-hour subway ride from the West Village, the heart of one of the largest and most vital gay communities in the world, but the two cultures could not be more different. During a decade when public display of a red ribbon to support unfortunate victims of AIDS became commonplace, the "gay disease" was the sickness that dare not speak its name at a ballpark near you.

The treatment of Paul Priore during the historic season illustrates the homophobic attitudes that saturate the Yankees. Priore, a clubhouse attendant and the son of a Yankee clubhouse man with over three decades on the job, was dismissed late in the 1997 season, accused of embezzlement. However, neither the team nor anyone connected to it brought charges against Priore. Paul's father Nick was released after the season; he immediately found work across town with the rival Mets. A year later, in July, Paul Priore filed suit against the Yankees' franchise, the team's general manager, Brian Cashman, and relief pitchers Bob Wickman (who'd since been shipped from the Yankees to the Milwaukee Brewers), Jeff Nelson, and Mariano Rivera for sexual harassment, slander, and wrongful dismissal. The lawsuit's allegations included the following encounters:

> That beginning in April of 1996 and continuing until June 1996, the Defendant Bob Wickman . . . on numerous occasions inside the clubhouse at Yankee Stadium, did expose his penis to [Priore], did rub his penis against [Priore], did grab and touch [Priore's] private parts, did expose his penis to [Priore] and did attempt to insert it inside [Priore's] mouth, did thrust his body up against [Priore's]

body and did repeatedly direct anti-gay remarks towards [Priore] and refer to him as a "faggot"....

That beginning in April 1996 and continuing until July 1997, the Defendants, Jeff Nelson and Mariano Rivera ... on numerous occasions inside the clubhouse at Yankee Stadium did repeatedly direct anti-gay comments toward [Priore] and call [Priore] a "faggot" and did threaten to perform assaultive and sexual acts to [Priore].

That on or about May 1996 ... in the clubhouse at Yankee Stadium ... the Defendant Wickman, while holding a baseball bat in his hand and waving it at [Priore], did say to [Priore], in sum and substance, "You know you want it you faggot, you know you like it," and the Defendants Wickman and Nelson did . . . pull on [Priore's] pants and . . . Wickman did say to [Priore], in sum and substance, "I'm going to stick this inside of you."

Priore further alleges that he told Yankee executives about the incidents and they failed to stop the harassment. Instead, he claims, they decided to accuse him falsely of stealing various items as a pretext for firing him. Priore, who had just received the news that he'd contracted HIV, also claimed that at the time the team found out that he was HIV-positive, they sought a pretext to fire him.

The media responded to the public dissemination of the charges in early August by asking Rick Cerrone, the Yankees' public relations man, about the allegations. Unsurprisingly, he vehemently denied all charges. Reporters also confronted the accused players. Rivera refused to comment. Nelson and Wickman (contacted by phone in Milwaukee) both claimed to be shocked, characterizing Priore as a former friend and the charges themselves as laughable.

The news cycle about the lawsuit lasted less than twenty-four hours. Stories summarized the charges, glossing over the ugly details of the alleged incidents, and recited the team's uniform denials. The *Post* was both fairer and more scurrilous than its rivals. The newspaper contacted the Priore household (the younger Priore still lived at home) seeking comment; Paul was unavailable, and the elder Priore refused to talk about the case. Happy to make anyone who would disrupt the great Yankee season look bad, a story in the *Post* claimed Priore was a "troubled young man" in search of a book contract in the wake of his dismissal and further accused him of seeking favors from celebrities in his pursuit of a budding acting career. Essentially, the *Post* turned Priore into a cross between Kato Kaelin and Linda Tripp. With such an easy villain at hand, one would have expected the tabloid to ride the story hard. Instead, the coverage ended as soon it started, and, according to Priore's lawyer, no one even tried to contact him or his client.

Some of Priore's most serious charges were leveled at Brian Cashman, the team's apple-cheeked general manager. No reporter, it seems, ever pressed Cashman about the case. Most of those covering the team wanted not to believe the allegations (and it is likely that some believed sexual harassment itself to be a crock). More troubling is the possibility of cronyism working to protect Cashman from any public scrutiny. The GM, who played second base at Catholic University, was also a high-school teammate of Lawrence Rocca, *Newsday*'s lead reporter on the Yankees. Since Mark Willes closed down its New York City edition, *Newsday* lags behind the other papers in circulation within the five boroughs, but the paper is frequently more aggressive in its local investigative reporting than the *Times*. Nevertheless, *Newsday*'s approach, like every other outlet in town, resulted in silence.

Sports talk radio, a more reliably conservative bastion than even the sports pages, never mentioned the lawsuit. Yankee fans I talked to about the case had a universal reaction of concern. Not for Priore, but for a lawsuit that might distract the team and frustrate its effort to break single-season records. Imagine a similar set of allegations involving a high-profile figure in any other aspect of public life, and it's hard to see the coverage dissipating so quickly. If these incidents occurred under the executive control of Donald Trump or Woody Allen, the news cycle would never end.

Without a McGwire or Sosa on the roster, the Yanks' success in 1998 was often presented as a testimony to the value of teamwork over individual glory. Dissecting the code of omertà suggested by Priore's allegations, which involved questioning an ethic that values the team's performance above all else, might have endangered the power of that myth. Sportswriters are notoriously lazy, and frequently serve as little more than house organs for management propaganda. Uncovering the truth behind Priore's allegations was an investigative journey no major media outlet (all of whom had hundreds of thousands of dollars of ad revenue tied to the Yankees' good fortune) was willing to take. Tightly bound groups keep secrets, and the always professional Yankees seemed especially good, with the exception of the blustery Steinbrenner, at maintaining their privacy. For example, reports of Bernie Williams's alienation from the rest of the team during the postseason triggered rumors that hinted at some personal, off-field problems. However, the rumors remained just that: vague, unsubstantiated, and, by season's end, forgotten.

A year earlier, bullpen ace Jose Mesa, Rivera's counterpart on the 1997 Indians, had been under an even darker legal cloud. He spent Opening Day of the 1997 season in a Cuyahoga County courtroom facing sexual assault charges stemming from an incident in Cleveland just before Christmas, 1996. The relief pitcher, a married man with five kids, and a friend picked up two women in the Flats and took them to a nearby motel. At that point, the stories conflicted, but all agreed that some sexual contact, along with an argument, had taken place. One of the women, stopped by police for making an illegal right turn shortly after leaving the hotel, had bruises on her face. Despite the physical evidence and compelling testimony, Mesa was acquitted on all counts, a surprising verdict by hometown umps who may well have been more worried about the Indians' fate than that of the victims.

After his acquittal, Mesa claimed, "God came through for me." The Indians' brain trust reinstalled Mesa in his role as the team's closer, the flamethrower pitched reasonably well throughout the season, and the expected fan disenchantment dissolved. In the playoffs, Mesa threw the final pitch as the Indians closed out the Yankees and then the Orioles. He was on the mound in the bottom of the ninth inning in game seven of the World Series with a one-run lead over the host Marlins when his undeserving dream season finally turned into a nightmare. With the Indians three outs away from erasing fifty years of disappointment, Mesa could not hold the lead. A half-hour later, the rent-an-All-Star Marlins finished off their stunning run through the 1997 playoffs. Cleveland's fans, generous about Mesa's off-field mishaps, turned brutal. Forty-five thousand booed each time Mesa took the field during the 1998 season until the Indians finally caved into their fans' wishes and dealt him off to San Francisco. Justice, in a sense, was served, but it was on-field failure that was needed to trigger universal censure.

When the Yankees started the postseason, anyone who found merit in Priore's charges watched closely to see whether Nelson and Rivera would suffer the same fate Mesa had endured a year earlier. Such individuals did not reside within the Yankee Nation. Fans embrace a "Just Win, Baby" belief system because they know, despite propaganda to the contrary, that the game contains no unique moral dimension that elevates it above other human endeavors. A bat doesn't know whether the man swinging it cheats on his wife; nor does a ball know whether the man hurling it believes blacks are inferior.

Baseball's action depends on physics, not metaphysics.

As the Yankees rolled through the postseason with eleven victories in thirteen games, Nelson and Rivera both played starring roles, leading the team in games pitched. Rivera pitched brilliantly in ten contests, surrendering no runs in more than thirteen innings. Nelson appeared in eight games, with only one bad outing in the Cleveland series blemishing an otherwise excellent record. When Andy Pettitte tired in the eighth inning of the fourth game of the World Series while protecting a three-run lead, Yankee manager Joe Torre put the ball in Nelson's hand with one out, two men on, and the dangerous Greg Vaughn at the plate. One mighty swing of Vaughn's fifty-home-run bat and the game would be even. Nelson struck Vaughn out, and Torre summoned Rivera to get the last four outs. Rivera gave up hits in the eighth and the ninth but worked his way out of both jams, closing the game by inducing the Padres' final batter to ground out to third baseman Scott Brosius. In the visitors' clubhouse, the Yankees celebrated the team's second title in three years with a clapping, singing tribute to the World Series MVP (*clap-clap, clap-clap-clap* SCOTT E BRO SHUS) that perfectly mimicked the Bleacher Creatures' own melody.

*         *         *

Despite the championship and their apparent inclusion in the celebration afterwards, something bothered the Creatures as the players and coaches who brought home the World Series trophy trekked up the Canyon of Heroes beneath a blizzard of paper. It wasn't the pack of truants (invited to play hooky by a mayor who said he learned more from baseball than school) vandalizing FBI cars, or the conflagration of shredded garbage that flared up and threatened to endanger spectators. It wasn't even the sight of the Mayor and the Boss, the dynamic duo apparently planning to move the team out of the Bronx, that raised their ire.

No, they felt cheated, believing that they deserved a float of their own, a chance to bask in the reflected glory that bathed over their heroes. The sight of innumerable state and city pols rolling up Broadway and grabbing a sliver of the wild devotion spilling over the Yankees must have rankled these true believers. Most disturbing was a vision of five heavyweights crammed in the back of one of the convertibles gliding through the parade. The thirtysomething men, their generous bellies and stingy hairlines confidently revealed, had a huge capital letter painted in blue on each of their midsections: A N S K Y. The five oversized men, the "Ansky guys," were actors in one of the most successful ad campaigns to hit New York City in a long time.

Adidas, the German sportswear and shoe manufacturer, had decided to challenge its longtime rival Nike by forming an alliance with the most recognized name in American sports, the New York Yankees. Initiated early in 1997, this partnership threatened every prior agreement among baseball's franchises to share national merchandising revenues. The Boss believed that other owners had no claim on any of his profits. The Adidas deal was yet another chance for Steinbrenner to make millions more than his rivals and destroy the healthy competitive balance the game had enjoyed just a decade earlier. When acting commissioner Bud Selig nixed the agreement, Steinbrenner sued, claiming that the other owners were acting as a cartel unfairly restraining trade (certainly an argument the players' union will find useful at some later date).

While the case was pending, Major League Baseball allowed the Yankees to run ads within the team's local region as long as they included no players, not even those with sponsorship deals with Adidas. The creative talent at Adidas America's advertising agency saw baseball's restrictions as a challenge. By necessity, they decided to organize their campaign around spectators. Recognizing the irrational devotion of Yankee fans, they created five fictional characters,

the "Ansky guys," to align their product with the most extreme exponents of consumer loyalty. The signature commercial in the first year
began by showing the back seat of a cab bulging with five beefy guys
who wore huge blue painted letters over their exposed midsections.
A cabby with a thick accent looks in the rear-view mirror and asks,
"What the hell is Ansky?" The guys look at each other and see
they're seated out of order. They then perform the amusingly difficult
task of crawling over each other until they have properly spelled out
YANKS, and the commercial ends with one of the heavyweights hollering "Yanks." For its precise ability to show consumer madness and
link it to Adidas, the campaign was rewarded with awards at the
Cannes Film Festival and a silver Clio at the world's largest advertising festival.

What were the Ansky guys, five fictional fans, doing in the middle
of a parade celebrating actual accomplishments? The Yankee celebration was sponsored entirely by corporations. Adidas, a primary
sponsor, was invited to use the party as yet another platform for
product identification, and the Ansky guys had become the company's link to the Yankees. Every local TV station presented hours of
coverage of the parade and gave the Ansky guys free airtime that
would have cost Adidas hundreds of thousands of dollars. One news-
cast even spent a few minutes interviewing the Ansky guys as if they
were real fans.

The inauthenticity of this display was overwhelming. Actual
fan devotion had been magically transformed into yet another way
to move product, and the media that presented those ads now
unquestioningly affirmed the actors' identification as real Yankee
fans. No wonder the Bleacher Creatures felt a little bit cheated.
Even though his own paper, the *Daily News*, had been one of the
event's biggest sponsors, Filip Bondy, the Creatures' own media
insider, could not find any way for his fellow loyalists to secure a
place in the celebration and instead chronicled their uncomfort-

able return to the space they had originally been assigned, on the outside looking in.

\*                    \*                    \*

Although the crowd in the bleachers will return home to their separate lives as soon as the game ends, for a few hours they inhabit a place where only one identity is acceptable: Yankee fan. Here Benedict Anderson's imagined community is very real indeed. Any statement that violates the group's one idea can prove dangerous. Fans wearing hats in support of the rival Mets or Red Sox are hounded by hundreds of fans pointing and chanting "Mets Suck" or "Boston Sucks."

The bleachers are an American Speakers' Corner, with an artless wit. Background crowd noise on baseball telecasts is as barren of meaning as a sitcom laugh track. The actual soundtrack out in the bleachers is loud, chaotic, often passionate, frequently vulgar, and occasionally funny. Any telecast that featured a live mike in the bleachers for a few minutes would probably increase ratings and certainly generate countless complaints at the FCC.

The bleachers at Yankee Stadium have open seating. Fans are not separated by team allegiance as they would be for precautionary reasons at English soccer games. The only protection offered is to the ushers. None are employed in the bleachers. During a Monday night game with Atlanta earlier in the season, three young African-American men, one wearing a Braves hat, took a seat high in the bleachers. They quickly began to exchange taunts with nearby Yankee fans who serenaded the traitors with a raunchy version of Atlanta's signature cheer, the tomahawk chop. To the same melody, hundreds swayed their arms with middle fingers extended and chanted "Fuck The Braves . . . Fuck The Braves."

As the tension escalated, a slim young white woman, seated a few rows back and emboldened in a way unimaginable in any other setting, approached the Braves' fan and screamed at him from no more than a foot away. When a white cop ascended from below to break it up, he confronted the Braves' fan, first telling him to shut the fuck up and listen. Then he assured the young man that if anything happened, the cop would hold him responsible and toss him out of the park. After the situation reignited, the cop sat the rest of the game amidst the hecklers in the last row to spot any problems.

During the same game, a gaggle of suburban kids lined the fence, high-school baseball teammates decked out in blue war paint that spelled out Y A N K E E S on their chests. After the key hit of a game against Ted Turner's Braves went over the head of young Atlanta center fielder Andruw Jones, the most extroverted member of the group rode the relaxed phenom, repeatedly hollering, "You suck cock, Andruw."

A few rows in front of the high-school kids, two Puerto Rican families raised their national flag and screamed wildly for Puerto Rican-born Yankees Ricky Ledee and Jorge Posada every time they came to the plate. The kids, second-generation Americans fluent in English, Sega, and pro wrestling, asserted themselves. Their parents were much more tentative in expressing their opinions, although the family patriarch criticized Paul O'Neill's "bad attitude" (clearly a response to the veteran's visible displays of anger at the plate) in a discussion with his eldest son. The fans in the bleachers appeared much more diverse in age and ethnicity than in the rest of the stadium. Even their tastes seemed more wide-ranging. In the field boxes, most fans wearing Yankee jerseys sported the numbers "21" and "23" for Paul O'Neill and Don Mattingly. The bleachers had a fair share of fans with those two jerseys, alongside fans wearing "2" and "51" and "39" for brothers Jeter, Williams, and Strawberry.

The worst behavior in the bleachers is mimicked by most fans, regardless of race, gender, or even age. Cap Day drew a huge crowd of over 48,000 for the last game before the All-Star break, a Sunday afternoon matchup in early July between the red-hot Yankees and the slumping Orioles. Just as the national anthem ended, I entered the park and found a few open seats in the sixth row of the left-field bleachers. As I sat my 6'7" frame down, I noticed a six-year-old boy seated with his family directly behind me. I scooted over one spot to avoid blocking the youngster's view. A few innings later, with the Yankees at bat, I noticed the boy climbing on to his seat. Before I could turn around, he started to heckle the struggling Orioles center fielder, Brady Anderson, a veteran with a vague resemblance to James Dean, by derisively chanting his first name. Rumors about Anderson's sexuality have flourished for years. In a macho world that has never been confronted with a major leaguer who is openly homosexual, Anderson's bachelorhood and lack of high-profile celebrity girlfriends with good looks to match his own has kept the pot roiling.

The kid yelled, "Brady, you're a faggot." The words were harsh, stunning. It's hard to believe he knew exactly what "faggot" meant, but he sure as hell knew it was an insult. In response to the youthful yelp, many seated nearby responded with laughter and shouts of approval. Nobody, myself included, confronted this candidate for the live road show of South Park. The child's exclamation reinforced the subculture's homophobia. Having gotten his opinion off his tiny chest, the young boy sat down and proceeded to watch the rest of the game without audible incident or censure.

Of course, self-censorship exists even in those bleachers. Yankee fans of all ages feel comfortable calling an opponent a cocksucker, a faggot, a pussy, a sissy, or an asshole, but they won't yell nigger at an enemy player. Once acceptable, racial slurs are no longer commonplace. This seems less an act of civility than a sense of pragmatism. That word could start a fight even with nine-inning allies.

## THE CROSS IS IN THE BALLPARK

*Why did they play during the Sacred Hours? I am told they insist-*
*ed they couldn't miss a single day of the season. Even the stock*
*market closes on Good Friday. Playing on Good Friday cheapens*
*our culture. I resent it.*

— John Cardinal O'Connor

The Yankees and the Catholic Church share a common ancestry. Both powerful civic institutions eagerly accepted the protective embrace of Tammany Hall. One of the leading figures at the dedication of St. Patrick's Cathedral in 1879, a defining event in the history of Catholicism in the city, was "Honest John" Kelly, who became the first Irish boss of Tammany in the aftermath of the Tweed scandals. Despite opposition from Giants' owner Andrew Freedman, the American League's entry into New York City was shepherded to a desirable home in Washington Heights in 1903. Freedman was well connected, but the new club's owners, Frank Farrell and Big Bill Devery, had equal pull within Tammany. The team's second owner, Jacob Ruppert, had represented New York in Congress on the Tammany line.

For nearly a century, the Yankees have often seemed to be an adult team in the city's Catholic-school league. The championship of that league's baseball tournament is played annually at the Stadium, and when the Yankees used a variety of pretenses to stop the title game from being played there in the spring of 1998, the furor leaked into the dailies. Funerals for nearly every major Yankee, from Babe Ruth to Thurman Munson and Billy Martin, have been held at St. Patrick's, the Midtown Manhattan home of the Irish American–controlled Archdiocese of New York. Yankee Stadium has played host to mass weddings, rock concerts, and a prolific number of non-Yankee sporting events, including title fights and the Giants-Colts

1958 overtime clash many consider the greatest football game ever played. However, the only plaque in Monument Park unrelated to the Yankees commemorates none of these affairs. It serves instead to remind fans walking among the flowers and the tributes to DiMaggio, Ruth, Mantle, and company that Yankee Stadium was the site of two papal masses.

How strange then to see Cardinal O'Connor, powerful Yankee ally and baseball fan ("I love the Yankees. I love the Mets. I love baseball," wrote the archbishop in *Catholic New York*), so upset that he refused to attend any game during the 1998 season and made that decision known to the public. Baseball's sin was playing on April 10, 1998. On that date the Yankees hosted the Athletics and drew a record crowd for the game, which started at 1 PM and opened the home schedule. That date was also Good Friday, when, according to the Church, Christ was crucified between the hours of noon and 3 PM. The idea of baseball in the Bronx during those hours mortified O'Connor.

The spokesman for the Archdiocese of New York assured everyone that the cardinal's column was not a call for a baseball boycott, a relief both to the Yankees and New York Catholics from Cuomo to Giuliani. More than a century earlier, New York's Catholics had pushed the Protestant establishment to allow Sunday baseball; now the Catholic establishment was calling for an end to Good Friday hardball. The conflict was in some ways unavoidable: every major-league team is scheduled to play each Friday during the major-league season. While the controversy demonstrates the limits of Church literalism (the crucifixion itself did not occur between noon and 3 PM Eastern Standard Time; temporally accurate services would occur in the early morning hours in New York City), the team could have avoided much of the furor. O'Connor praised the archenemy Red Sox because they chose to start their game at 3:05 PM, after the time in question, and banned alcohol sales. The Red Sox schedule also accommodated Jewish fans who needed to get home before Passover began at sundown. Although he asserted that the Yankees had a long tradition of playing home openers during the day, Yankee spokesman Rick Cerrone said, "With the respect that we have for Cardinal O'Connor, we will certainly give consideration to his concerns and his suggestions in the future."

During the 1998 season, the Mets and Yankees combined to draw well over 5 million fans. Apparently, O'Connor's principled stand inspired few followers among the hundreds of thousands of baseball-loving Catholics in New York City. By the end of baseball's season of resurrection, O'Connor would reestablish his faithful connection to the national pastime. Even if he refused to go to the games, he could invite a few ballplayers to his home turf.

The Catholic Church has been the key private source of services for immigrants to New York City, offering, among other things, food, shelter, legal aid, job placement services, and English courses. Beyond providing services, the Church's strategy for appealing to recent arrivals involved the development of churches with priests and nuns who would minister to immigrants in their own language. Looking to expand, the Church rejected the seductive lure of nativism at nearly every turn. A history of anti-Catholic discrimina-tion—the churches of antebellum Irish and German immigrants had been targets of America First attacks and the Johnson-Reed Act insured that every European group entering the U.S. lost ground except the Protestant British—also grounded the Church's position. Even after the Irish and German Catholics had become successful third-generation immigrants by the turn of the century, the Church welcomed millions of new arrivals from Italy. A half-century later, as one of the nation's most powerful institutions serving a primarily suburban, completely assimilated parish, the Church expanded to make room for hundreds of thousands of new members from Puerto Rico who replaced Italians, Irish, and Germans in urban neighbor-hoods and churches.

Cardinal O'Connor, seeking a way to put himself back in the good graces of baseball fans, understood Sammy Sosa's popularity among the Church's emerging Dominican parishes and appreciated the slugger's good works for his suffering countrymen. O'Connor, along with Giuliani (who was attempting to broaden the always uncertain appeal of Republicans in New York City), invited Sosa to the city during the opening weekend of the World Series being hosted by the Yankees. The evening before the Series started, O'Connor honored Sosa during a special Spanish-language mass at St. Patrick's Cathedral to celebrate the twentieth anniversary of the papacy of John Paul II. As O'Connor awarded the Medal of John Paul II to Sosa for his charity and sportsmanship, most of the worshippers gave the Cub slugger a standing ovation. A few even waved Dominican flags.

Placing a red skullcap on Sosa's head, O'Connor joked in Spanish, "You were once a little Cub, now you're a big Cardinal." Sosa then climbed the pulpit to offer brief remarks. He recalled his difficult childhood—washing cars and shining shoes to help his family get by after his father died—and marveled at receiving a tribute from the cardinal. He concluded by offering himself as a beacon for others: "If you keep going, you can accomplish anything." The Church's interaction with Sosa demonstrated a continuing respect for the ethnic diversity of its worshippers, not to mention a command of public relations. O'Connor's embrace of Yankee hero Hernandez a week later, and the Church's behind-the-scenes effort to coax Castro into allowing the Hernandez family to leave Cuba and join El Duque were even more masterful. The Church, frequently attacked for its rigidity, continues to benefit from an acute understanding of the rapidly changing demographics of the city.

## A CITY DIVIDED AGAINST ITSELF

*You see, the Mets are losers, just like nearly everybody else in life. This is a team for the cab driver who gets held up and the guy who loses out on a promotion because he didn't maneuver himself to lunch with the boss enough. It is the team for every guy who has to get out of bed in the morning and go to work for short money on a job he does not like. And it is the team for every woman who looks up ten years later and sees her husband eating dinner in a T-shirt and wonders how the hell she ever let this guy talk her into getting married. The Yankees? Who does well enough to root for them, Laurence Rockefeller?*

—Jimmy Breslin

*Suddenly the Mets fans made sense to me. What we were witnessing was precisely the opposite kind of rooting that goes on across the river. This was the losing cheer, the gallant yell for a good try—antimatter to the sounds at Yankee Stadium. This was a new recognition that perfection is admirable but a trifle inhuman, and that a stumbling kind of semi-success can be much more warming. Most of all, perhaps, these exultant for the Mets were also yells for ourselves, and came from a wry, half-understood recognition that there is more Met than Yankee in every one of us. I knew for whom that foghorn blew, it blew for me.*

—Roger Angell

While the Dodgers and Giants left a city full of Yankee haters empty-handed after the 1957 season, New York did not remain a one-team town for long. The threatened Continental League and congressional hearings into baseball's antitrust exemption forced the game's owners into the first expansion in six decades. The Mets, who sought baseball fans abandoned by the Dodgers and Giants, were born. Despite an underdog status, the Mets outdrew the Yankees by their third year in existence. During the 1964 season, the Yankees won 99 games and the American League while the Mets lost 109 games but claimed the hearts of millions of self-identified outsiders.

During the thirty-seven years the two franchises have shared the city, the Yankees have made the postseason twelve times, and the Mets just four. Shea Stadium is no pleasure palace, and its site is hardly convenient. Nonetheless, the Mets have drawn more fans than the Yankees during twenty-one seasons, solid evidence that Steinbrenner is failing in his efforts to draw fans to Yankee Stadium. In 1988, the last year the Mets led the major-league fan race, the crosstown rivals combined to draw nearly 5.7 million spectators. Ten years later, with the Yankees breaking league records and the Mets in playoff contention until the final weekend during "baseball's greatest year," the two teams drew half a million fewer patrons. The midseason trade for future Hall-of-Famer Mike Piazza nearly doubled Met attendance during the remainder of the season, and, with both franchises likely to be in playoff contention in 1999, a renaissance at the gate for major-league baseball in New York is probable. Such a trend will not be welcome beyond the Lincoln Tunnel given the history of suffering by the rest of major-league baseball during boom periods in Gotham.

The Yankees could draw three million fans every year with one simple change: more home games against the Mets. The Subway Series, which started as a result of the introduction of interleague play a few years ago, sells out the first day tickets are available in the dead of winter. The Mets hosted the series during the summer of '98 and drew three straight crowds of over 50,000 for the first time in franchise history. Tabloids ran special sections, scalpers charged prices that would have been outrageous even during the playoffs, and, in anticipation of trouble between fans, police security was increased tenfold. Save for Paul O'Neill's homer off the abysmal Mel Rojas and a subsequent squabble between Met manager Bobby Valentine and a mocking press corps, the 1998 games were far from memorable. Yet the TV ratings were the highest for any baseball games in New York City all year. By any measure, the Mets against the Yankees is exactly what the public wants. Steinbrenner responded to the demand by saying that three games a year against the Mets was more than enough. Cognizant that the Mets drew 3 million fans for consecutive seasons during their last boom and that the city's undecideds may be drawn to his rivals, Steinbrenner is happy to duck games against the crosstown team. Fortunately for New York baseball fans, major-league baseball doubled the number of games between the Mets and Yanks despite Steinbrenner's wishes.

The Boss' Nixonian paranoia about the Mets trickles down to haunt the whole team. His players and manager do everything they can to deflect this pressure. Public statements playing down the contests with the Mets as just three more games on the calendar were mere spin. The Yanks' conspicuous relief after winning the first two games was a more accurate gauge of the team's feelings. During a season drained of tension by a huge lead on all rivals, the Mets performed a useful service for the 1998 Yankees. For three games, the Yankees felt playoff pressure and could walk through a dress rehearsal for the important games a few months away.

It is safe to say that the Met Nation of old, described above by Angell and Breslin, no longer exists. Met fans, like their Yankee counterparts, believe they deserve a quality product. Given the team's irregular postseason appearances, averaging once every nine years, it's hard to understand where this faith springs from. Perhaps such expectations are unavoidable during boom periods on Wall Street. The swaggering Mets of the late eighties (how much more dynamic Mookie, Darryl, and Doc, Carter, Hernandez, Darling, Cone, and Dykstra seem than the members of the town's best team now) have cast a long shadow, and, in it, the once-famed Met loyalty has waned.

What remains of the old days is an appealing cheesiness in the way the Mets deliver product to their fans. The orange-and-blue color scheme alone is enough to move the Mets outside the realm of life-and-death seriousness inhabited by the Yankees. Add between-innings entertainment that mimics minor-league fare, complete with a goofy mascot and cheerleaders bearing rocket launchers that fire cheap freebies into the furthest reaches of the upper deck, and it's clear we're not in Yankee Land anymore. Unlike their coolly efficient older brothers across town, the Mets, like younger siblings everywhere, aim to please their audience in any way they can.

## NEED TWO?

*Because of scalpers' practices of reselling tickets to events at exorbitant prices, New York fans have found it next to impossible to obtain World Series tickets at face value prices. Understandably, baseball fans get caught up in the fervor of the moment, particularly when you have the Yankees in the Series. They become easy prey for the scalpers and find themselves forking over huge sums to those cashing in on the loyalty of baseball fans.*

—Dennis Vacco, New York State attorney general during
   the 1998 World Series

Tickets to the 1998 World Series were harder to find than a disinterested response to the Clinton scandal. Tabloid headlines blared with reports of tickets selling for $5,000. While scalpers were more than willing to take advantage of scarcity, they had not created this condition. The policies of the Yankees and major-league baseball were responsible. Fewer than 10 percent of the seats at Yankee Stadium were sold to the general public during the '98 Series because the team allowed season-ticket holders, even those with partial plans, to snatch up most of the seats, and the Yankees and the league distributed thousands of seats (some free) to sponsors, local politicians, editors, and publishers. Tickets were scarce not because of those free-

marketeers outside the park, but instead thanks to Steinbrenner and
Selig, who wanted all their influential friends at the party, and Rupert
Murdoch, who needed to battle tabloid rumors that his network's
star Calista Flockhart was starving herself to death by making
America watch the poor girl stuff a hot dog into her mouth. The
director did not linger long enough to see if she swallowed.

The scarcity created by New York's First Scalper, Steinbrenner,
allowed him to charge $300 per ticket for field boxes to the World
Series, four times what he'd demanded just two years earlier. Torre,
Steinbrenner's loyal $2 million-a-year employee, brushed aside con-
cerns about the price hike with a comparison to the even more inflated prices for front-row seats at Knick games. As Phil Mushnick noted
in the *New York Post*, the increase meant that a family of four with
season tickets in the field boxes paid over $20,000 for tickets alone
by the time the season was over. One fan complained to Mushnick, "I
shouldn't be expected to pay that much for baseball tickets. No one
should. It's as if they found out what scalpers could get, then attached
that price to the face of the ticket."

New York State attorney general, Republican Dennis Vacco,
blamed scalpers rather than Steinbrenner for ticket scarcity–the
equivalent of blaming bank robbers for long lines to see tellers. Poor
passionate Yankee fans became Vacco's Victims, "easy prey" who
"find themselves forking over huge sums of money." Vacco, in the
midst of a difficult reelection campaign, spoke out boldly against lais-
sez-faire capitalism (which is what a secondary market for baseball
tickets—like a secondary market for common stock, say, the NYSE—
faithfully delivers). When Republicans advocate price ceilings in New
York City, the world must be nearing the millennium.

The election drove Vacco's grandstanding efforts to "root out corruption" and paint ticket brokers as a social threat akin to organized
crime and drug dealers. In New York, the attorney general has very
limited jurisdiction. Without show trials in which to make a name

for himself, Vacco had few ways to attract positive public attention. Unfortunately for the streetwalkers who represent the second tier of the resale market (the upper class set up brokerages in New Jersey where scalping is legal and buy and sell from the comfort of their own offices), ticket scalping is under the attorney general's domain. Vacco, needing as much free media as possible, especially in New York City where Republicans struggle, could find no better issue for populist appeal than outrageous Yankee ticket prices. The knee-jerk media ran stories about scalpers and Vacco for a few news cycles, thereby aiding brokers, by advertising their product, even more than they helped the attorney general. In the midst of his heated effort to purge New York City of all ticket brokers, Vacco sat down for an interview about his candidacy (with the same Jewish weekly in the city that reported D'Amato's costly "putzhead" remark about opponent Chuck Schumer) and asserted that he was tough on crime, but couldn't just execute all the banditos standing in front of bodegas. Vacco's implication that all the city's Hispanic Americans who hung out on the streets were criminals betrayed an ignorance about the cramped conditions of New York City life and a racist stereotype about the criminality of an ethnic group. When he tried to back away from his remarks by asserting that he said "bandits," not "banditos," he only buried himself further, triggering the largest Hispanic turnout for an election in city history. Those new voters refused to become Vacco's future victims, and their overwhelming support for Democratic candidates not only elected Vacco's opponent but also helped push D'Amato to a stunningly large defeat.

Perhaps it wasn't just the Hispanic vote, maybe it was the scalpers, too. For what it's worth, I never paid above face value and usually paid less than half. Scalpers, like other true entrepreneurs, suffer in a soft market; they scarf up a tremendous amount of tickets for the whole season (in part to secure access to postseason tickets), betting that most nights they will make out. During the week or when poor teams are in town (especially as game time approaches and passes), little demand exists and prices dip rapidly to the point where any money a scalper receives represents a ticket he didn't have to burn.

City law makes the resale of tickets even at or below face value illegal within a thousand feet of the Stadium. The purchaser is treated like some sort of innocent bystander; although it takes two to make a market, the law sees no reason to punish Vacco's Victims. This statute allowed Vacco and Giuliani to sic undercover cops on anyone trying to resell tickets at any price throughout the playoffs, indiscriminately arresting hundreds, including one attorney in the office of the city's corporation counsel, the legal muscle behind the mayor's relentless battles, caught capitalizing on an office perk.

*           *           *

In 1977, the Yankees beat Kansas City to reach the World Series for the second straight year. The tens of thousands of World Series tickets made available to the public that year were distributed through a mail-in lottery. Two rising stars in the public sector, friends and devoted Yankee fans, agreed to share their tickets if either hit the jackpot. That year, they got lucky and saw all the games in person. The Yankees returned to face the Dodgers in the fall classic again the following season. This time, the buddies, Rudy Giuliani, future mayor, and Peter Powers, future head of the mayor's Stop the Yankee Stadium Referendum charter review commission, were not as fortunate. Nevertheless, as Giuliani tells it, the two men scrounged around among their already numerous contacts and found tickets for every game. The corruption reflected in this sort of networking is so routine that Giuliani, who jealously guards his image as Mr. Clean, told this story without prompting or shame to a live radio audience. Most Yankee fans, lacking insider connections, were not so lucky.

Twenty years later, fewer than 5,000 of the 57,000 seats for the Series were made available to the public. On the night the Yankees won the American League title, the team announced plans for a ticket lottery that would occur two days later. Between 7 AM and noon, randomly numbered wristbands would be distributed to those who wanted to buy tickets to the first two games of the World Series. A half-hour later, a number would be drawn, the person with that number would head the line, and those with subsequent numbers would follow until the tickets ran out.

The lottery was created in response to the unparalleled demand for tickets in 1995, when the Yankees reached the playoffs after the longest drought since they'd moved to the Bronx. The "first-come, first-served" policy that year attracted hundreds of fans who camped out at the stadium for days waiting for the tickets to go on sale. During the 1996 World Series a similar ticket distribution policy nearly caused a riot outside the Stadium. Rewarding intense dedication with tickets seemed just, but the Yankee front office and city officials feared what would happen if more fans camped out the next time.

With a lottery, no advantage would be gained by sleeping out. In theory, a fan who arrived at the stadium just before noon and secured a wristband would have as good a chance as someone who slept out in order to secure the first wristband. In practice, this system worked well in the first two rounds of the playoffs when demand was within reason. I arrived at the stadium in the middle of each of those lotteries and received a wristband a few minutes later.

The Series was another matter entirely. The lottery was announced on a Tuesday night, with wristbands to be handed out on Thursday morning. Nevertheless, a handful of devoted fans secured their places in line immediately. As the media coverage escalated, the crowds at the stadium grew. By Wednesday night, hundreds of Yankee fans had camped out, just like under the prior system, merely for a chance to secure the lottery bracelets.

Conditions were miserable. To control the huge crowd, the NYPD set up dozens of holding pens, massive blue police sawhorses corralling the patient loyalists. The pens, packed with tired, dirty, agitated bodies, extended all the way around the Stadium and down River Avenue. The smell of urine was everywhere. No one in the Yankee organization had announced that the number of wristbands would be limited, but these fans weren't taking any chances.

When I arrived at the Stadium mid-morning on the day of the lottery, all the cops assured me that my chances were nil, not only of getting a ticket, but of securing a wristband. The campers had been right in not trusting the Yankees to run a fair lottery. I was annoyed, but my frustration was nothing compared to that of the people who'd been confined by police barricades for hours with nothing to show for it.

The next day, one unhappy participant in the Yankee cattle drive called the mayor's radio show (broadcast on WABC, home to Rush Limbaugh and the Yankees' flagship station) to complain about the way ticket distribution was handled. The disappointed fan told Giuliani that cops at the stadium had told her that if she had any complaints she should take them to the mayor. "I didn't do it," Giuliani, secure in his boatload of tickets, alibied. "The city didn't sell Yankee tickets. The Yankees sell their tickets. I don't think there's any perfect way to do it."

The lottery was manifestly unjust. Back near the entrance to the promised land where bracelets were being doled out, I watched two cops approach a car that had just double-parked. I assumed they would tell the driver to move along, but instead the cops exchanged pleasantries with what seemed to be a friend. The cops asked the driver if he wanted their help. Sure enough, a passenger emerged and was immediately escorted to the front of the line. When a Yankee fan lucky enough to secure tickets through the lottery called WABC to complain about a similar incident he'd witnessed, macho talk-show host and professional vigilante Curtis Sliwa accused the caller of fab-

ricating the story, then attacked the man's credentials as a ticket holder and fan before hanging up on him.

This kind of corruption abounds at Yankee Stadium, especially in
the netherworld of the bleachers. This section doesn't generate much
revenue for Steinbrenner, and he makes getting tickets in the cheap seats
almost as hard as purchasing World Series tickets. Bleacher tickets
aren't sold in advance unless the rest of the stadium is already sold out.
They are sold at a single window to the walk-up crowd before game
time. The Yankees normally employ only one ticket seller for the bleachers, which creates a line that snakes hundreds of feet up River Avenue.

This reproduction of the Disney experience in the Bronx forces
bleacherites to wait at least a half-hour for seats. The less patient have
three options: buy a higher priced ticket for another part of the stadium, buy a bleacher ticket from one of the scalpers working the
nearly static line, or slip some money to one of the security guards at
a bleacher gate. Well, they also have a fourth: watch the game at home
or in a neighborhood bar. Steinbrenner can't maximize attendance
when he puts a chastity belt around the bleacher entrance.

The scalping that exploits these conditions is truly offensive.
During the season, bleacher seating is open: once you've made it past
the bleacher entrance, you can sit anywhere you want. Theoretically,
no ticket should be better than any other. Of course, the sooner you
get in, the better your chance of obtaining a good seat, which creates
pressure to buy early. Understanding this phenomenon, a handful of
homeless people work the lines, offering to sell tickets for a few dollars over face value. But these grifters are amateurs; the real action is
in the parking lots and along the south wall of the stadium, where
the pros try to move box seats.

Nevertheless, anyone waiting on line has to wonder about the origins of this seemingly bottomless supply of unattainable ducats. The
scalpers sometimes convince people at the front of the line to buy
extra tickets for them with sob stories or a little cash. Most of the

tickets get placed in the scalpers' hands by the ticket seller himself. The guy working the window lets the grifters cut the line in exchange for a share of profits from the illicit sales.

But you don't even need a ticket. During the weekend series with the Red Sox in May, the games on Saturday and Sunday were sell-outs. Tickets could not be found, and scalpers wanted three or four times face value. Although only one entrance to the bleachers was open, the adjacent garage door had been raised to reveal a barricade guarded by a pair of security guys. A handful of fans milled around the gauntlet, only a few yards away from a thicket of police. Every so often, a fan would offer the guard a green handshake, a Hamilton if he was flying solo or a Jackson if he'd brought along the kids, and walk into the park. The cops did nothing.

During the playoffs, those same cops, pressured from above by Giuliani and Vacco, took a much more active role fighting corruption in Yankee ticketland, arresting roughly fifty people every night outside the Stadium. Vacco made lots of noise about insuring ticket distribution would be fair and then found evidence of no corruption whatsoever in the Yankee ticket office. He did not examine where the vast majority of tickets not on sale to the general public had gone. Perhaps Steinbrenner or his agents directly sold huge blocks of tickets at higher than face value to ticket brokers. Even if Steinbrenner didn't engage in this kind of petty corruption himself, dozens of the insiders who got tickets turned around and resold them right away. Because the secondary market thrives legally just across the river, prices were incredibly inflated for playoff games. The anti-scalper law and its enforcement insured only that access to streetwalking scalpers was limited. Thanks go to Giuliani and Vacco for protecting the profits of their pals and ticket brokers in Jersey, while the rest of us watched the games on TV.

## COPLAND

*Anybody who thinks he gets the privilege of calling me all sorts of nasty names when he pays 50 cents to go into the bleachers is in for another thought. If any fan in the future uses indecent language, either to me or any other Yankee, I will stop the game, call a policeman, and have the fan thrown out of the park. I am going to be my own law from now on.*

—Babe Ruth

*Thousands poured out of the stands and onto the field like a torrential flood … Many of the fans began tearing across the field, ripping out bases, snatching caps from the heads of players, stealing baseballs and bats. It was an all-out riot!*

*… I saw fans tearing at uniforms, grabbing for players' arms, trying to leap up on the Yankees' backs. Then, cops on horseback began galloping across the field and swinging heavy black nightsticks at teenagers and exuberant fans. Clubs came down with full force, whacking and threshing at heads and legs. The fans were amok everywhere: up flagpoles, backstops, and scoreboards. The police moved in with determination to turn them away.*

—Danielle Gagnon Torrez, describing Yankee Stadium after her husband won the final game of the 1977 World Series

*I was really proud of you the other night at the game … You showed what New York is really all about now: respectful. We root for our team and we get on the other team in a respectful way.*

—Rudy Giuliani, addressing Yankee fans on his radio show after the Yankees beat Cleveland in the 1998 playoffs

Thanks to the lack of competition, every Yankee fan was looking forward to the playoffs by June. When the Texas Rangers finally arrived on a Tuesday night in late September, so did the biggest crowd of the

year, decked out in their team jerseys for a brisk fall night. In the
bleachers, the assembled thousands seemed even more boisterous
than normal. The media presence was oppressive, cameramen everywhere: in the extended dugout pits, behind the outfield walls, wan-
dering through the stands, and (could it be?) even atop the decorative
facade that loomed over the bleachers. When the fans in the right-
field corner noticed men and women with their video cameras a hundred feet above them, they started a chant, "Jump! Jump! Jump!"

The cries for flight were ignored. Upon closer examination, it
became apparent these were no run-of-the-mill lensmen. They were
wearing dark uniforms and nightsticks and guns. Either Rupert
Murdoch had hired a new, more aggressive breed of cameraman or
we were being watched. By cops. When the crowd recognized the
identity of the voyeurs, the chant quickly changed, "Five Oh Sucks,
Five Oh Sucks."

Although the crowd follows the game closely, the bleachers act
like an early warning system for off-field action, instantly sniffing
out any confrontations. Thousands rise as one onto their seats to seek
a glimpse of impending brawls. During the regular season, the police
presence is large and organized. Observers at the edge of the adjacent
reserved seating in the second deck scan the bleachers, communicat-
ing by walkie-talkie with their colleagues amidst the fray. The city
spends roughly ten to fifteen thousand dollars per game on security.
This is hardly the vaunted civility in Rudy Giuliani's vision of New
York City; the police presence can seem slightly reassuring in a community with more than a hint of menace in the alcohol, the intoler-
ance, the youth, the machismo, and the tribalism displayed by the
huge group.

But those cops in the rafters were too much, taping all of us for
posterity in case something ugly broke out. Had New York City, with
its constant buzz of surveillance, become a land of watchers and
secret police like East Germany? Sure, we were out in public and,

thus, according to our own laws and judges, asking to be monitored by law enforcement officials, but the cops' furtive behavior (they avoided being photographed as earnestly as they watched us) made it plain that they did not want us to be aware of their activity. If Rudy said that he was proud of us, that we were respectful, evidence of a better New York, well, that seemed doubtful to those in the midst of the crowd, but he had the videotape record. What was certain was, gushing public words or no, the mayor didn't trust us.

*              *              *

Baseball fans did not suddenly become dangerous in the last few years. The national pastime has inflamed American passions for more than a century. In 1887, at a key late-season game between Red Bank and Freehold in northern New Jersey, Red Bank's players and supporters became so agitated at what they thought were bad calls by the umpire (one ump worked the games in those days) that they took the field in protest. Fearful the situation would get worse, the umpire's father, a prominent lawyer from Freehold, secured a revolver and threatened everyone in the crowd with it. Order was eventually restored without a bullet being fired.

Such incidents did not occur everyday, but they were hardly exceptional. In 1907, a new New York City police commissioner (appointed by a reform administration that had replaced the corrupt Tammany bosses) decided to follow the law that barred use of city police within private property except during an emergency. The owners of the New York Giants, who had received free protection from their Tammany cronies, nevertheless announced that they would not hire their own private security for Opening Day in the hopes that the cops would be forced to offer protection. A near riot resulted as a restless crowd of 17,000 took the field during the top of the ninth inning. Despite appeals by the team's owners, city police refused to enter the Polo Grounds. Private security was soon secured.

Most incidents involved a direct interaction between player and fan. A confrontation at Hilltop Park, the Yankees' first home, on May 15, 1912, was typical. En route to the visitors' dugout after the end of the third inning, Tiger superstar and lifelong racist Ty Cobb became enraged at hearing a Yankee fan call him a "half-nigger" and jumped over the railing along the third-base line to go after the heckler. Cobb reached the man, Claude Lueker, a printing press worker who'd lost his hands in a workplace accident, and proceeded to beat him up until Yankee security guards restrained him. Cobb was ejected from the game. A day later, American League president Ban Johnson suspended baseball's best player indefinitely. However, when the rest of the Tigers decided to strike to show their support of Cobb (the only game in major-league history involving scabs and the real thing was a rout; the pros, the Philadelphia Athletics, won 24–2), the league itself almost imploded as Johnson threatened permanent suspension for the strikers and Cobb had to intervene. Rewarded for his uncharacteristic role as peacemaker, Cobb's suspension for the criminal beating of a paying customer was reduced to ten days.

Cobb was hardly alone in taking on his hecklers. Babe Ruth visited the stands nearly as often as he hit home runs. During his first spring training as a Yankee, Ruth quickly became the central focus of fan interest. At a game in Jacksonville, a bleacherite rode Ruth for striking out during his previous at-bat, calling the slugger a "big bunch of cheese." The inning over, Ruth confronted the heckler, who challenged the giant to come into the stands. The Babe rose to the challenge, the fan pulled a knife, and Ruth's new teammates had to pull him out of the stands before something serious happened.

The vision of Yankee Nation as mob dates back to the era of Ruth's wild appeal. The Roaring Twenties witnessed death at the ballpark three times during Yankee home games. Every baseball fan knows Ruth's teammate, Carl Mays, beaned Indian shortstop Ray Chapman at the Polo Grounds during the Yankees' first pennant race in 1920, the only death of a ballplayer during major-league play. The other two incidents are long forgotten. Two years later, at the end of their last season at the Polo Grounds, the Yankees hosted a double-header against the Philadelphia Athletics. Eager to see the Babe's final games at the Polo Grounds, a huge crowd gathered, tens of thousands more than the old ballpark could hold. Told the game was sold out and urged to go home, many in the crowd instead decided to rush the turnstiles and force their way in. The resulting crush left one fan dead and dozens of others injured. Although the game had to be stopped repeatedly to clear fans off the field and parts of the ball-park were torn to shreds, the next day's story in the *New York Times* was buried in the sports section. It included the subhead "Crowd Is Handled Well," claiming that "in spite of the huge gathering there was little if any disorder . . . for the most part, the crowd was well behaved and orderly."

On May 19, 1929, just across the river, the House That Ruth Built hosted an even sadder incident. In the middle of an afternoon game, a sudden storm with heavy gusts and torrential rains hit the Bronx. Play was called, and fans in Ruthville, the always crowded right-field bleachers where the Babe's most ardent followers gathered, raced for the section's one exit. The vicious weather created a panic as hundreds rushed to find cover. What should have been an orderly procession instead became a stampede that left two dead and dozens injured.

This time, the *Times* headlined the incident. The cover story featured allegations that the Yankees had made the situation worse by keeping the exits locked so that Yankee owner Jacob Ruppert would not have to give out rain checks, and that the bleachers lacked adequate facilities to care for those injured. In what appears to be an illustration of the team owner's power at City Hall, the Yankees were cleared of any wrongdoing by the city's district attorney in less than forty-eight hours. The DA attributed the death not to negligence but instead to a "wild rush of people down a narrow chute with no apparent reason." According to a *Times* story two days after the incident, the Yankees did not even plan to make any improvements to the bleacher exits. With that information, the story disappeared as quickly as it had erupted and has now been forgotten. It does not appear in the official history of Yankee Stadium published on its seventy-fifth anniversary, nor was it mentioned in the aftermath of the fallen expansion-beam joint.

These incidents occurred because of lax security policies, bad planning, and poorly trained employees. A letter writer to the *Daily Mirror* during the 1927 season complained about a similar if less tragic event two years earlier:

> May I call your attention to a disgraceful occurrence at the Yankee Stadium Sunday. When it started to rain, the bleacher fans started for cover, and, of course, as there was a large crowd, it caused some confusion. But, not satisfied with that, the Keystone Kops ordered those fans who tried to stay under the stands to move on and, after being shoved and pushed like a herd of cattle, they were put out in the rain, a few of the policemen using strong arm methods.

Forty years later, the more things had changed, the more they looked the same. The Yankees were caught flat-footed when thousands of teens turned out for a double-header with the Tigers in April 1969. Without enough security to control them, the bored adolescents amused themselves by throwing stuff at the visitors: peanuts, apples, bananas, and rubber balls. Anything within reach was thrown at the nearest Tiger. One young fan entered the diamond itself. Heading over to right field, he exchanged greetings with Tiger Al Kaline before swiping the cap off the head of the stunned star.

For those who think Met fans are better behaved, ask any member of the 1973 Reds how they were treated after the fight between Bud Harrelson and Pete Rose during the final game of the playoffs. The Met fans, like their Yankee forebears, tossed everything but the kitchen sink at their rivals. When the game ended with Rose on base, thousands of Met fans surged onto the field. Uncertain if their teammate would escape alive, two dozen major leaguers waited in the dugout, bats in hand, ready to take on all comers.

*                    *                    *

From a distance, the crowd in the bleachers at Yankee Stadium appears to be monolithic, linked by a bond that would be perceived as frightening if redirected to the political arena. The significant police presence at the playoff opener was a sign of respect for the crowd's size and the increased electricity of the occasion. The cops generally have an understanding with the Bleacher Creatures: stay within certain boundaries, and we will leave you alone. Disputes flare up among the Creatures, and suddenly two friends will be wrestling with each other like a pair of bear cubs. As the gentle rumble continues, the cops instead turn their attention to someone smoking a cigarette a few rows back. However, during the postseason, the Creatures were warned that they were on public display and very little would be tolerated.

Three hours later, a Yankee victory tucked away and the speakers cranking out "New York, New York," the raucous bleacherites celebrated the win at a volume designed to wake up the neighborhood. The joy of most fans seemed boundless, at least until they looked back at the field where the Yankees' quiet celebration was quickly overshadowed by another kind of display. Less than a minute after the final out was registered, hundreds of police in full riot gear, dozens on horseback, took the field and lined the perimeter.

Decades earlier, the warning track (now trod on by giant stallions bearing armed policemen) had served as a commoners' boulevard after games, a route for fans to take as they passed out of the stadium. To walk over the hallowed grounds was a pleasant reminder to fans that they were an integral part of the community of baseball. They could almost reach out and touch a Yankee.

Go up to the Bronx three or four hours before game time some day and walk to the southwest corner of the Stadium. On the promenade between the press gate and the Yankees' private parking lot, dozens of fans lean against blue police sawhorses, waiting for one glorious moment. At Yankee Stadium, the walk from SUV or sports car to the media entrance is the only time the players cannot avoid being exposed to the desire they create. Fans snapping photos and begging for autographs are routinely dissed by the players as they enter the ballpark, but that only increases the longing.

While the desire to reach out and touch a Yankee is punishable by up to ninety days in jail, almost all offenders are let off with a minor fine. Some are treated even more leniently. A pair of teenage girls who lusted after Derek Jeter ran onto the Stadium field one afternoon at the end of infield warm-ups to get a closer look at the object of their desire. They gaped at the Yankee shortstop, mumbled a few words, and were gently escorted off the field where they were warned not to do it again. You couldn't punish a girl for loving Jeter too much—that could cut attendance by one-third overnight.

Later in the summer of 1998, a young man who worshipped Ken Griffey, Jr., and boldly wore his Seattle colors in the hostile Yankee bleachers, jumped onto the grass in the left-field corner and raced toward his favorite. The fan beat the security guards to Griffey and tossed a baseball and pen to his hesitant hero. As Griffey signed the orb, the fan was arrested. While he was being escorted off the field, Junior handed him the ball. Later, in the tunnels under the stadium, Yankee security stripped the man of his souvenir.

Some Yankee fans are more equal than others, as twenty-two year-old Paul O'Grady sadly learned. O'Grady ran onto the field during the sixth game of the 1996 World Series against the Atlanta Braves, his shirt tossed aside, revealing "Howard Stern for Mayor" inked on his chest. His back read "Mayor Giuliani, Kiss My" with an arrow below pointing to his posterior. This message apparently enraged the otherwise content mayor in the midst of his favorite leisure activity. No matter that the Yanks won the Series that night and all was well in RudyLand, no punk kid was going to get away with a display like that. Pressure from City Hall insured that O'Grady was prosecuted like no one before him. Despite his defense lawyer's complaints about the arbitrary nature of the prosecution, O'Grady was convicted of criminal trespass and sentenced to thirty days in prison. It was the harshest punishment ever handed out for running on the Yankee Stadium sod. The verdict against baseball's first political prisoner remains on appeal.

*The disparities between successful and unsuccessful Clubs have produced significant conflicts of interest in the operation of Major League Baseball. . . . While the Yankees and many other Clubs have embraced competition between the Clubs for fans, player services, and sources of revenue as the legal, efficient, and proper way to insure fan interest and league success, Clubs such as the Expos and Brewers have repeatedly and aggressively campaigned for the imposition of revenue sharing arrangements in which the revenue of the more successful Clubs is shared with the less successful Clubs.*

*. . . The Yankees' success on and off the field, and their advocacy of greater competition, has led to envy and retaliation by the less successful Clubs, and other Clubs aligned with them.*

*The marks of a small number of the larger and more successful Clubs—including the Yankees—account for the great bulk of the income generated each year by MLB Properties. Despite the wide disparity between the contributions made by the marks of these Clubs, each Club receives an identical distribution of the MLB Properties income. As a result of this distribution of income, the operation of MLB Properties deprives the individual Major League Clubs of incentives to promote and protect their own Club's marks. The equal distribution of revenues from MLB Properties diminishes the incentives for individual Clubs to promote and invest in their marks and in the success of their own Clubs.*

—From the Yanks' 1997 lawsuit against Major

League Baseball

*There was a standing gag around the league that Kansas City had been a Yankee farm club for years—and it still was. We did make more than our share of one-sided deals with A's . . . the reality was that the A's were a bad team in a small market and hurting for money. It wasn't hard for the Yankees to take advantage of them.*

— Mickey Mantle

# 2
# THE DEATH OF COMPETITION

## STEALING FROM THE POOR

Few may remember today, but Yankee dominance emerged in the aftermath of a lawsuit. In the middle of the 1919 season, the great young Boston hurler Carl Mays walked off the mound without explanation after the second inning of a game in Chicago and caught the next train home to Boston. He was uninjured but refused to continue to play for his current employers. Having faced innumerable player rebellions over the past decade, American League president Ban Johnson, a notorious hard-liner, immediately declared Mays ineligible to play for any other team until he resumed his place on the Red Sox roster. Red Sox owner Harry Frazee was already in financial trouble. As the Boston team that had won three of the past four World Series slipped dramatically despite Babe Ruth's unprecedented home-run pace, Frazee hoped to unload Mays to the highest bidder. The Yankees, under new owners Ruppert and Huston, were looking to make inroads on the hold McGraw's Giants had over New York and offered Frazee a couple of mediocre pitchers and $40,000 for Mays. But Mays's walkout so enraged Johnson that he canceled the trade and suspended the player indefinitely.

Most team owners would have respected the ruling of the league boss, but the Yankee lords refused to bow to a higher authority. Instead of working within the partnership, the Yankees went to court to enjoin Johnson from nullifying the trade. A New York court sided with the Yankees (home-field advantage before the bench has a long tradition in the national pastime) and ruled that Johnson had no authority to interfere with contracts between players and owners. After Mays left the Red Sox, his old teammates fell out of the pennant race and could only wonder what might have been as Mays went 9–3 with a 1.65 ERA down the stretch (shades of Randy Johnson in 1998) to lead the Yankees into contention for the first time in a decade. Boston's long-dreaded Curse of the Bambino began a year before the Babe left town.

One Red Sox employee saw the forthcoming devastation. Manager Ed Barrow had guided the 1918 Red Sox to a title. The following year, Barrow gave in to the Babe's desire to move from the mound to the outfield where he would change the game forever. When the Yankees bought Ruth himself from the Red Sox during the 1919 offseason for the unbelievable sum of $125,000 (none of the transfer fee went to Ruth), Barrow jumped ship. After the 1920 season, he was hired by the Yankee owners to run the club's business affairs. The Yankees had never won the pennant, and the team's aggressive owners needed a winner to escape the long shadow of John McGraw. Barrow knew he'd put together a champion in Boston, and he simply lured the best of his players a few hundred miles south.

By 1923, half the Yankee roster consisted of former members of Boston's championship squads. Not coincidentally, the Yankees won three straight pennants while the Bostons slipped into the cellar, where they would languish for a decade. Imagine the 1999 Red Sox winning the World Series thanks to the purchase of seven members of the 1998 world champion Yankees and you will understand why those thefts—the kind of salary-dumping deals that Bowie Kuhn blocked the Oakland As from making a half-century later—started a rivalry that still burns.

The Yankee rise culminated in a 1923 World Series victory in their new stadium over McGraw's Giants. Not only did Ruth's three roundtrippers lead the Yanks to their first title, but ex–Red Sox hurlers Herb Pennock, Sad Sam Jones, Bullet Joe Bush, and Waite Hoyt pitched forty-six of the fifty-four innings played. The brilliant veteran Wally Schang, another former Boston, caught every pitch they tossed. Curse? More like a mugging.

The next victim, too, had close relations with the Yankee bosses. Arnold Johnson was a businessman who saw an opportunity in the uncertainty created in the fifties by New York domination of the national pastime. He entered the playing field by purchasing Yankee Stadium, as well as a ballpark and minor-league team in Kansas City, from the team's owners in 1952. A few years later, as the fortunes of major-league teams continued to falter, Johnson was among those given a chance to purchase the once-proud Philadelphia As. Others may have bid more, but Yankee owner Dan Topping secured the necessary approval from other owners for Johnson.

New ballclub in hand, Johnson moved the operation to Kansas City, where he drew healthy crowds for a few years before it became clear to everyone in town that they still had a minor-league franchise. The

Athletics finished sixth out of eight teams in their initial year in Kansas City and never moved any closer to contention. Even worse, Kansas City served as little more than a trading post along the Yankee Trail. Now led by Barrow's heir, George Weiss, the Yankees fleeced Johnson's team repeatedly, sending cash and well-known veterans on the verge of breakdown to Kansas City in exchange for rising young stars. The list of acquisitions included key performers like Ralph Terry, Hector Lopez, Art Ditmar, and, most notably, Roger Maris, who broke Ruth's single-season home-run record in 1961 in a Yankee uniform.

When the Yankees could not exploit conflicts of interest, they exercised the best of manners. A January 16, 1926, letter from Ed Barrow to Cincinnati president August Herrmann after he unloaded Wally Pipp, an over-the-hill first baseman who'd hit .230 with just three homers the prior season and been more than adequately replaced by young Lou Gehrig, reveals the power of politeness:

> The Baseball Writers here all seem to think that the acquisition of Pipp makes your club a sure contender this season for the National League pennant. Personally, I quite agree with them.

> It is too bad you did not make a deal with Manager Huggins for Wallie Schang. He is still a splendid catcher and his arm is as good as it ever was. His batting, speed on the bases, and his hustling spirit would have made him a valuable addition to your club.

> Trusting this finds you well and happy and wishing you good luck for the coming season, I remain, with best regards,

> Sincerely yours,

> E. G. Barrow

In person, Barrow was curt and a bully, but his politesse on the page enabled him to pilfer on behalf of the Yanks for a quarter-century. Barrow dumped the unwanted Schang on the miserable St. Louis Browns, but one can be certain that he made them feel good about the deal. Pipp did play well for the Reds the next season, and the Reds fought the Cardinals for the pennant until the final week of the season. However, the next year, the first baseman resumed his inevitable decline, leaving the Reds again searching for an answer at first base.

By the start of World War II, the initial outlay of a few hundred thousand to import the best of the Red Sox to New York City had turned the Yankees into sport's wealthiest franchise. That money bought talent, as the Yankees repeatedly outbid other teams for the best young high-school, college, and minor-league players in the country. The Yankees would even sign college players on the sly before they'd exhausted their eligibility and secured their degrees.

A generation later, the Yankees continued to fleece their rivals, but the methods had changed. In the seventies and eighties, Steinbrenner lacked the baseball expertise to recognize other teams' best players and the people skills to allow his rivals to feel good about dealing with him. Meanwhile, players had finally secured a fair chunk of the owners' revenue under a less restrictive collective bargaining agreement, and money replaced loyalty as players shifted rapidly from team to team. Longtime Yankee fans had watched their heroes Gehrig, DiMaggio, Berra, Ford, and Mantle wear only the black-and-white pinstriped uniform during their careers. Now they adapted to a brave new world of mobility. If capital could race wildly around the planet, then so too could labor—at capital's beck and call. The fans rooted passionately against Reggie Jackson for a decade, cheered him on for five years in the Bronx, and then turned against him when he left town and finished his career elsewhere.

With few friends to abuse, Steinbrenner instead exploited this new system of free agency with huge contracts that brought Hall-of-Famers Jackson, Catfish Hunter, Goose Gossage, and Dave Winfield to the Bronx. A natural geographic advantage, which gave the Yankees a potential local audience in the tens of millions, generated revenue streams to support Steinbrenner's free-spending ways. His "win at any cost and do it now" approach pushed salaries up by leaps and bounds. The Boss scared fellow owners who until then had taken a more gentlemanly approach to the baseball business.

The Yankee machine in the mid-nineties established a new reign of terror across the American League: 125 victories in 1998 may have been historic, but the Boss had only just begun. After signing all the central players and every member of the supporting cast save one from the title team, Steinbrenner was not satisfied. When Roger Clemens, baseball's best pitcher over the last fifteen years, came on the trade market after the 1998 season, Steinbrenner turned the heat up on Brian Cashman, the Yankee general manager. The Yankees would secure the object of the Boss' desire or, at the very least, Cashman would monitor the situation closely to make sure the rival Indians did not snatch up the staff ace that might pull them even with the Yanks. If the Yankees secured Clemens, it would make Andy Pettitte, the league's best young lefthanded pitcher, no better than the team's fifth starter. This hardly seemed fair, but somehow the media would figure out a way to convince New Yorkers that the Yankees' accomplishments were a testimony to the value of teamwork instead of bemoaning the life sucked out of the sport by Steinbrenner's voracious acquisitiveness.

Nobody had explained why, soon after Steinbrenner took over, the Yankees had risen only to fall back during the ultra-competitive eighties before reclaiming their elevated perch. Some claimed the Yankees were winning again because Steinbrenner had mellowed. Those who worked under the Boss would be quick to refute such an idea but, even if it were true, it would not explain Steinbrenner's success during the early days when no self-respecting journalist would dare suggest the Boss was calm and detached.

The actual story involved a number of changes in baseball's economic structure that affected the Boss' ability and willingness to spend the big dollars required to sign the best baseball mercenaries. In the mid-eighties, the owners crafted a response to the first era of big free-agent spending by Steinbrenner and a few others. Management decided to violate their collective bargaining agreement with the players' union and unfairly restrain trade. In an attempt to increase their profits, the owners, including the maverick spenders, reached an accord not to pursue free agents.

In the mid-eighties, the Yankees had put together an offensive juggernaut that featured Rickey Henderson, Don Mattingly, and Dave Winfield. Although they could score runs with anyone in the league, their pitching was always shaky. They lacked an ace to front the uncertain staff. At the end of a tantalizing but disappointing 1986 season, the Yankees looked to be one pitcher away. Furthermore, the Mets had just won the World Series and drawn more fans than any Yankee team ever, which normally would have triggered an overreaction by Steinbrenner.

That winter, the game's best pitcher, Jack Morris, was on the market. Morris, who had just turned thirty and had averaged eighteen wins a year over the prior seven seasons, wanted to become a Yankee. His agent, Dick Moss, recognized the impact of the violation of the collective bargaining agreement and devised a way he thought would allow the Boss to acquire Morris without annoying his fellow owners. Moss offered Morris to Steinbrenner through an arbitration deal for one year. The player and owner would each propose a salary for the 1987 season, and an independent arbitrator would choose the figure that he felt was fair. Moss understood the Boss would pay Morris a generous salary once he became part of the Yankee fold; the trick was getting his client into a Yankee uniform. But a variety of threats

from the other owners and then-commissioner Peter Ueberroth halted Steinbrenner's aggressive acquisitiveness. Steinbrenner would not
break with his partners and refused to take the deal.

In 1987, Morris won eighteen more games for the Tigers and led
them to a division title while the Yankees' pitching staff fell apart
again in the heat of the pennant race. Morris finally left the Tigers
after the 1990 season, and Steinbrenner was able to see what might
have been. From 1991–93, Morris's first three seasons after he left
Detroit, the ace pitcher won three straight World Series with two
different teams. Meanwhile, Steinbrenner and the Yankees struggled
to recover from an era when collusion forced them to compete with
their rivals on an economically even playing field.

This glorious period of competitive balance would not last long.
The labor agreement signed after the 1994 strike maintained limits
on the revenue that the big-market owners shared with the small-
market owners during a period of tremendous earnings growth for
the league's most successful teams. Then the Yankees caught a lucky
break that helped them rebound by the mid-nineties. Steinbrenner's
manic impatience insured that the proper nurturing of young talent
rarely occurred on his watch. If the front-office men built up a player too much, the Boss would naturally want to rush him along and
get him to the majors as soon as possible. That was dangerous
enough, but any kid that wasn't hyped was likely to become trade
bait in the effort to secure the object of Steinbrenner's latest crush. At
the precise moment that the Yanks needed to restock their farm system, Fay Vincent, baseball's commissioner, made that mission possible by suspending Steinbrenner from baseball.

\*                    \*                    \*

Baseball's ownership cartel served two of Steinbrenner's basic needs.
The league provided a schedule filled with opponents, raw meat for

his carnivorous players to devour. Even more importantly, the cartel, with its unique antitrust exemption, protected Steinbrenner's geographic advantage, the main element in his franchise's value. The baseball monopoly fought proposed rival major leagues (any of which would consider invading the Boss' territory), and the power of the cartel was so great that no serious attempt at a new league had been made in the four decades since the majors' first expansion. The cartel also kept expansion teams out of his territory and stopped any of the weaker franchises from moving to New York City.

Nevertheless, like Ruppert eighty years earlier, Steinbrenner felt unnecessarily constrained by the cartel. In January 1996, the owners unanimously approved baseball's agency agreement. That pact delineated how national marketing deals would be made and how the revenue produced by those deals would be shared among the teams. While Steinbrenner had skipped that meeting, his son-in-law Joe Molloy, a general partner, and David Sussman, the team's general counsel, had been present and agreed to the deal on behalf of the Boss.

About a year later, Adidas, the second largest maker of sporting goods in the world, was looking to challenge Nike and its aggressive marketing campaign revolving around superstar athletes like Michael Jordan, Tiger Woods, and John McEnroe. By linking its product with iconic franchises like Notre Dame football and Yankee baseball, Adidas hoped to break Nike's grip on the American market. Just prior to the 1997 season, Adidas and the Yankees announced a ten-year, $95 million deal that allowed the company to advertise all over Yankee Stadium and outfit the players rising through the Yankee minor-league system.

When Steinbrenner saw then-Yankee Wade Boggs wearing a turtleneck with a Nike swoosh under his jersey during warm-ups, the Boss called down to the clubhouse and ordered Boggs, who had a contract with Nike, to change clothes. The future Hall-of-Famer refused and remained in the Boss' doghouse until he was released after the season. At the same time, the grounds crew at the Stadium, which was required by league contract to wear gear sponsored by another manufacturer, was wearing Adidas. And the team was selling Yankee T-shirts that featured the Adidas label. Two weeks into the season, the league ordered the Yankees to cease and desist.

The Yankees, fresh off their first World Series triumph in two decades, already had gross revenues that exceeded more than half the league's teams by at least $50 million. All baseball observers agreed that the increasing income disparity between the haves and have-nots was making the very idea of competition untenable. Steinbrenner, who didn't see anything wrong with a new era of Yankee domination, sued, challenging the league's decision to stop him from entering a partnership with Adidas as an unfair restraint of trade and accusing the owners of collaborating in a merchandising cartel. His suit essentially claimed that what was good for the Yankees was good for baseball.

Rather than split the Adidas money among his partners (which would produce an extra half-million dollars a year for each team), Steinbrenner preferred to keep the $9.5 million per year that he had already contracted for. The other owners wanted a piece of the action to be sure, but they also wanted to protect the sanctity of their exclusive agreements with Majestic for batting practice gear, New Era for caps, Russell for game uniforms, and Starter for jackets. If the Yankees took the field clothed in Adidas from head to toe, the Yankees and Major League Baseball would be slapped with a lawsuit before that day's starter could toss the first pitch. Steinbrenner, who'd been around long enough to weather two suspensions and still secure a seat on the executive council that ruled over the game, was in danger again. His partners immediately suspended him from the council, and anonymous insiders claimed that investigations were under way that might trigger a third suspension from ownership of the Yanks. Such a threat seemed serious given the team's exalted status. The Boss surely did not want to miss more postseason heroics, yet the Yankee lawyers persisted in their efforts.

What pushed the parties to a settlement was the trial's relocation. The case, originally scheduled to be heard in Tampa (Steinbrenner's residence and a place where he could expect a more favorable result), was moved to New York City, a venue where the judges had a tendency to look askance at any claims by the man who repeatedly threatened to move his Yankees across the river to Jersey. Feeling a renewed pressure, Steinbrenner and his counsel found a way to settle the case while preserving the Adidas deal. The terms of the agreement remained private. If Nike had turned the American sportscape into an endless sea of swooshes, Adidas now struck a blow by transforming the premier theater in sports into the Land of Three Stripes. Meanwhile, the Boss' counsel restored their man to his powerful seat on the executive council, where he could resume his self-interested battle from within on behalf of large-market teams already fat with profits and playoff appearances.

## THE MADNESS OF KING GEORGE

*George Steinbrenner and Ted Turner and the burger and beer barons who run major-league baseball love to go on the rubber-chicken circuit and tell America's young idealists about the glories of the free-enterprise system, but the truth is that they have spent their entire baseball lives trying to avoid it.*

—Marvin Miller

*This is all Psychology I, understand, but Steinbrenner had a very tough and very rich daddy. And in the dark of his shredded soul, I believe Steinbrenner wonders, wonders fiercely, would he have made it had he not been born so rich and so privileged? And what rips at him, of course, is this: He'll never know. I know, though. Not a chance.*

— William Goldman

*I won't be active in the day-to-day operations of the club. I've got enough headaches with the shipping company.*

—George Steinbrenner, at a press conference

  announcing his purchase of the Yankees in 1973

*How do you know when George Steinbrenner is lying? When his lips are moving.*

—Jerry Reinsdorf

At the time he acquired the Yankees from CBS for $10.8 million in the winter of 1973, the sole male heir in the fifth generation of a family of wealthy German shipbuilders from Cleveland was unknown beyond the world of government contracts. When George Steinbrenner said that he would be an absentee owner of the Yankees a quarter century ago, only those who already knew him understood how empty that promise was. To gain control of baseball's most prestigious franchise during a period of management neglect, Steinbrenner used Mike Burke, a well-liked CBS executive, as his front man. From the day he secured ownership, he took an active role, quickly pushing aside Burke and longtime front-office man Ralph Houk. However, Steinbrenner's initial years of aggressive participation would be short-lived. His unrestrained pursuit of government contracts on behalf of his shipbuilding interests soon came back to haunt him.

After he graduated from Williams in the mid-fifties, George Steinbrenner dabbled in college coaching and minor-league team ownership, while occasionally working for his father. In his late twenties, Steinbrenner took over a larger role in the family business and eventually expanded Kinsman Marine through the acquisition of American Ship from Tampa. In 1969, seeking a greater ability to influence the awarding of huge government contracts, Steinbrenner, who came from a family of Republicans, became chairman of the annual Democratic Congressional Dinner, a huge fundraiser that brought in about a million dollars a year. His efforts were quickly rewarded. In 1970, Congress, controlled by a Democratic majority, authorized over $300 million in new shipbuilding contracts for the Great Lakes, an unprecedented amount for an area which had been relatively neglected.

Steinbrenner's efforts on behalf of the Democrats did not preclude him from seeking assistance from the Nixon White House. Amship had problems with cost overruns on one project and several concerns about antitrust enforcement. They needed to work with the administration. When Herbert Kalmbach, Nixon's moneyman for the Committee to Re-Elect the President, approached Steinbrenner about the possibility of donating $100,000 to the campaign, Steinbrenner leapt at the opportunity to ingratiate himself. Campaign finance laws did not allow gifts so large to be given directly by one individual to one committee, but Steinbrenner circumvented the restriction by giving his employees bonuses that they turned over to the Committee to Re-Elect.

On April 5, 1974, opening day of the Boss' second season as Yankee owner, he was indicted on five counts of violating campaign contribution laws, four counts of obstruction of justice, two counts of obstructing a criminal investigation, two counts of making false statements to the FBI, and one count of conspiracy. Steinbrenner, the first corporate official charged with felony during the Watergate scandal, was looking at up to fifty-five years in prison. Although Steinbrenner would later try to convince everyone that the incident was trivial ("I believe the matter of illegal campaign contributions has been blown somewhat out of proportion due to its identification with the Nixon presidency."), the charges were apparently serious enough to convince him to plead guilty to one count of obstructing an investigation. He faced as much as six years in jail, however, character witnesses convinced the judge to be lenient. Steinbrenner faced no jail time and was fined a mere $15,000. Nevertheless, Steinbrenner, who is highly patriotic, was distressed by being labeled a felon and losing his right to vote. Over the next fifteen years, he petitioned repeatedly for the presidential pardon that he eventually received from Ronald Reagan during his final days in office.

Baseball's boss, commissioner Bowie Kuhn, issued a harsher sentence. Kuhn warned that Steinbrenner's attempts to influence employees to behave improperly could undermine public confidence in the national pastime and then suspended Steinbrenner from baseball for two years. Even from the ineligible list, Steinbrenner was the most hands-on absentee owner baseball had ever seen. His impetuous, erratic conduct made the Yankees one of the least stable franchises in sport despite their success. From the time he took over in 1973 until he was suspended from baseball for a second time in 1991, the Boss went through 13 general managers, 15 pitching coaches, and 19 managers.

In 1991, the Boss was punished for his involvement with Howard Spira, a gambler. Spira offered Steinbrenner information that would embarrass veteran Dave Winfield, the Yankee All-Star who had sued Steinbrenner over his refusal to deliver promised money to Winfield's charitable foundation. When Major League Baseball decided to investigate Steinbrenner's actions, the Boss claimed that he had given the informant $40,000 to help him start his life over again. On July 30, 1991, Commissioner Fay Vincent concluded that Steinbrenner paid Spira the money to dig up dirt on Winfield and placed the Yankee owner on baseball's permanently ineligible list. Steinbrenner, who had become a high-ranking official with the United States Olympic Committee, agreed with that language because he was afraid that a suspension might produce a similar action from the U.S.O.C. When Vincent's decision was announced in the middle of a Yankee home game, 24,000 fans responded with a standing ovation that lasted for more than a minute.

No matter how many times he got caught breaking the rules or violating the boundaries of decent conduct, the Boss refused to change his ways, especially when it came to matters involving influence. A telling example involved the Boss' effort to muscle the Hall of Fame into honoring Phil Rizzuto, a Yankee icon for decades on the field and in the broadcast booth. Bill James devoted dozens of pages to the question of Rizzuto's qualifications in *The Politics of Glory* and felt that the Yankee shortstop did not deserve a plaque at Cooperstown. Furthermore, James believed it wasn't a close call. For years and years, the voters—sportswriters and veterans committee members alike—agreed and refused to name Rizzuto.

When Pee Wee Reese, the Brooklyn Dodger shortstop who had been Rizzuto's peer, was selected in 1984, the New York media was outraged. Through the nostalgic haze of memory, the two players were seen as equals, although Reese had delivered almost three times as many homers and 600 more hits than Rizzuto. Steinbrenner accused the veterans committee of favoritism and wondered if there were enough ex-Yankees included among the voters. Within a year, Steinbrenner announced that the Yankees would boycott the annual Hall of Fame game that was part of the induction ceremonies weekend each year until Rizzuto was chosen. Steinbrenner's petulant action might seem insignificant in retrospect, but the plurality of visitors to the Hall of Fame every year are Yankee fans. If the Yankees stopped cooperating with the Hall or encouraged their fans to stay away until the Scooter got in, they could affect Cooperstown's business significantly.

Steinbrenner lives in a world where arms are twisted and people are manipulated. The veterans committee voted in Rizzuto in 1994, ten years after Reese. It seemed that Steinbrenner believed that all it took to get the Scooter to Cooperstown was the right friends in high places. On the same day that Yogi Berra accepted Steinbrenner's apology for having sent a subordinate to fire the Yankee manager some fifteen years earlier, the Hall of Fame announced the selection of George Brett, Nolan Ryan, and Robin Yount. As the adversaries reconciled, at least tentatively, Steinbrenner had the following exchange with Berra about Rizzuto's admission to the Hall of Fame:

BERRA: I'm on the veterans committee. We got the hard ones. We got the tough ones, boy ...

STEINBRENNER: But [you] got Rizzuto in ...

BERRA: No, I did not.

STEINBRENNER: And he deserved to be in.

BERRA: I'm only one vote.

STEINBRENNER: Yeah, but he was your pal.

BERRA: We've got sixteen other guys.

Whether the veterans committee's decisions are politicized or not, Berra gives the impression that either he believes that they are solely a function of merit or that they should be. Steinbrenner, on the other hand, is thanking Berra for being a loyal Yankee. In essence, the Boss is suggesting Yogi acted in a manner that reeks of favoritism and cronyism, but in this context, that is a compliment, as far as Steinbrenner is concerned.

# BREAK UP THE YANKEES

*It is baseball's double misfortune that Steinbrenner is not just an owner, but the owner of the Yankees. Damn them to your heart's content, they have been important to the game's health. Steinbrenner's mismanagement of the Yankees matters much more than the mismanagement of the Braves. The Yankees, the source of so much of baseball's most stirring history—Ruth, Gehrig, DiMaggio, Mantle—are simply irreplaceable as carriers of a tradition that lends derivative glory to teams that compete against them.*

—George Will (1990)

*Been watching Ken Burns' epic about Baseball on PBS? I have, and something's been eating at me. At times it seemed that all the stories, all the commentators were New Yorkers.*

*The players most mentioned all played on New York teams— Babe Ruth, Lou Gehrig, Joe DiMaggio, Mickey Mantle, Jackie Robinson, Willie Mays, Murderers' Row, Roger Maris. The people on camera talking were nearly all New Yorkers—Billy Crystal, Roger Angell, Mario Cuomo, Doris Goodwin Kearns, Stephen Jay Gould.*

*Subliminal message: the history of baseball is the history of the joys and sorrows of New York fans rooting for New York teams. Forget about us hayseeds out here—our joys and sorrows, played out to smaller audiences, with less press coverage, don't cut it.*

*Grrr.*

*George Steinbrenner represents everything about New York that the rest of the country is sick to death of.*

*The melodrama. ("Joe loved Marilyn as no man ever loved a woman.") The self-centeredness. ("Phil Rizzuto was the greatest shortstop to play the position.") The big money. ("So what if I get paid more than President Hoover?" Babe Ruth said. "I had a better year.")*

—Michael Finley

The reemergence of Yankee hegemony as exemplified by the 1998 edition's cruise through the regular season and playoffs is surely a joy to the team's players, front office, and fans. Despite George Will's belief in a need to measure oneself against greatness, that coronation does not bode well for baseball. What is good for New York is not, in this case, good for America. Between 1936 and 1964, the Yankees won the American League twenty-two times in twenty-nine years. During World War II, the Yanks lost two of four pennants when the rosters were radically altered. Excise those four years, and the Yanks dropped just five pennants in a quarter-century. By the last decade of that run, the citizens of a wealthy nation with increasing leisure time at their disposal stopped going to major-league ball games. Yankee dominance had eliminated hope in all but a few of the outer provinces, and the game soon plunged into the most severe turmoil it had faced in half a century. That Yankee machine is back, better than ever, and more than a dozen overwhelmed teams across the league know months before the season commences that any hopes they foster are false.

*          *          *

The initial advent of Yankee domination afield spurred an advantage at the gate in a time when local media revenues were negligible. There have been three periods of Yankee dominance at the box office. The first (1920–27) can be directly attributed to Babe Ruth. No one in any sport has ever changed a game the way Ruth transformed baseball. The argument can be made that Babe wasn't the greatest home-run hitter in baseball history. McGwire advocates will point to his higher home-run per at-bat ratio, Josh Gibson supporters offer tales of eighty-plus homer seasons and moon shots even longer than Ruth's, Aaron fans note his durability, and Sadaharu Oh devotees assert his unparalleled career numbers. What is beyond question is that Babe Ruth invented the home run. Don't be fooled by the nick-name of Ruth's elder, Frank (Home Run) Baker. Baker won four home-run titles just before World War I, but in 1921, the first year Baker and Ruth were teammates, the Sultan of Swat smacked fifty-nine roundtrippers while Home Run belted just nine.

The longball, a symbol of the new global power felt by the United States during a postwar era of good feeling, brought people out to the ballpark as never before. Major-league attendance had peaked near 7 million fans annually between 1907 and 1913. The war effort, and the loss of some of the game's top players to the upstart Federal League, caused the turnstile count to drop off by one-quarter over the next half-decade. Even as the Black Sox scandal erupted late in the 1920 season, Ruth's invention pushed turnout over the 9 million mark, a new record. Prior to 1920, the Yankees had never been able to draw even 10,000 fans a game over an entire season. Before Ruth's arrival in New York, no team, not even McGraw's mighty Giants, had ever surpassed the million mark for attendance. Now, with the Bambino on display, the franchise topped that figure every year from 1920–24 and again from 1926–28. Although no other team would draw more than a million fans until 1927, attendance surged in both leagues as players everywhere copied the Babe's new toy.

During the 1921 season, which was capped off by the city's first Subway Series, one in three fans attending major-league games went to a ballpark in New York City. A similar ratio during the 1998 season would have required 23 million fans to turn out for Yankee and Met games. The current Met and Yankee share of baseball's local broadcast revenue approaches Gotham's attendance dominance during the Roaring Twenties. In an era before television, radio, and deals to sell the naming rights to stadia, revenue at the box office was the only significant source of a team's income. The Yankees' ability to rule at the box office during this era insured that they could afford to replace aging players with rising young stars who remained beyond the means of most teams.

The second era (1933–38) coincides with the Yankees' first peri-od of on-field dominance. As great as Ruth was, the Yankees lost more World Series than they won during the twenties. The fran-chise's reversal of fortune occurred during the Yankees' sweep of the attendance kings from the north side of Chicago during the 1932 World Series. Ruth's legendary called shot highlighted the easy vic-tory that started three decades featuring seventeen titles in nineteen World Series appearances. During the century's greatest economic crisis, millions of New Yorkers had an unwelcome abundance of time on their hands, but those living in shantytowns along the Hudson River could hardly afford to buy a ticket to support their neighbor Babe Ruth. The first $100,000-a-year ballplayer, Ruth watched the nightly bonfires along the Hudson from his Riverside Avenue apart-ment. Little wonder that baseball's box-office appeal dropped by 40 percent. To hold the Yankees responsible for baseball's decline dur-ing the Depression would be misguided, but the American League lacked good pennant races, instead featuring miserable teams in Philadelphia and St. Louis that finished more than forty games back year after year. An unfair playing field in the American economy proved too much for even America's elite to bear. FDR's New Deal stanched capitalism's bleeding with a steady dose of Keynesianism and, as consumers reclaimed some buying power, baseball erased some of its losses.

During the Yankees' final era of box-office superiority (1946–52), initially the league was phenomenally successful. While the Yankees won five titles in seven years, their huge numbers at the gate were equally attributable to the efforts of a man who never set foot on the field. Larry MacPhail, the turbulent general manager who threw alcoholic tantrums and fervently defended the color line, was one of the few brilliant promoters in the history of major-league baseball. Like his much better humored and more humane rival Bill Veeck, MacPhail was a hustler. The MacPhails and Veecks are few and far between; a century of antitrust exemption has enabled the major leagues to survive despite being run by generation after generation of risk-averse, do-nothing owners and their lackeys.

Anticipating another postwar boom (major-league attendance went up 39 percent the year after World War I ended), MacPhail battled the penny-wise, dollar-foolish philosophy of front-office rivals Ed Barrow and George Weiss. As World War II ended, MacPhail prevailed temporarily and used his resources to renovate the club-owned Yankee Stadium prior to the 1946 season. Lights were installed, new box seats brought in to replace the grandstand, a new clubhouse added, and MacPhail unveiled the first stadium club in sports history, a gathering place for the city's movers-and-shakers. MacPhail kept his eye on the masses, too, by running an endless string of promotions and giveaways designed to appeal to those attracted as much by spectacle as the game itself. MacPhail had pre-game fashion shows (with free nylons passed out to all ladies in attendance) and contests of skill, including a memorable duel between his fastest ballplayer and a racehorse.

The new lights also allowed MacPhail to appeal to working-class New Yorkers who didn't have the luxury of attending day games during the work week. On a damp, cold Tuesday night in May 1946, the Yankees' first night game drew nearly 50,000 fans to the Bronx. If the traditionalists in the front office looked down their noses at MacPhail's means, they could hardly dismiss his results. Across the country, attendance went up by an astonishing 71 percent, a record to this day. The Yankees did even better, boosting their turnout by over 150 percent and becoming the first team in baseball history to draw over 2 million fans. That year, the three New York major-league franchises drew well over 5 million fans, 28 percent of the major-league total. If one includes the crowds that watched Negro League games hosted by the Black Yankees and the Cubans, professional baseball games in New York City were witnessed by more than 6 million fans during the summer of 1946, a million more than turned out to watch the Mets and Yankees during 1998.

As the Yankees continued to dominate at the gate and on the field, the game stagnated. The Yankees plowed their annual million or so in profits back into scouting and buying up the best players on other teams in order to maintain their rule while all their rivals lost a step. If the Yankees had been great before the war, now they were obscene, losing the American League just twice in sixteen years. Their hegemony spurred a Yankee hater named Douglas Wallop to pen *The Year the Yankees Lost the Pennant,* an update of the Faustian myth in which an average Senators fan makes a deal with the Devil so he can lead his beloved team to the title. *Damn Yankees,* a play and movie adapted from Wallop's novel, proved appealing to the general public even as fewer went out to the ballpark to watch Yogi, Whitey, and the Mick wipe the floor with outclassed opponents.

The fifties are remembered by many as the golden era of baseball, a time of stickball and arguments about Willie, Mickey, and the Duke. The flood of books (fan memoirs, oral histories, and biographies) that cover this period could easily fill a typical New York City apartment. What the authors and Manhattan-based editors and publishers seem to have missed is that their Camelot turned the national pastime into a five-borough diversion. But despite five Subway Series in six years, attendance levels in New York City fell, and the game was devastated elsewhere, erasing more than half the postwar gains. Fans of perennial losers in Boston, Philadelphia, Pittsburgh, St. Louis, and Washington stopped going to the ballpark when they lost hope that their teams had even a prayer of beating the Dodgers, Giants, or Yankees. During the subsequent economic chaos, exacerbated by salaries that had risen during the expansion, a contraction in spending on baseball in the face of national abundance overwhelmed a number of franchises. For the national pastime, the fifties proved more difficult than the Depression-era struggle.

The Yankees sailed blissfully along with little competition on the field in the American League. The Yankees were pushed from the major-league attendance throne only after the first franchise move in major-league baseball since the Orioles deserted Baltimore to set up shop at Hilltop Park in Manhattan fifty years earlier. After a surprising pennant in 1948, the Boston Braves struggled to play .500 baseball for the next five years and watched their attendance drop by more than two-thirds. When Lou Parini, the Braves' owner, was offered the chance to move his franchise further west and escape the long shadow cast by the Ted Williams–led Red Sox across town, he did not hesitate. The reign of New York City baseball left owners at more distant outposts with no hope and few ideas. The Braves packed their bags and headed for Milwaukee, where the first city to see a new major-league team in half a century went appropriately nuts. In their first year in Milwaukee, the Braves outdrew the Yankees by 300,000 fans and every other team by at least a half-million. Their dominance at the gate was immediately reflected on the field in the brilliant play of two prodigies, Eddie Matthews and Henry Aaron.

When baseball's economy collapsed, New York City's two weaker teams chose to escape the Yanks' shadow by moving across the country. Milwaukee's sudden resurgence threatened the family who owned the Brooklyn Dodgers. Walter O'Malley's decision to leave Brooklyn is often blamed on local politicians who refused to do what they considered a bad deal at the time. However, the truth is far more complex. Whether motivated by greed or a desire to maintain a competitive edge, Walter O'Malley looked at the untapped markets west of the Mississippi longingly as he remained in the second tier of box-office draws, a good million behind the Braves every year. The declining fortunes of the Athletics and Browns, second bananas in Philadelphia and St. Louis (as the Braves had been in Boston), turned around, at least temporarily, after their respective moves to the baseball-starved towns of Kansas City and Baltimore. Having seen further proof of the positive effects of franchise relocation, O'Malley decided that he must either get exactly what he wanted from the city, given the wider appeal of the Yankees, or move on to much greener pastures.

The economic crisis caused by the lack of competition, a direct result of New York dynasties, triggered the most chaotic period in the game's history. Had the first decade after World War II featured an era of relative balance, the game would have been healthier and new markets could have been opened through a less haphazard process that worked to preserve successful teams like the Dodgers and Giants in the cities they already inhabited. The events of a half-century ago should serve as a warning about the likelihood of franchise relocation during eras like the present one when tremendous economic disparity intertwines with structural inequality on the playing field. Desperate owners trying to keep up with Steinbrenner may well seek greener pastures, or, at least, leases so favorable that they are little more than corporate welfare. Those same struggling owners will try to take a piece out of the players' hides in the next collective bargaining sessions when, in fact, the villain is one of their own.

## DOWN BY LAW

... Flood *stands as a notable example of judicial powerlessness in the face of a self-created dilemma, an object lesson in conservative principles run amok, and a textbook example of the limits of the reform power of public institutions. The Supreme Court should not bear the entire blame. Congress had many opportunities to alter the course of baseball's antitrust exemption or to reaffirm its correctness, but it sat quietly in the dugout.*

*The* Federal Baseball, Toolson, *and* Flood *trilogy is a remarkable example of the Supreme Court's incapacity to address legal issues arising out of the national pastime. Whatever the mer-*

*its of the individual decisions, the Supreme Court cannot be proud*
*of an outcome so many have found inexplicable and indefensible.*
—Roger Abrams

For decades now, baseball's barons have defended their antitrust exemption as if their very livelihood depended upon it. That exemption gives baseball's owners powers unlike those in any other business. Without the antitrust exemption, the owners would have been unable to maintain the reserve clause that tied players to one team for so long, or to secure a stranglehold over the formerly independent minor leagues. Even the owners of other professional sports franchises are subject to antitrust laws. Baseball's exemption was created not by an act of Congress or an affirmative decision by a stalwart Supreme Court, but instead came into being through a series of omissions. That decades-long collection of errors, far worse than the blunders committed afield by the 1962 Mets, has created a body of case law and legislative inaction so irrational that these documents should be placed under the pillow of every practicing Critical Legal Theorist just before bedtime.

The first miscue came in 1922 when Ned Hanlon, a longtime player and manager, brought an antitrust suit against baseball after the renegade Federal League collapsed, thereby killing the team he owned in Baltimore. Hanlon alleged that the major leagues had broken the Federal League through a series of wild payoffs that induced some of Hanlon's partners to sell off their best players. The facts supported Hanlon's allegations that the owners' actions were an unprecedented example of "ruthless conduct toward a competitor, or of shameless disregard of his fundamental property rights," and a jury awarded Hanlon $80,000, which was then trebled under the terms of the antitrust laws. Major-league baseball won an appeal before the U.S. Court of Appeals for the District of Columbia on two counts. Antitrust laws required interstate commerce for enforcement, and the appellate judges ruled that baseball was local (and, therefore, not "interstate") and sport rather than business (and, therefore, not "commerce").

At this point, Hanlon brought his appeal before the Supreme Court. The chief justice, former President William Howard Taft, had played third base at Yale, initiated the custom of the President throwing out the first pitch on Opening Day in 1912, and been offered the position of baseball commissioner prior to Judge Landis. After declining to recuse himself, Taft, along with the other eight justices, chose to extend an unjustified antitrust exemption to baseball's owners. Taft was wise enough to pass along the chore of writing the opinion to another justice.

The specious reasoning for the decision was offered by Oliver Wendell Holmes, who labeled the interstate travel required for the Yankees to meet the Red Sox as "a mere incident, not the essential thing." Even more improbably, Holmes claimed that baseball was not commerce because "personal effort, not related to production, is not a subject of commerce." Thank God Holmes found his resting place before the service economy exploded. Otherwise, we'd probably have to read decisions claiming that fast-food chains and movie studios are not engaged in commerce, but rather in "personal effort," whatever that vague term meant. The truth according to Holmes seemed to be that ballplayers were not in fact working and, if any money was being made, well, better not to think about that.

Congress never specifically excluded baseball from the antitrust laws when they were written, and to this date has yet to create such an exclusion, yet Holmes and his eight peers created their own strike zone. A later court inquiring into the antitrust exemption would describe May 29, 1922, the day the *Federal Baseball* decision was issued as "not one of Mr. Justice Holmes' happiest days." You couldn't tell by the parties thrown in baseball front offices across the land. Apologists for Holmes have claimed that his decision reflected the novelty of antitrust laws that were less than ten years old. The court, apparently, was still finding its way as it looked to protect business interests. All that analysis suggests is that later decisions to uphold Holmes's original error by judges with decades of experience working with antitrust law are even worse.

*                    *                    *

In the late forties and early fifties, the Yankee dynasty was in full force. A young pitcher named George Toolson worked his way through the low minors to the Newark Bears, the top of the Yankee farm system during that period. Try as he might, Toolson could not crack the major-league roster that was winning the World Series every year. The pitcher believed that he belonged in the majors: if not with the Yankees, then with some other team. Under the reserve clause, however, the Yankees could keep as many Toolsons in the minors as they wanted for as long as they wanted no matter how talented.

The reserve system has always been justified by the owners as necessary for competitive balance. In fact, it has enabled the best teams to squirrel away talented players in the minors where they can serve as insurance in case of injury and, more importantly, be kept off the rosters of potential rivals. The 1937 Newark Bears, the top Yankee farm club, were one of the great teams in minor-league history, and surely could have finished ahead of the weakest American League squads. Before the NCAA severely limited the number of scholarships allowed, college football suffered from a dynastic stasis similar to the one baseball has lapsed into repeatedly over the years as the Nebraskas, Notre Dames, and Southern Cals fielded second and even third teams stronger than some of their opponents.

When the Yankees decided to send Toolson back down to a weaker minor-league club, the pitcher balked. After refusing to go, he brought suit, claiming the reserve system violated the antitrust law. Lower courts merely followed the *Federal Baseball* precedents and turned

Toolson down cold. The Supreme Court issued a per curiam opinion in 1953, a procedure which allows a short anonymous majority opinion to be published. This is the judiciary at its most gutless, hiding behind a process that allows it to avoid accountability even to history.

None of the seven justices that denied Toolson his rightful freedom to contract were willing to go on the record. The justices decided to toss the ball back across the street to their legislative counterparts. The opinion read:

> The business has been left for thirty years to develop, on the understanding that it was not subject to existing antitrust legislation. We think that if there are evils in this field which now warrant application to it of the antitrust laws, it should be by legislation.

A vituperative dissent by Harold Burton noted that Congress had considered four bills to continue baseball's antitrust exemption in 1951, but it had passed not a single one. This legislative inaction, which indicated a lack of support for baseball's special status, was misread completely by the Toolson majority as a ratification of Holmes's earlier error. Whether they were misled by a duplicitous reading of the legislative history by baseball's counsel or merely searching for any pretext for their decision, the Supreme Court had booted another easy one. For his part, Toolson was blacklisted after he filed suit and never pitched an inning in the majors.

## CASEY AT THE BAT

*I have never known in my thirty-five years of experience of as great a lobby as the organized baseball lobby. They came upon Washington like locusts.*

— Emanuel Cellar

*A man who walks in and sees you get fair compensation and if*
*you are great, be sure you get it because the day you don't report*
*and the day you don't open a season you are hurting the major*
*league and hurting yourself somewhat, but you are not going to be*
*handicapped in life if you are great in baseball. Every man who*
*goes out has a better home than he had when he went in.*

—Casey Stengel, testifying before Congress in 1958

during hearings exploring the antitrust exemption


Senator KEFAUVER: Mr. Mantle, do you have any observa-
tions with reference to the applicability of the antitrust
laws to baseball?

Mr. MANTLE: My views are about the same as Casey's.

By the late fifties, Congress had grown increasingly dissatisfied with
baseball's owners. For more than half a century, the number of major-
league teams remained fixed at sixteen. The minor leagues, which had
been thriving just two decades earlier, were in a state of collapse
thanks to the tight reins of major-league bosses. The Negro Leagues
had faded away. Worst of all, franchises that seemed stable (no major-
league team had moved for fifty years) were packing up and heading
west in search of excitable new audiences, leaving behind angry, dis-
located fans who turned to their politicians with hostile demands for
action. Fans in Brooklyn and Manhattan, along with their comrades
in Boston, Philadelphia, and St. Louis, sought some kind of relief.
Feeling the political heat, Congress put aside their usual apathy and
tried to squeeze some justice out of the owners.

With their vaunted exemption in jeopardy, baseball's bosses chose
to send the game's clown prince up to the Hill. Anyone doubting
Casey Stengel's intellectual gifts need only glance at the precise
scouting reports that the Yankee manager sent to George Weiss over
the years, but the Ol' Perfesser never needed to show off his keen

mind to anyone. He preferred to play possum. His appearance in 1958 before a Senate Anti-Monopoly Committee investigating antitrust violations by major-league baseball was the ultimate expression of that art. At times, the exchanges between Casey and the senators resembled an Abbott and Costello routine:

Senator KEFAUVER: Mr. Stengel, I am not sure that I made my question clear.

Mr. STENGEL: Yes, sir. Well that is all right. I am not sure I am going to answer yours perfectly either.

Senator KEFAUVER: I was asking you, sir, why it is that baseball wants this bill passed.

Mr. STENGEL: I would say I would not know, but would say the reason why they would want it passed is to keep baseball going as the highest paid ball sport that has gone into baseball and from the baseball angle, I am not going to speak of any other sport. I am not here to argue about other sports, I am in the baseball business. It has been run cleaner than any business that was ever put out in the 100 years at the present time. I am not speaking about television or I am not speaking about income that comes into the ballparks: You have to take that off. I don't know too much about it. I say the ballplayers have a better advancement at the present time.

Senator CARROLL: I am not talking about that fund.

Mr. STENGEL: Well, I tell you if you are going to talk about the fund you are going to think about radio and television and pay television.

Senator CARROLL: I do not want to talk about radio and television, but I do want to talk about the draft clause and reserve systems.

Mr. STENGEL:  Yes, sir. I would have liked to have been free four times in my life; and later on I have seen men free, and later on they make a big complaint "they wuz robbed," and if you are robbed there is some club down the road to give you the opportunity.

Senator CARROLL:  That was not the question I asked you, and I only asked you on your long experience—

Mr. STENGEL:  Yes, sir. I would not be in it 48 years if it was not all right.

Senator CARROLL:  I understand that.

Mr. STENGEL:  Well, then, why wouldn't it stay that?

Senator CARROLL:  In your long experience—

Mr. STENGEL:  Yes.

Senator CARROLL:  Do you feel—you have had experience through the years—

Mr. STENGEL:  That is true.

Casey kept ducking and moving, dancing a rope-a-dope to match Ali at his peak. Stengel concluded his remarks to Senator Carroll by asserting that baseball did not want the proposed legislation, the converse of what he'd said just a few minutes earlier:

Senator CARROLL:  With the draft system, and the reserve clause in the contracts. Do you think you could still exist under existing law without changing the law?

Mr. STENGEL:  I think it is run better than it has ever been run in baseball, for every department.

Senator CARROLL:  Then, I come back to the principal question. This is the real question before this body.

Mr. STENGEL: All right.

Senator CARROLL: Then what is the need for legislation, if they are getting along all right?

Mr. STENGEL: I didn't ask for the legislation.

Senator CARROLL: Your answer is a very good one, and that is the question Senator Kefauver put to you.

Mr. STENGEL: That is right.

Senator CARROLL: That is the question Senator O'Mahoney put.

Mr. STENGEL: Right.

Senator CARROLL: Are you ready to say there is no need for legislation in this field, then, insofar as baseball is concerned?

Mr. STENGEL: As far as I'm concerned, from drawing a salary and from my ups and downs and being discharged, I always found out that there was somebody ready to employ you, if you were on the ball.

Senator CARROLL: Thank you very much, Mr. Stengel.

Casey's obfuscation was necessary. The senators were asking good questions. They just couldn't get a straight answer out of the beloved Yankee skipper. Senator Kefauver asked how many players the Yankees controlled, exactly the right question in light of George Toolson's lawsuit. Stengel begged off ("I do not know how many players they own as I am not a scout and I cannot run a ball club during the daytime and be busy at night and up the next day and find out how many players that the Yankees own.") and avoided further direct inquiries into whether the number of pro baseball players had expanded during his forty-eight years in the game.

Senator Langer expressed concerns about the impact of pay-per-view TV. Casey dissembled some more, babbling about how TV hurt the movie business. Senator O'Mahoney pressed Stengel on the lack of expansion by the major leagues, and Casey digressed even further into a discussion of per diem, salaries for star players, and his numerous firings. Stengel's meandering did not anger the senators in the slightest. After Casey avoided his questions for ten minutes, a bemused Senator O'Mahoney concluded, "Mr. Chairman, I think the witness is the best entertainment we have had around here for a long time and it is a great temptation to keep asking him questions but I think I better desist."

After Casey's wizardry, it was little surprise that the senators put aside any thoughts of revoking the major league's antitrust exemption. The Ol' Perfesser's efforts helped preserve the exemption for at least forty more years. This service to his employers at Yankee Stadium was likely worth millions, but they showed the limits of their gratitude just two years later. When the Pirates stunned the Yankees in the 1960 World Series, the team's owners gave Casey his walking papers.

## LET THEM MAKE ICE

*Why don't people support their team? Maybe they just care about hockey.*

—George Steinbrenner

*I found out a long time ago that there is no charity in baseball, and that every club owner must make his own fight for existence.*

—Jacob Ruppert

*Where have you gone, Ninety-Four Expos?*
*A cartel expresses no regrets to you [hey, hey, hey]*
*What's that you say, Mr. Steinbrenner?*
*Those Expos should pack and move away [woe, woe, woe]*

Not that long ago small-market teams had a chance against the big boys. The eighties featured the greatest competitive balance in the history of the sport. No National League team repeated as division champ during the entire decade. The American League was nearly as even with just three repeat winners in twenty tries, the most hard-fought period in the history of that league. Incompetent management doomed the big-market teams to inconsistency, and then collusion restrained the Turners and Steinbrenners from buying titles when their limited patience ran out.

From 1987 to 1991, the Minnesota Twins and the Oakland Athletics represented the American League in the World Series. Seven years later, the combined payrolls of the two depleted franchises may not reach half the Yankee payroll. Neither team has posted a winning record during any of the last five years, and both franchises are rumored ready to relocate. Loyal Oakland fans suffered as their beloved slugger Mark McGwire annihilated the single-season home-run record a year after he moved halfway across the country as a result of a salary-dumping trade.

Twins fans were rewarded for their faith with a chance to witness history during the 1998 season, too. A lineup that featured Paul Molitor and little else faced David Wells on a Sunday afternoon in mid-May before a huge crowd drawn to the Stadium by a Beanie Baby giveaway. Add the salaries for the nine Twins together, and they were still millions shy of the money earned by Wells and his center fielder Bernie Williams. The Yankee starting lineup featured five players hitting over .300 and three others above .260. The Twins, by contrast, could boast no starters batting over .300 and only two regulars above .260. Few teams would field such a weak nine all season: Brent Gates, Alex Ochoa, Jon Shave, Javier Valentin. On this day, the cast of unlikely immortals found their place in history by showing why they still belonged in the minor leagues. Wells had his good stuff, stayed ahead of the hitters all afternoon long, and waltzed his way to the easiest perfect game baseball has ever seen.

The list of fifteen perfect game twirlers featured as many Mike Witts and Len Barkers as Sandy Koufaxs and Catfish Hunters, proof that the level of competition was at least as important as the quality of starting pitcher in creating history. Nevertheless, the media celebrated Wells's triumph, reflexively revealing the conventional belief of most sports-writers in a great-man theory of history. The truth behind Wells's per-fect game was that the Twins sucked at least as much as the Boomer shined, but the media was more interested in creating a hero than ana-lyzing the structural inequality which has emerged in the game.

Any serious analyst looking at baseball before the 1998 season could have predicted extreme performances, both by teams and indi-viduals. The gap between the haves and have-nots was widening dra-matically every year and the addition of two expansion teams could only further dilute talent in a way that would increase the number of one-sided contests. Whether the statistics for hitting or pitching would improve was an open question because as many minor-league hitters would have jobs as minor-league pitchers, but miracles were surely about to be witnessed.

Leave Sosa, McGwire, and the Yankees out of it and 1998 remains a baseball freak show. Roger Clemens finished his year by winning fifteen consecutive decisions. Tom Gordon topped that by closing out forty-two straight saves to set a major-league record. In just his fifth career start, young Kerry Wood struck out twenty Astros to tie a major-league record. Wells, of course, tossed his perfect game.

The best hitters exploded, too. Alex Rodriguez became only the third player in major-league history (and the first infielder) to steal forty bases and jack forty homers. Craig Biggio stole fifty and slashed fifty doubles, the first player to do so in nearly a century. Juan Gonzalez spent the first half of the season knocking in well over a run a game, a pace unseen since World War II. Manny Ramirez, a Dominican-

American slugger from Washington Heights, smacked eight home runs in five games to tie a major-league record. Rickey Henderson, at the age of thirty-nine, became the oldest man ever to steal fifty bases. Ken Griffey, Jr., swatted fifty-six homers, and Greg Vaughn popped fifty. A record thirteen players hammered forty or more homers.

And the Florida Marlins registered the third most precipitous single-season fall in baseball history. At least Marlin fans had their memories of the 1997 title to comfort them during the crash. As fans of the Montreal Expos watched their team prepare another generation of phenoms—led by ace reliever Ugueth Urbina and amazing young outfielder Vladimir Guerrero—for their eventual departure to much greener pastures, Expo rooters could only remember the abrupt end to their last good season.

When a strike halted the season in 1994, the Expos, despite a low payroll, had the best record in baseball. Other have-nots competed, too. The Royals were over .500 and three games out in the wild-card race. The '94 Athletics were playing badly at the time of the strike but trailed the Rangers by just a game in the miserable AL West.

The Expos were led during their great abbreviated season by seven brilliant young players: outfielders Moises Alou, Marquis Grissom, and Larry Walker, starting pitchers Pedro Martinez, Ken Hill, and Jeff Fassero, as well as relief ace John Wetteland. Of the seven, only Fassero, thirty-one, had reached his thirtieth birthday. The other six were between twenty-five and twenty-eight years old. No other team could boast such a youthful, talented core of players.

The '94 Yankees had the best record in the American League at the moment play stopped, yet their seven best—Paul O'Neill, Bernie Williams, Danny Tartabull, Mike Stanley, Jimmy Key, Melido Perez, and Steve Howe—looks far less impressive than the Expo Seven through the rear-view mirror. Of the '94 team, only O'Neill and Williams remain on the Yankee roster five years later. Four of the other five players have retired.

Since the collective bargaining agreement that reinforced baseball's class structure took hold in 1995, the Yankees have carefully cultivated an image as working-class champs who build from within. In reality, they have maintained their edge because they make and therefore can afford to spend the most money. Key veterans including David Cone, Tino Martinez, Jeff Nelson, David Wells, Chuck Knoblauch, Scott Brosius, and Chili Davis arrived in the Bronx during the last few years from all over the league because Steinbrenner was willing to pay them more than their prior teams. Because baseball's draft of young players only covered Americans, the Yanks could also use their financial muscle when acquiring offshore talent. Orlando Hernandez, Hideki Irabu, Jorge Posada, and Mariano Rivera were Yankees because Steinbrenner had outbid his less prosperous competitors.

Since 1995, the year the strike was settled, three teams—Atlanta, Cleveland, and the Yanks—have made the playoffs every season. The Braves, Indians, and the Yankees have claimed three of four World Series titles and six of eight league crowns while every other team has missed the playoffs at least twice. The trio has established themselves as the Terrible Three, but it should have been the Fantastic Four. The Expos were every bit as loaded as the other teams when baseball took its unwelcome sabbatical.

What happened to the Expo Seven? The team that should have emerged as a permanent contender for the championship never made the playoffs, instead becoming ore for the affluent teams to mine. Larry Walker was lured to Denver by Jerry McMorris's millions. He led the Rockies to a wild card in 1995 and won the National League MVP two years later. Marquis Grissom left Montreal in 1995, too, and found himself as the center fielder and leadoff man for three straight World Series teams. First, Grissom headed south to aid Ted Turner's dynasty in Atlanta. His huge postseason performance helped the 1995 Braves claim the franchise's first title since moving to Atlanta. Again in 1996

Grissom led the Braves into the World Series, and the following year he reached the Series again with the Indians. No other major leaguer could claim a record of three pennants in three years. In the 1997 Series, Grissom ran into his old mate Moises Alou, possibly the best everyday player on the 1997 World Champion Marlins. Alou then witnessed the second clearinghouse sale of his career but landed on his feet in Houston, where he's one of the key players on a serious title contender. Ken Hill skipped town in 1995 in time to help pitch the Indians into the World Series. The next year he became ace of the 1996 Rangers' pitching staff. Hill left the mound with a lead in game two of the first-round series at Yankee Stadium and Texas already up a game, but the bullpen blew the first of three late-inning leads to that year's eventual champs. Pedro Martinez hung around Montreal long enough to win the 1997 NL Cy Young in Montreal before signing what was then the sport's richest contract ever with the Red Sox and leading the 1998 edition into the playoffs. Jeff Fassero helped the 1997 Mariners make the playoffs. John Wetteland became relief ace of the Yankees in 1996 and claimed the World Series MVP trophy after getting four saves. Wetteland then moved to Texas, where he was the closer for the 1998 division champs.

### TABLE 2.1 1998 Wins, Payroll, Media Revenues, and Home Attendance

(payroll, attendance, and revenue in millions)

|  | WINS | PAYROLL | MEDIA | ATTENDANCE |
|---|---|---|---|---|
| Yankees | 114 | 63.5 | 52.5 | 3.0 |
| Boston | 92 | 51.6 | 20.0 | 2.4 |
| Toronto | 88 | 48.7 | 17.0 | 2.4 |
| Baltimore | 79 | 69.0 | 25.0 | 3.7 |
| Tampa Bay | 63 | 25.3 | 15.0 | 2.5 |
|  |  |  |  |  |
| Cleveland | 89 | 59.6 | 18.4 | 3.5 |
| Chicago | 80 | 36.8 | 21.0 | 1.4 |

| | | | |
|---|---|---|---|
| Kansas City | 72 | 33.0 | 6.8 | 1.6 |
| Minnesota | 70 | 26.2 | 7.0 | 1.2 |
| Detroit | 65 | 22.7 | 9.0 | 1.4 |
| | | | | |
| Texas | 88 | 55.3 | 16.0 | 2.9 |
| Anaheim | 85 | 38.7 | 24.2 | 2.5 |
| Seattle | 76 | 52.0 | 13.7 | 2.6 |
| Oakland | 74 | 20.1 | 13.5 | 1.2 |
| | | | | |
| Atlanta | 106 | 59.5 | 47.0 | 3.4 |
| Mets | 88 | 49.5 | 33.0 | 2.3 |
| Philadelphia | 75 | 34.3 | 14.5 | 1.7 |
| Montreal | 65 | 9.2 | 5.7 | 0.9 |
| Florida | 54 | 33.4 | 16.5 | 1.8 |
| | | | | |
| Houston | 102 | 40.7 | 15.0 | 2.4 |
| Chicago | 90 | 49.4 | 49.0 | 2.6 |
| St. Louis | 83 | 52.6 | 15.0 | 3.2 |
| Cincinnati | 77 | 22.0 | 8.5 | 1.8 |
| Milwaukee | 74 | 32.4 | 8.0 | 1.8 |
| Pittsburgh | 69 | 13.4 | 6.0 | 1.6 |
| | | | | |
| San Diego | 98 | 45.3 | 8.5 | 2.6 |
| San Francisco | 89 | 40.6 | 14.5 | 1.9 |
| Los Angeles | 83 | 48.0 | 23.5 | 3.1 |
| Colorado | 77 | 47.4 | 14.5 | 3.8 |
| Arizona | 65 | 30.6 | 19.0 | 3.6 |

The Expo Seven could certainly be called Montreal's Mercenaries, but the billionaires paying them millions had little to complain about. Each man helped lead his new team into the playoffs, most in their very first year in town. In fact, Grissom, Alou, Hill, and Wetteland had each played key roles in getting two teams into the playoffs. For their efforts, the Expo Seven were well rewarded during the 1998 season. Houston, Seattle, Milwaukee, and Anaheim paid Alou, Fassero, Grissom, and Hill, respectively, $5 million apiece for the 1998 season. Their ex-teammates did even better. Wetteland pulled in $5.75 million from Texas. Walker drew $5.875 million from the Rockies. And Pedro Martinez topped the list with $7.5 million from Boston during the 1998 season.

As a unit, the Expo Seven earned roughly $39 million during the 1998 season, four times the payroll of the 1998 Expos. No small-market team could afford to hire all seven or even four of the seven, yet such an investment is required just to show up at the beginning of the season with a chance of winning.

\*                    \*                    \*

Some poker games require "jacks or better" to open. In 1998, baseball demanded forty million or better to compete. Table 2.1 shows that the Houston Astros and San Francisco Giants were able to fight for playoff spots with $40 million payrolls. Most of their competition spent significantly more. The table is misleading because it captures a snapshot of payroll information at the beginning of the season. It, therefore, undercounts the expenditures by good teams and over-counts the payrolls of bad ones. Both the Astros and Giants restocked by acquiring veterans during the season. Players like Randy Johnson don't come cheap, and those moves put millions more on the debit side of their ledgers. On the other hand, the Marlins may have opened the season with a payroll around thirty-three million, but they dumped high-salaried players like Bobby Bonilla and Gary Sheffield in the early part of the season, and cut their payroll under twenty million, down toward Expo territory. Their performance afield descended accordingly.

Many of the small spenders had two good reasons for their limited operating budget: local media revenues below ten million annually and home attendance under two million. Kansas City, Detroit, Minnesota, Montreal, Cincinnati, Milwaukee, and Pittsburgh each found themselves in that relatively impoverished state. With seventy-seven victories to their credit, the Reds were kings of the beggars last year. The have-nots averaged just seventy wins during 1998, and none finished anywhere near contention.

As mentioned above, Atlanta, Cleveland, and the Yankees have established dynasties in the years after the omitted 1994 World Series. Table 2.2 reveals the nature of that domination. Not only have the elite trio made the playoffs each year. They also own the best record during each regular season. Their nearest competitors—the Astros, Dodgers, and Red Sox—have been ten games back each year on average.

In all the divisions except one, performance on the field reflected media contracts and box-office appeal during the 1998 season. The natural order was overturned only in the National League West, where the paupers from San Diego rose up to conquer titans from Los Angeles, Denver, and Phoenix. Do not expect the Padres to return to the playoffs in 1999. They lost their best pitcher, ex-Marlin Kevin Brown, right after the season when Murdoch's Dodgers gave him the richest contract in baseball history. They also lost their third baseman, Ken Caminiti, 1996 NL MVP, to the wealthier Astros, and their rivals kept on spending.

Lording over a system deeply in need of reform, George Steinbrenner behaved like a good reactionary. In early December, Steinbrenner told reporters gathered to witness the signing of Bernie Williams that it might be time for the Montreal Expos to move. Montreal's small payroll bothered Steinbrenner, who wanted to control how his transfer payments were spent. "If that goes into player development, fine. If that goes into owners' pockets, that's wrong," the Boss complained. "I want to see results. I don't mind helping Montreal."

**Table 2.2 Team Winning Percentages and Playoff Appearances (1995–98)**

[Underlined = League Leader; Asterisk = World Series Champion]

|              | 1998  | 1997  | 1996  | 1995   | %WON | PLAYOFFS |
|--------------|-------|-------|-------|--------|------|----------|
| Yankees      | .704* | .593  | .568* | .549   | 60   | 4        |
| Boston       | .568  | .481  | .525  | .597   | 54   | 2        |
| Toronto      | .543  | .469  | .457  | .389   | 46   | 0        |
| Baltimore    | .488  | .605  | .543  | .493   | 53   | 2        |
| Tampa Bay    | .389  |       |       |        | 39   | 0        |
|              |       |       |       |        |      |          |
| Cleveland    | .549  | .535  | .615  | .694   | 60   | 4        |
| Chicago      | .494  | .497  | .525  | .472   | 50   | 0        |
| Kansas City  | .447  | .416  | .469  | .486   | 46   | 0        |
| Minnesota    | .432  | .420  | .481  | .389   | 43   | 0        |
| Detroit      | .401  | .488  | .327  | .417   | 41   | 0        |
|              |       |       |       |        |      |          |
| Texas        | .543  | .476  | .556  | .514   | 52   | 2        |
| Anaheim      | .525  | .519  | .435  | .538   | 51   | 0        |
| Seattle      | .472  | .558  | .525  | .545   | 53   | 2        |
| Oakland      | .457  | .401  | .481  | .465   | 45   | 0        |
|              |       |       |       |        |      |          |
| Atlanta      | .654  | .617  | .593  | .625*  | 62   | 4        |
| Mets         | .543  | .544  | .438  | .479   | 50   | 0        |
| Philadelphia | .463  | .420  | .414  | .479   | 44   | 0        |
| Montreal     | .401  | .481  | .543  | .458   | 47   | 0        |
| Florida      | .333  | .569* | .494  | .469   | 46   | 1        |
|              |       |       |       |        |      |          |
| Houston      | .630  | .519  | .506  | .528   | 55   | 2        |
| Chicago      | .552  | .419  | .469  | .507   | 49   | 1        |
| St. Louis    | .512  | .451  | .543  | .434   | 49   | 1        |
| Cincinnati   | .475  | .469  | .500  | .590   | 51   | 1        |

| | | | | | |
|---|---|---|---|---|---|
| Milwaukee | .457 | .485 | .451 | .461 | 46 | 0 |
| Pittsburgh | .426 | .488 | .451 | .403 | 45 | 0 |
| | | | | | | |
| San Diego | .605 | .469 | .562 | .486 | 53 | 2 |
| San Francisco | .546 | .556 | .420 | .465 | 50 | 1 |
| Los Angeles | .512 | .544 | .556 | .544 | 54 | 2 |
| Colorado | .475 | .512 | .512 | .535 | 51 | 1 |
| Arizona | .401 | | | | 40 | 0 |

Steinbrenner expressed his disapproval of the recent expansion, asserting that existing clubs in trouble should have been allowed to move to Phoenix and Tampa Bay. He claimed he was against expansion when owners voted in March 1995 to award franchises to those two cities, but went along as a favor to his friend Bud Selig. "I think expansion ultimately was a mistake," the Boss said, although he didn't volunteer to return the millions he'd received as a share of the expansion clubs' entry fee. "Relocation and stabilization was the answer."

Don't mistake Steinbrenner's words. He believes the O'Malley solution—take the Dodgers wherever one can find the municipal government most ripe for the picking—is justified in response to his empire. The Boss likely believes he's the leading exponent of social Darwinism of our time. His success is not his own, but instead almost entirely a function of environmental conditions. What is good for the Bombers is bad for baseball, and the Boss is the prime beneficiary of the most unhealthy competitive climate that baseball has seen in at least forty years.

## APOCALYPSE NOW

*The Yankees are certainly the team to beat. The Yankees have the most money of anyone in baseball, and they can be active in the international market and the free agent market. There are no limitations for the New York Yankees.*

—John Hart, Cleveland Indian general manager, looking to 1999

*What if commissioner Bud Selig canceled spring training for any baseball team with a payroll of less than $50 million next season. And what if he explained it this way: "There's no point in practicing since those teams don't have a chance at making the playoffs. They might as well spend the money on some new mascots."*

*In the past month, baseball has become a competitive joke. The rich clubs are getting richer and the poor ones are signing guys you couldn't pick out of a lineup ... The pockets of the top dozen or so clubs are lined by local television contracts and stadium revenues. They don't even miss the $10 million or so they dole out to cover their revenue-sharing and luxury-tax obligations. As a result, the disparity between the rich and the poor is greater than ever.*

— Associated Press

*I don't think revenue sharing's right. Do you want to reorganize the United States? We're not in a socialistic country. We're in a democracy. We're in free enterprise.*

— George Steinbrenner

A quarter-century ago, *Forbes* magazine proclaimed the ill health, if not future demise, of the national pastime. Jeremiads proclaiming the death of baseball have been a recurrent theme in baseball literature for over a century, but this article emanating from capitalism's house organ carried particular weight. Joseph Durso, then and now a *New York Times* sportswriter, told the article's author that "Baseball is already overextended. The kill ratio of franchises is going to be high." Twenty-four teams were in the majors at the time. None of the endangered species perished and only one moved during the past quarter-century—the Washington Senators set up shop outside Dallas. All the more reason to be careful before we echo the alarmist proclamations about the present game. We should not assume that franchises in Oakland and Montreal and Kansas City will require life-support systems. Team owners are always quick to ask for corporate welfare, but they are never quite desperate enough to open their books for public appraisal.

When Wayne Huizenga shredded the World Champion Marlins right after Miami chose not to give the billionaire a ridiculously generous deal for a new stadium, his lackeys claimed that the owner had lost tens of millions even during a championship year and was just doing what was necessary to insure the team's economic viability. Break up the Marlins, the numbers asserted, and so Huizenga did. The decimated roster finished dead last in the season following a title, and the scattered Marlin veterans made their presence felt at the All-Star game (sponsored by the suddenly generous Huizenga through his Blockbuster corporation) and later on in the playoffs. Toward the end of the Marlins' sad season, Andrew Zimbalist, author of the brilliant *Baseball and Billions* (easily the most comprehensive exploration of franchise finances ever written), took a closer look at the team's finances in the *Times* and revealed that Huizenga still made a sizable profit on the season, though he would have made more if he hadn't thrown a tantrum. The disparity between Zimbalist's numbers and the team's claims were so staggering that no owner claim of misery should ever be relied upon again without independent verification. Treating a patient that won't even allow a cursory examination is worse than bad medicine; it's malpractice.

All the owners have done lately is weaken the game. After the strike that they prompted killed the World Series, they abandoned the pennant races that longtime fans had lived and died with for a century. The new wild-card races didn't erase fan bitterness over the lost World Series so the owners decided that they needed another novelty to attract fans to the park: interleague play. Although I prefer the leagues stay in their respective corners until the postseason because it makes the World Series special, that has not kept me from watching the Braves-Yankees contests religiously the last few years. Anything that forces the few remaining heavyweights to slug it out more often can't be all bad.

However, as it was originally designed, interleague play was balanced. Each division was supposed to play a different division every year. That idea has been thrown out the window. The promised Yankee-Dodger matchup has yet to materialize because the owners realized they couldn't make sufficient money from games such as Tampa Bay against Arizona. During the 1999 season, the owners' greed will affect the game's sense of fair play. The schedule has been unbalanced so that each team plays its greatest rival in the other league twice as often as the other teams. The Yankees play the Braves, Marlins, Expos, and Phillies three times apiece during the 1999 season, but they will face the Mets six times. This may thrill local fans and line the pockets of Steinbrenner and Wilpon, but it has little to do with equity. While the Mets face the powerful Yanks three more times, their 1998 rivals for the wild card, the Giants and Cubs, have extra games against the feeble Athletics and White Sox. This system was put into place without any public notice, which is so typical of the lords of baseball. Make a decision in a back room somewhere and assume that we fans will learn to live with it.

*     *     *

Three solutions can alleviate some of the problems created by baseball's present economic structure. First, increasing the amount of local media revenue shared by the franchises would have an immediate impact on the ability of teams to compete. In a period of great wealth, the revenue disparity creates an unhealthy condition: the poor teams can't win, however, they can make a profit if they are very prudent. Enough revenue is shared already that a team can keep its payroll under $20 million, draw a million fans, and still break even or make a few bucks. If the same team doubles its expenditures, then it will be at much greater risk of losing money and may have only a slightly greater chance of winning anything. Obviously, that situation creates all the wrong incentives by punishing those weaker teams that try to compete. Greater revenue sharing would address this problem by creating a more level playing field. Steinbrenner, as a big-market owner, is naturally opposed to that kind of cooperation.

Despite his claims to the contrary, he isn't ready to embrace free enterprise, either. He opts in and out of the cartel's embrace as it serves his interest. Another way to make things fair again is to allow expansion in large-market cities without penalizing new teams with a relocation fee. If I was awarded a major-league expansion team and the right to put the franchise anywhere I wished, I would plant roots in New York City. The massive population base—even split three ways—cannot be matched anywhere else. But the Boss isn't looking for real competition in New York City. "Now, if somebody says, 'Well, we want to bring another team into New York,' no way.

It's crazy," Steinbrenner has said. "There are two teams here already."

The final technique to increase competition on the field comes from British professional soccer. The major leagues should adopt relegation, a system that drops the worst teams in the highest league to the league below them at the end of each season and replaces them with the top teams from that lower league. A relegated team immediately sees a decrease in attendance, a loss in television revenues, and a migration of its top players to teams in the elite leagues. The threat of relegation insures honest competition by forcing mediocre and poor teams to fight hard all season long. Even better, it creates a second pennant race where the league's losers play meaningful matches until the last match of the season.

In a baseball world with relegation, what Wayne Huizenga did to the Florida Marlins would never happen. In 1997, the five-year-old Marlins rode a roster of expensive free agents to an improbable World Series victory. Nevertheless, South Florida taxpayers refused to foot the bill for a new baseball-only stadium for the billionaire owner, while Huizenga complained about how much money he'd lost during the season without opening his books. The bitter owner then acted like a three-year-old having a fit, punishing local fans by trading away all of his high-salaried players in less than ten months. While six ex-Marlins showed up for a reunion at the 1998 All-Star Game, the defending champs slipped into the cellar of the National League. Huizenga destroyed his own team so willfully because he had nothing at risk. No matter how badly the Marlins performed, they would remain a major-league club. Huizenga, who paid just $95 million to buy the franchise in 1992, could turn around and unload the team for at least $150 million.

Relegation would have kept Huizenga honest. Huizenga would not have shredded his team if he faced the risk that most of his asset's value would slide away before he could sell it. The owners don't embrace relegation because they don't want to take any risks that they can avoid. No lockout or collusion or franchise dismemberment excludes an owner from showing up the following season as a full partner in the multibillion-dollar oligopoly.

*I never have slept under the same roof with a nigger, and I'm not going to start here in my own native state of Georgia.*

—Ty Cobb, on sleeping in the same hunting lodge with Babe Ruth, who he believed to be part black

*I have felt deep in my heart that the Yankees for years had been giving Negroes the runaround.*

— Jackie Robinson

# 3
# ANYONE BUT JACKIE

## THE NATIONAL PASTIME

American institutions that dare to be great must be democratic and inclusive. During the first half of the twentieth century, the national pastime was not open to all comers. More than fifty years after Jackie Robinson broke baseball's color line, the grand old game remains a landscape littered with injustices large and small. A lower percentage of African Americans play in the majors than did on the day Robinson retired from the game in the late fifties. There are a handful of black coaches, a few black managers, and not a single black general manager or owner in the major leagues. Given that abysmal record, it's little wonder that the fiftieth anniversary celebration of Jackie Robinson's entry into the majors left no visible, positive residue.

As mediocre as baseball's record on race has been nationwide, the Yankee record has been even worse. The Yankees have not represented well a city that sees itself as cosmopolitan and progressive. They have repeatedly behaved not as if they resided in an urban center famed for its diversity but instead in a backwater determined to maintain the old ways at any price. They have often acted as if they were being run by George Wallace or Bull Conner.

Baseball's racial problems spring from the rancid cultural soil in this country. In 1911, the Cincinnati Reds signed two Cuban players, Armando Marsans and Rafael Almeida, during a period of intense racial hostility. Almeida and Marsans were to be the first Latin Americans in the majors, and their arrival caused a furor. Journalists and opponents wondered openly if the Cubans were black. The Reds were forced to prove that the Cubans were 100 percent Caucasian, and they sent a man down to Cuba who returned with the necessary affidavits. Although both men had barnstormed in the States against Negro League teams, their light complexion allowed them to pass. One local paper referred to the Cubans as "two of the purest bars of Castillian soap ever floated to these shores."

The American fascination with race persists to this day. Baseball's Hall of Fame maintains a database that includes the self-reported ethnic backgrounds of the inductees. No similar material of sociological interest to researchers has been compiled on religion or the wealth or employment history of the inductees' parents. For Babe Ruth, the Hall offers a detailed family tree. Ty Cobb's slurs notwithstanding, the Babe appears to have been a descendant of German ancestors on both sides.

In 1938, Yankee left fielder Jake Powell told a radio audience that he kept in shape during the offseason as a policeman in Dayton,

Ohio, by "cracking niggers over the head." His remarks went generally unremarked by the white press. The comments, however, triggered protests by blacks across the country and outrage from the black press. Sensitive to the concerns of black baseball fans, Judge Landis, the commissioner of baseball, suspended Powell for ten days. The Yankees sent Powell on an apology tour of black newspapers and Harlem bars. Both the Reds' satisfaction of a racist requirement a quarter-century earlier and the punishment of a Yankee for racist remarks emanated from baseball's desire not to offend its audience.

Fifty years later, what was controversial had become iconic. A photograph of Jackie Robinson in his Dodger uniform showed the first black major leaguer touching home plate with his right foot while reaching out with his right hand to shake the hand of a white teammate who was otherwise cropped out of the shot. That image, suggesting moral courage and racial harmony in the world of sports, graced the backs of a number of glossy magazines toward the end of 1998. The photo's quietude was disrupted by the imposition of the insignia of Apple Computers, along with the address of the company's website and the corporate slogan "Think different." Absent the details of Robinson's struggle (comments like the one quoted above caused many white sportswriters and their readers to turn on Robinson for a lack of submissiveness), that slogan seemed exceptionally empty. Floating apart from any historical context, Robinson's image could now move product in a manner similar to that of Michael Jordan, the thoroughly apolitical heir to his athletic throne.

## STEALING HOME

*Greenberg and DiMaggio came to be seen as more than exceptionally gifted players: they were "American" role models, whose behavior apparently embodied model characteristics for ballplayers of that era. They appeared as humble, hard-working, patriotic individuals who took their ethnic heritages seriously but did not exhibit stereotyped ethnic characteristics. They were seen as ballplayers first, Jews or Italians second. They were, in short, not only star players but confirmations of the melting pot theory of ethnicity in America.*

—G. Edward White

*In a democratic, catholic, real American game like baseball, there has been no distinction raised except a tacit understanding that a player of Ethiopian descent is ineligible. No player of any other "race" has been barred. The Mick, the Sheeny, the Wop, the Dutch and the Chink, the Cuban, the Indian, the Jap or the so-called Anglo-Saxon—his nationality is never a matter of moment if he can pitch, or hit, or field.*

—*The Sporting News*, 1923

The emergence of the Yankees after World War I coincided with a resurgence of American nativism. The 1924 Johnson-Reed Act turned a massive European influx into a mere trickle. Officially called the Permanent National Origins Quota Act, Johnson-Reed froze the demographics of the American population by doling out visas in proportion to the ethnic makeup of the country at that moment. Eugenics dominated the national discourse. Hundreds of thousands of Jews and Italians seeking freedom and opportunity they'd been denied on the continent were no longer welcome.

Almost 90 percent of the 36 million Europeans who migrated to the United States between 1820 and the present arrived before 1924. If the door was no longer open, the room inside was hardly warm for those already here. Violent economic cycles placed recent immigrants, primarily Jews and Southern Europeans, in the most jeopardy. With one avenue for social mobility gone—staying ahead of more recent immigrants within their neighborhood—the first-generation Jews and Italians had to look elsewhere to find ways to gain a toehold in the American mainstream.

For some, baseball offered that promise. My maternal grandfather, a Jewish farmboy whose father migrated from Central Europe to Rhode Island, escaped his agrarian childhood at least in part on a ballfield. His athletic talents, as an outfielder and a state champion wrestler, enabled him to "win friends and influence people" long before the world had heard of Dale Carnegie. Although he never played professionally, the contacts and interpersonal skills he developed on the diamond accelerated his assimilation and helped foster six decades of success as a salesman.

Only one-third of the first generation of New York ballplayers were blue-collar or unskilled workers. The leisure time demanded by baseball at the elite level was beyond the means of recent immigrants toiling long hours just to survive. The few who had the skill and opportunity to develop into professional players moved into the middle class. Upon retirement, however, almost all of them reverted to their earlier status.

American-born Protestants, Irish Catholics, and German Catholics dominated that first generation of ballplayers. Of those three groups, the Irish alone remained fixed in a lower socioeconomic position at the turn of the century. During the first decade of this century, the number of Italian and Jewish major leaguers could be counted on one hand. As immigration patterns changed over the next two decades, hundreds of thousands of Jews and Southern Europeans arrived in New York City, and baseball would slowly reflect those demographic changes. Of course, blacks, whether American or Cuban, were excluded from the major leagues.

The ethnic makeup of the Highlanders reflected the first two sets of owners, wealthy men of Irish and German origin with deep ties to the Tammany bosses. Their more successful neighbors in Washington Heights, the Giants of the National League, assembled

rosters with a similar composition. Although the two teams coexist-
ed in the neighborhood for a quarter-century and even played in the
same park for a decade, the Giants never suffered at the gate thanks
to the excellence of the teams John McGraw managed. In this period just before the explosion of advertising and the mass media, neither team worried greatly about the ethnicity of the thousands of
men in suits and ties that poured in to see the games.

*       *       *

If baseball was one point of entry, a much more traditional means of
uplift was education. The early sequences of the Lou Gehrig biopic
*Pride of the Yankees* beautifully illustrate the tension between the generations over diamond dreams. In the film, the young Gehrig smash-
es a home run that breaks a plate-glass window. Arrested by an Irish
cop, the boy is taken home to face his German parents. The cop and
the weak father exchange heavily accented small talk while they wait
for the dominant mother to appear and allocate justice.

This baseball narrative is not one of fathers and sons playing catch
but instead a story of mothers and sons negotiating power. When
Ma worries about how they'll pay to fix the window and complains
about the time young Lou wastes playing ball, the boy offers to quit
school and get a job. Ma becomes apoplectic; in her agitation, she
explains she and Papa are a cook and a janitor because they didn't go
to school. Lou must stay in school and eventually go to Columbia so
that he can become an engineer like his university-educated uncle.
When he complains that he "ain't cut out to be an engineer" (the
"ain't" signifying working-class roots is the only time the mythic
Gehrig uses a colloquialism), Ma asks him what he wants to be. The
boy lovingly eyes the baseball in his hand but stammers that he doesn't
know. She again urges him to be an engineer like his uncle, and the
boy capitulates, "Sure, mom, sure. Whatever you want me to be."

Mom kisses him, and, after a quick dissolve, the film relocates Gehrig to Columbia University. All is well until Ma gets sick and Gehrig quits school and turns pro to pay for her hospital stay. When Gehrig later returns from a stint in the minors to play for the Yankees, his unhappy mother wishes that she'd died rather than see him give up on engineering in order to play ball. He coaxes her to attend a game where she demonstrates her scant knowledge of American culture by asking her husband what the groundsmen are doing with the pillows (bases) and wondering how so many Americans have so little to do that they can watch games. By the end of the reel, her son's success has transformed her into the most sophisticated fan, a vocal critic of the Yankee manager's strategies, and she dismisses the role-model uncle as nothing compared to her Lou.

The real Gehrig was an icon of durability and class, the perfect immigrant with a life story that would be used to inspire patriotic feelings at the outset of a war against the country where his parents were born. Gehrig was an Ivy Leaguer, quiet, well mannered, a mama's boy, a loyal husband (his wife was the first woman he'd ever loved besides his mother, according to legend), and a man without any reported vices. He was, in other words, fully assimilated, and served as a counterpoint to his teammate and fellow German American, the boundless Ruth.

\*             \*             \*

When the Yankees imported Babe Ruth, they became the game's box-office champs overnight. The Giants, who owned the Polo Grounds where the Yankees played, wanted to escape the Babe's shadow and threw out their suddenly prosperous tenants. The Yankees built the massive ballpark across the Harlem River from their rivals and, in their first season in the Bronx in 1923, proved they could attract even more fans to their new home. The Giants countered their rivals' overwhelming success with a young second baseman, Andy Cohen. A part-time player for two years, Cohen replaced Rogers Hornsby, a future Hall-of-Famer, before the 1928 season. The Washington Heights neighborhood near the Polo Grounds had become increasingly Jewish over the preceding two decades, and the buildup before the Giants' home opener was over-whelming. The *American Hebrew* predicted "if Cohen comes through as the manager expects him to, it is felt that he will rival Babe Ruth as a drawing attraction."

On opening day, 30,000 fans, most Jewish, streamed into the Grounds to witness Cohen's brilliant debut. The second baseman knocked in two runs, scored two more, and played great defense as the Giants beat Boston, Hornsby's new team, 5–2. When the game ended, thousands of fans surged onto the field to celebrate. They put Cohen on their shoulders like a new Jewish groom and carried him around the Grounds until his teammates dragged him away. This stunning display moved reporters into a rhapsody of praise for the growing number of Jews in New York. During Cohen's initial sea-son, the Giants finished just short of the pennant and drew more fans. The following year, Cohen's performance slipped, and, a year later, he was sent back down to the minors.

Having seen Cohen's appeal, the New York teams continued their search for "the great Jewish ballplayer." Ironically, the man who was to fulfill that role was a young Babe Ruth fan who lived in the Bronx and waited after games just to watch the Bambino walk to his car. Hank Greenberg was right under the Yankees' noses, but Detroit snatched him away. He would draw huge crowds to Yankee Stadium during each visit, but he also led the Tigers to four pennants during a twelve-year stretch when the Yankees featured Gehrig and DiMaggio and won seven of the other eight pennants up for grabs. Had the Yankees signed the boy from their hood, they likely would have won two or three extra pennants. The Brooklyn Dodgers drafted the other great Jewish ballplayer from the five boroughs, but Sandy Koufax did not harness his talents until they had moved to the West Coast. Like Greenberg a few decades earlier, Koufax would return to his hometown to beat the Yankees, striking out fifteen Yanks during the opening game of the 1963 World Series.

Despite lacking a great Jewish ballplayer, the Yankees made every attempt, honest or otherwise, to appeal to the hundreds of thousands of Jews in the city. Many lived in the Grand Concourse neighborhood of the Bronx within a few miles of the Stadium; in fact, the land on which Yankee Stadium stood had once been home to a Young Men's Hebrew Association (YMHA) that provided an athletic and cultural center for nearby Jews. In 1942, the Yankees thought about using Ed Whitner, a young Irish Catholic, to plug the hole at first base that had existed ever since Gehrig retired in 1939. They asked Whitner to use his stepfather's last name, Levy, to help the team draw Jewish fans from the neighborhood. Shirley Povich, a Jew and longtime sports-writer for the *Washington Post*, reported that Yankee president Ed Barrow told the first baseman, "You may be Whitner to the rest of the world, but if you are going to play with the Yankees you'll be Ed Levy." New York reporters also made their readers aware of the Yankee scam. Call him Whitner, call him Levy, call him overmatched, he was out of the majors after hitting just .215 in fifty-four games.

The growing Italian-American community, with players like Poosh 'Em Up Tony Lazzeri, Frankie Crosetti, and Joe DiMaggio, had better representation in the game. Lazzeri broke in during the 1926 season and received his nickname for his seeming ability to foul pitches off ad infinitum. In the years after Yankee Carl Mays killed Indian Ray Chapman with a beanball in 1920, fans had been allowed to keep balls hit into the stands. Chapman's inability to see a base-ball dirty after innings of use had been at least partly responsible for his death, and baseball's owners decided that they would provide a greater supply of balls for each game. Lazzeri's skill in generating souvenirs deepened his appeal among the Italian Americans who came to the Stadium from the Bronx, northern Manhattan, and even Little Italy to support their kin.

During Lazzeri's first two years manning second base, the Yankees reached the World Series easily. Across the river, the once-proud Giants lost their perch atop the National League and a large number of their fans to the Murderers' Row Yankees of 1927. During that season, Ruth and Gehrig put on a home-run race to match Mantle and Maris, as well as McGwire and Sosa. The team won 110 games and swept the World Series, a display so overpowering that they continue to be considered among the greatest that ever played the game.

Sixty years ago, Yankee Stadium served as a site of assimilation for first-generation Italian Americans, a weigh station on the path to whiteness. The franchise had already cemented a strong bond with the better established Germans and Irish as they became the favorite team of New York City's powerbrokers. Wall Street bankers didn't venture up to the Bronx to see ball games every day, however, and the Italians who inhabited the Belmont neighborhood around Arthur Avenue a few miles from the Stadium provided a natural audience. Lazzeri, the first hero in the Italian markets, soon shared an infield with Crosetti. It was easy for the new Americans to get on the bandwagon because the Yankees were winners. The arrival of DiMaggio in 1936 to play alongside Poosh 'Em Up and Cro during back-to-back title runs clinched the deal. DiMaggio's impact on the field was immediate. He hit 29 homers, knocked in 125 runs, and batted .323 as a 21-year-old to win the Rookie of the Year and help the Yanks to their first title in four years. The next year he was even better, adding 17 homers and 42 RBI to his tremendous first-year total while leading the league in runs scored, slugging, and homers. The Yankees won four titles in Joltin' Joe's first four years in the majors, and the mild-mannered DiMaggio became baseball's answer to Sinatra.

*Life* magazine ran a big story on DiMaggio in the spring of 1939

that was laced with backhanded compliments full of racial stereo-
types. DiMaggio was "lazy, shy and inarticulate," and he was a great
ballplayer, according to the author, because "Italians, bad at war, are
well-suited to milder competitions." Despite the slurs, the article
attempted to paint DiMaggio, like Gehrig, as a fully assimilated
American, a good immigrant:

> Although he learned Italian first Joe, now 24, speaks
> English wiithout an accent and is otherwise well adapted
> to most U.S. mores. Instead of olive oil or smelly bear
> grease, he keeps his hair slick with water. He never reeks of
> garlic and prefers chicken chow mein to spaghetti.

With DiMaggio firmly established as the new Yankee superstar,
the third man in the line that started with Ruth and Gehrig, Italian
Americans throughout the city, even in Brooklyn where they had to
turn their back on the beloved neighborhood team, embraced the
Yankees the way African Americans would root for the Dodgers a
decade later. Those Italian Americans became a central part of the
team's identity. The Yankee Clipper shared the honors with Phil
Rizzuto before the Scooter passed the torch to the universally loved
Yogi Berra. Yogi handed it to Joe Pepitone who booted it before it
was rekindled by Lou Piniella, Dave Righetti, Mike Pagliarulo, and
Joe Girardi.

For seventy-five years, first-generation immigrants have occu-
pied the most distant seats at the Stadium. As Italian Americans took
on smaller roles afield for the Yankees, their kinsmen certified their
growing power through a progressive downward mobility at the
Stadium. Those grandchildren of Italy, seated among the great-
grandchildren of Ireland, cheer Tino Martinez and Paul O'Neill from
the box seats that are proof of their elevated social status.

While the team has never been owned or run by an Italian
American, every Yankee championship team except the first includ-

ed at least one Italian American on the roster. Joe Torre, an Italian American with a sister who teaches at a Catholic school in Queens, reflects that history perfectly in his middle-management role as the team's field boss. In slugging first baseman Constantino (Tino) Martinez, a Cuban American from Tampa, the Yankees have even found an analog to Ed Whitner Levy. Despite his Caribbean roots, Tino has been embraced by the grandchildren of DiMaggio fans who chant his name faithfully during every at-bat.

## MACPHAIL GUARDS THE LINE

*Broke the color line—it sounds like me crossing a finish line, like I broke the tape. He didn't break the color line—he shattered a myth which was prevalent in those days that a major league baseball team with a black athlete was not going to win, couldn't win. Or if it was going to win, it was going to have to carry him.*

—Branch Rickey's grandson

*I was in high school when Jackie Robinson broke the color line, so the full drama of that time didn't really register on me. Still, the Yankees were one of the last teams in baseball with an all-white roster. This didn't go unnoticed, but there was no explanation that I ever heard. I don't think Del Webb and Dan Topping, who owned the club, or George Weiss, the general manager, were bigots. But the Yankees were winning, and Casey felt no pressure to seek out the gifted players who were available as the Negro Leagues faded away.*

—Mickey Mantle

*I will never allow a black man to wear a Yankee uniform. Boxholders from Westchester don't want that sort of crowd. They would be offended to have to sit with niggers.*

—George Weiss

The July 1997 issue of *Yankees* magazine, the team's house organ, featured an article written by John Ralph, the head of public relations for baseball's Hall of Fame, that detailed the day Jackie Robinson broke into the majors. The piece had the warm, fuzzy glow of predigested history, a moment of actual conflict in national history embedded so deeply in amber that Robinson's triumph occurs in the absence of any real opponents. Had Jackie faced down no enemies, his heroism would be pure spin, but Robinson and Branch Rickey had to fight to smash the old segregationist mindset.

Of course, sanitizing the true story was necessary in *Yankees* magazine because the leading villain was a Yankee boss named Larry MacPhail. Why MacPhail was such an adamant defender of the color line is not entirely clear. The Yankees were making tens of thousands annually when they rented the stadium to Negro League teams. MacPhail may have feared that many of his white customers would boycott a team that included black players. Furthermore, MacPhail had a long rivalry with Rickey and reflexively opposed nearly every move the Brooklyn Dodger boss made.

Over the years, MacPhail attacked integration from every angle. First, he claimed that there was no color line and that blacks were welcome to play in the majors. This was nonsense. Then he argued integration would decimate the Negro Leagues, which meant fewer opportunities for black ballplayers (here MacPhail was prescient). MacPhail then claimed that no Negro was good enough to play in the majors. As Robinson's entrance loomed on the horizon, MacPhail put together a cadre of owners to write a secret report condemning integration as bad for the sport. Fifteen of sixteen owners (all save Rickey) signed the report co-authored by MacPhail, but Rickey persisted in the face of the bitter anger of his peers. Ironically, his co-owners pushed out MacPhail, an alcoholic and a mean drunk, after he picked a fight during the celebration of the Yankee victory over Jackie and the Dodgers in the 1947 World Series.

In April 1947, Herb Pennock, the former great Yankee pitcher and then Phillie general manager, told Rickey he would keep the Phillies off the field if Robinson was on the roster May 9. "You just can't bring the nigger here, Branch. We're just not ready for that sort of thing yet," Pennock said. Jackie showed up in uniform, and the teams played despite Pennock's threats. Robinson got a pair of hits in a Brooklyn loss. Pennock died a year later, but the Phillies would not have a black player for ten more years.

Fifty years after his death, during the summer of 1998, Pennock became a figure of controversy once again. The Historic Commission in Kennett Square, Pennsylvania, Pennock's hometown, wanted to erect a statue in honor of the golden anniversary of his induction into the Hall of Fame. They tried to raise $80,000 in contributions, setting off a firestorm in the little burb of 6,000. "If he was a racist, I don't think he should have anything done for him," said Russell Brown, an African American. Mayor Charles S. Cramer, also African American, supported the statue. Cramer explained, "The man was a great pitcher. I don't want to hurt his image, but back in those times, those things were said." The tribute to one of Robinson's leading antagonists today remains on hold.

By the time Mantle reached the Yankees in the early fifties, MacPhail was long gone, but the Yankee color bar remained. When Larry Doby joined the rival Indians in 1948 and won the rookie of the year award while leading Cleveland to the pennant as the first black player in the American League, the Yankees knew that players from the Negro Leagues could not only compete but excel. Nevertheless, the Yankees maintained their reactionary ways for as long as they could get away with it. Mantle mentions Doby, the AL's best black player during his early days, just once in his memoirs, in the context of offering a spirited defense for teammate and pal Enos Slaughter against accusations of racism.

## POWERLESS

*I really thought that if I played for the Yankees I could piss, too.*
—Vic Power

*If the Yankees weren't guilty as charged, they were certainly going out of their way to look for trouble.*
—Dan Daniel

Yankee icon Bernie Williams suffered more than a few slings and arrows from an occasionally doubtful owner and an unsympathetic press during the nineties. But it was nothing compared to what his fellow Puerto Rican Vic Power encountered forty years ago. Power, a black man, joined the Yankee organization in 1951 before the team had integrated at the major-league level. Power's experience in the minors was hardly sublime. While subtler forms of racism surely existed in Puerto Rico, there were no Jim Crow laws in place. Power, as a member of the Yankees' Kansas City farm club, had to live in a town with dozens of establishments that served only whites.

At the time Power joined the Yankee farm system, the other two teams in New York City featured elite black players like Jackie Robinson, Roy Campanella, Don Newcombe, and Willie Mays. The Yanks may have continued to win, but they were becoming a civic embarrassment. When Ruben Gomez, another black Latino in the Yankee farm system, bought back his contract so that he could offer his services to the more inclusive Giants, Power wondered about his possibility for advancement but persisted nonetheless. Gomez won thirteen games for the team across the river in 1953, but Power, who led the American Association in hitting that same year, still received no callup from the Yankees. Power refused to believe the worst, assuming his righthanded swing was a poor fit for Yankee Stadium. However, when the Yankees called up another righthanded-hitting first baseman, Moose Skowron, who was a much worse fielder, he knew he'd reached the end of the line. He was traded not long afterwards.

The Yankees were hardly discreet. Traveling secretary Bill McCorry promised to keep all niggers off his trains. Beyond that, the Yankees spread a variety of negative stories about Power. One vague report alleged the Puerto Rican had a bad attitude, the basis for this judgment being the team's belief that Power was involved with a white woman. It was a case of mistaken identity: Power's wife frequently wore blond wigs.

No matter. Yankee boss Dan Topping claimed that Power could not be called up to the big leagues because he was not much of a fielder. When he finally reached the major leagues after leaving his Yankee nightmare behind, Power would eventually collect seven straight Gold Gloves for his brilliant play at first base.

## GIVE ME AN ASTERISK

*My colleagues are not usually thought of as the last of the liberal Democrats. By and large, the umpires are conservative, salt-of-the-earth guys, traditional in American values, flag-waving patriots ... None of that is intended as criticism ... I'm just making the point that I wasn't exactly umpiring the annual softball game at the NAACP picnic.*

—Eric Gregg

*I have little doubt that Josh Gibson was probably one of the most talented men ever to strap on the ol' shin guards. Same goes, essentially, for [Judy] Johnson and [Pop] Lloyd, and Oscar Charleston and Satchel Paige, too.*

*The problem is where do they rank? Like it or not, the lingua franca of these discussions is statistics, and the truth of the matter is the statistics we have for the Negro Leaguers are essentially worthless. I mean, they can tell us roughly how good the black players were, relative to each other. But relative to the American and National Leaguers of the day?*

*We can only guess. And I'm doing enough guessing here, without making that giant leap out into Unknown Gorge. So while I freely acknowledge that some pre–Jackie Robinson black players were quite possibly good enough to rank among the all-time greats, I can go no further than that.*

— Rob Neyer

In 1961, Roger Maris and Mickey Mantle chased the single-season home-run mark Babe Ruth established thirty-four years earlier. The expansion prior to that season had not only diluted pitching in the American League but also forced a change in the league's schedule. Teams had played 154 games a year, but during the expansion era, teams would play 162 contests each season. In the middle of the summer, when it became apparent that both Yankee sluggers had an excellent chance to break the game's most famous record, a debate arose. If either man broke the record by the hundred and fifty-fourth game, he would become the record holder, but what if the mark was toppled after that point in the season?

Ford Frick, baseball's commissioner in 1961, was responsible for handling the dispute. Frick, a former sportswriter who had been the Babe's close friend and occasional ghostwriter, announced that the record would have to be broken in 154 games. Anyone reaching 60 after the hundred and fifty-fourth game would always be remembered with an asterisk after his name in the record book, a sign the accomplishment was less worthy. Frick's action embittered the two Yankees, but they had little recourse. When Mantle was injured late in the season, Maris stood alone in his pursuit of the fabled mark with 58 home runs entering the critical game. He hit his fifty-ninth homer during that game, but he would not tie the Babe until four games later. Maris hit home run number sixty-one on the final day of the season. In fact, no asterisk was listed in league records, but for thirty years, the major-league record for home runs in a single season was officially listed as follows:

61 **ROGER E. MARIS, AL: NY,** 1961 (162 games)
60 **GEORGE H. RUTH, AL: NY,** 1927

Finally, in 1991, Fay Vincent, then baseball's commissioner, declared Maris the record holder and erased Ruth's name from the books six years after Maris's death. Frick's decision created the most famous controversy involving statistical records ever seen in baseball, however, a far more heated brawl rests just beneath the surface of the current discussion of the game's history.

Rob Neyer, a sportswriter for ESPN.com who used to help Bill James with his books, regularly pens well-reasoned columns that challenge baseball's conventional wisdom in a way that would make his mentor proud. But when it comes to an extended argument about the greatest players in the history of the game, his decision to exclude Negro Leaguers from consideration while including Caucasian Leaguers because the stats for the Negro Leagues are spotty reinforces a questionable status quo. Neyer is far from alone when he makes the assumption that the white game was played at a higher level than the black game without offering any proof.

In fact, it can be argued that the assumption should be reversed because the black game was better. Ty Cobb, an avowed racist and a vicious competitor, would hardly have let up when competing against black players. However, when the eleven-time American League batting champion played in the Cuban winter league in 1910 at the peak of his career, he was outhit by three black Americans: Pop Lloyd, Judy Johnson, and Bruce Petway. Josh Gibson, who was considered the black Ruth (although comparisons to Mike Piazza seem more apt), did something no one else, not even the Babe, accomplished. He hit a ball clean out of Yankee Stadium. He also hit over eighty home runs one year. Although the majority of Gibson's schedule involved non-league games and weaker opposition, he frequently hit home runs at a Ruthian pace during the abbreviated Negro League schedule. The growing compilation of records of exhibitions between Negro Leaguers and major leaguers show a clear advantage for the Negro Leaguers. Satchel Paige pitched especially well in these contests and was considered by the best major-league pitchers to be their equal if not their superior.

The argument need not rely on such anecdotal testimony. We can look at the statistical record after integration. In the first generation of players after Jackie, just one of the top ten hitters in career batting average was white and only two of the top ten career home-run hitters were white. If anyone appeared inferior, it was the white players. Only eleven men whose careers began after the game was integrated have hit 500 home runs. Seven of that esteemed eleven (Hank Aaron, Willie Mays, Frank Robinson, Reggie Jackson, Willie McCovey, Ernie Banks, and Eddie Murray) are African American. If the black ballplayer has had this much success on the field since Jackie, it is reasonable to assume the top black players of the first half of the century would have been similarly dominant.

While this data may not be quite as dramatic as the difference between a segregated and an integrated professional basketball league, it is clear that the level of competition in the major leagues was much lower before integration. The decades before integration and after Ruth popularized the home run represent the greatest offensive era in the history of the majors. Those performances are largely due to two effects of segregation. The first, a weaker talent base, meant the difference in the level of play between the superstar and the average player was greater than normal. Those accentuated disparities were reflected in statistical aberrations, i.e., great performances like Hack Wilson's 190 RBI in 1930 and Ted Williams's .406 batting average in 1941. The odds that either of those performances would have occurred in an integrated league are much lower. The top thirty-four single-season performances in batting average and the best thirty years in runs batted in occurred during baseball's apartheid era.

Those absurd numbers also reflect the weakest fielding era in the game's history. Improved equipment has certainly made a huge difference, but so has the influx of new players. Ten years after Jackie broke the barrier, defensive geniuses like Vic Power, Luis Aparicio, Roberto Clemente, and Willie Mays, men who would have been restricted to the Negro Leagues, were transforming the way the game was played in the field. If present-day hitters were not foiled by the defensive efforts of players like Ozzie Smith, Omar Vizquel, Rey Ordonez, Derek Jeter, the Alomar brothers, Kenny Lofton, Devon White, Marquis Grissom, Ray Lankford, Barry Bonds, Bernie Williams, Ken Griffey, Jr., Charles Johnson, and Pudge Rodriguez, batting averages and run production would climb dramatically for the best remaining players.

Insert those same players into the major leagues in the twenties and thirties, and offensive production (except for those home runs no gloveman can reclaim) would decline significantly. The idea that the statistical data that emanated from the major leagues' apartheid era should be regarded with the same degree of respect as later numbers because a rational accounting system was in place is naïve. The numbers aren't inaccurate due to sloppiness; they're just juiced on the steroid of weakened competition.

Any record performance in the majors during the first half of the century should come with a big fat asterisk attached and a note explaining the weaknesses of hardball for whites only. Those records that demand reconsideration include the greatest performances in Yankee history. Although his single-season and career home-run records have been surpassed, Babe Ruth continues to own the single-season records for walks, runs scored, total bases, and slugging percentage. Jack Chesbro, an ace during the franchise's early days, still holds the mark (at least in the twentieth century) for wins and complete games pitched in one season. While there's no obvious reason to believe integration would have shortened Lou Gehrig's consecutive-game streak, the increased quality of pitching and defense would have made Joe DiMaggio's hitting streak much more difficult.

If you're going to leave out the Negro Leagues when you're discussing the greatest players in the history of the game, then you should exclude the white players from the apartheid era, too. They did not play the best competition—an integrated league—either. And, if this seems unjust, then include the great Negro League players in this serious discussion or comfort yourself by remembering not a single major leaguer was among the agitators for integrated baseball before Jackie broke the line.

*         *         *

Baseball's statistical analysts are often tripped up by their unyielding belief in the game's overarching rationality, a faith that the numbers represent something objective. This may be true in some areas, but not at the subjective heart of the game: the strike zone. Critics have shown with numbers and videotape that umpires are not robots. Eric Gregg, one of the few black umpires, describes his peers as having a very specific mindset. An umpire's cultural background is very likely to influence his judgment.

Mickey Mantle and Willie Mays, rival center fielders during New York's last golden era of baseball, ended their careers with the same slugging average, but many experts give Mantle a large advantage because he drew significantly more walks than Mays. Bases on balls, of course, are dependent on the decision of the home-plate umpire, and each ump has his own personal strike zone. While black players won league titles in runs scored, runs batted in, stolen bases, batting average, and home runs soon after integration, Jim Gilliam did not secure the first walks crown until 1959. Dick Allen did not become the first black to win the walks title in the more slowly integrated American League until a full quarter-century after the color line had been broken. If some, or even most, of the white umpires called more strikes on black ballplayers, it is safe to assume Mays adapted to this discrimination by choosing to be less patient at the plate than Mantle. Analysts should not punish Mantle or his peer Ted Williams for their fine batting eyes, but if the key difference between two players of different color is their ability to take a walk, experts should be cautious when making historical judgments.

That goes double for Latin American ballplayers. Over the last quarter-century, dozens of African-American players have been able to draw huge numbers of walks as the old patterns have largely dissolved. However, no Latino has ever led the league in walks, and only a few of the hundreds who have played in the majors have ever drawn one hundred walks. Baseball lore has it that Latinos are undisciplined hitters, free swingers who think that "you can't walk off of the island." While there is certainly a cultural difference in the game in the tropics that fosters a reluctance to take a pitch, the absence of any Latino walk kings may stem from the inability of ballplayers to be fully understood by the home-plate umpire. A lawyer who spoke only in Spanish in an American courtroom to a judge who had no fluency beyond English would not expect to receive a fair hearing. A Spanish-speaking hitter in the majors is in a similar situation with the vast majority of umpires.

## FOR WHITES ONLY

*Everything that comes out of Europe . . . is already an American,
and as long as you and I have been here, we are not an American yet.*

—Malcolm X

*I can honestly say racism is worse today than it's ever been in the
years I've played. You have to hear it, and live it, every single
minute of every single damn day. That's why you don't see black
managers. If you had black managers, they might hire their black
friends as coaches. And if you have black coaches, they might get
black players.*

*You want to know why there aren't any black players? Because
you've got to be twice as good as anyone else. If you're not, you just
won't make it. Why do you think you hardly ever see any black
bench players? You better be a star, or you're not making this team.
They don't want a black player sitting on the bench making money.
You got to be white.*

*People talk about blacks not coming to games, why should they?
They're not going to come see a team of white players all of the
time. They'd like to see at least some black players. And why should
they go to a game, like in San Francisco, when all you're going to
hear is that one black guy [Barry Bonds] being booed.*

—Gary Sheffield

Steinbrenner and his minions seem trapped in yearning for a return
to a distant era of civility, a fever dream of powerful white men in
suits and ties respectfully cheering their Yankees on. This vision
informs Steinbrenner's oft-expressed desire to move to Midtown,
where he can raise his already outrageous ticket prices and exclude
the people he considers undesirables. A 1994 article called "Yankee
Imperialism" in *New York* magazine revealed the Yankees' barely hidden racism toward their fans. Former Yankee great Tony Kubek

noted that blacks and Latinos outnumbered whites by three to one in the Bronx, but that management did not promote its minority players, especially outfielders Danny Tartabull and Bernie Williams. Kubek registered the following complaint:

> These are the guys that the Yankees should be marketing to that populace. All I heard out of the front office is "Bernie can't do this" or "Danny won't play hurt." I mean, if that's not a veiled form of racism ...

No rabble-rouser, Kubek is so square he makes Kevin Costner seem like Dennis Rodman. But unlike Steinbrenner, who has regularly trashed the neighborhood where his team resides, he was sensitive to Yankee Stadium's surroundings. Richard Kraft, Steinbrenner's college roommate and, at the time of the article, Yankee vice president for community relations, revealed the Yankee idea of neighborliness when he complained about the unkempt state of the neighborhood park bordering Yankee Stadium with its graffiti and broken basketball rims: "It's like monkeys ... Why do they do this to themselves? These things are for them." After his tirade, Kraft basked in nostalgia and wistfully showed the author a photo of Yankee Stadium in the twenties with its better dressed clientele. In doing so he concisely presented the motives underlying the Yankee vision of a new home in Manhattan. However, Steinbrenner was forced to let his old pal go in the face of public outrage when Kraft's remarks were published.

Despite their staunch defense of the color line, the Yankees could not afford to alienate all the black baseball fans in New York City. After all, the New York Black Yankees had occasionally outdrawn the New York Giants when the two teams were playing right across the river from each other, and big Negro League games frequently drew crowds of over 20,000 to major-league ballparks. However, when the Dodgers brought up Jackie Robinson, the Giants Willie

Mays, and the Yankees continued to hold the line, the animosity of most black fans was assured.

To this day, games at Yankee Stadium reflect the demographics of the city forty years ago with white suburbanites massively outnumbering the scattering of African Americans in the crowd. Although African Americans continue to be slightly overrepresented among major-league players relative to their percentage in the overall population, the same is certainly not true in the stands. According to one demographic research company, whites are more than three times as likely per capita to attend baseball games than blacks. When four of five NBA players and two of three NFL players are black, watching a game where only one in six players are black may be less compelling for the average African American sports fan.

While there are countless black infielders and outfielders, black pitchers and catchers remain the exception, evidence of an unspoken racism that believes that blacks can't be trusted to perform in the central roles on the diamond. Rarer than black pitchers and catchers are part-time black players. With even token front-office jobs rarely available to African Americans, it is not surprising that visitors to baseball's Hall of Fame in upstate New York, where the exploits of Aaron, Mays, and Gibson are celebrated alongside those of Ruth, DiMaggio, and Mantle, are almost entirely white.

Given the hundreds of thousands of African Americans in the New York metropolitan area, the lack of black faces at Yankee Stadium (except as concession workers) is telling. For years, Howard Rubinstein, Steinbrenner's spokesman, has claimed that team research shows most Yankee fans come to games from outside the five boroughs and that less than 2 percent of ticket buyers come from the Bronx. But the methodology used by the team is flawed in that it counts only season-ticket holders, and not walkup buyers, who are much more likely to live in the city. The complaints of Steinbrenner and his hirelings about the lack of interest in the neighborhood are a signal to the heart of his audience, New Yorkers who embraced white flight and residential racism while retaining their affection for an urban institution, the New York Yankees.

It's hard to believe today that fifty years ago Yankee and Italian-Catholic icon Phil Rizzuto and many of his teammates lived just up the block from the Stadium at the Grand Concourse hotel. During his career, Rizzuto would sometimes spend his off-days playing stick-ball with the local kids at the park next to the Stadium. Decades later, as a broadcasting legend during the Steinbrenner reign, Rizzuto often complained on the air about being stuck in traffic during his commute across the George Washington Bridge. Rizzuto had evolved from a neighborhood legend to a suburbanite annoyed by urban sprawl. His emotional and physical voyage away from the city mirrored the journey of millions of Yankee fans and did nothing to diminish his acceptance as the perfect Yankee.

As prices have escalated, baseball's ticket holders have less and less accurately reflected their community. More than one in five adults with a household income of at least $75,000 in 1995 attended baseball games. They were twice as likely to attend games as the average American and more than five times as likely as the average African American. Given the Yankees' high ticket prices, this imbalance is likely to be more extreme in the capital of income diversity, New York City.

Because of the nature of his product, Steinbrenner caters to those who fled the city. Having that audience at Yankee Stadium is hardly essential to increasing the team's worth. His profits are not produced primarily at the Stadium but instead over the airwaves. The wealthy suburbanites watching Paulie and Derek and Tino and Boomer on Charles Dolan's MSG cable network and Rupert Murdoch's Fox affiliate generate tens of millions in revenue that no other team can accumulate. These couch-potato fans remain the primary reason the value of the franchise has escalated over the past quarter-century. By design, the Yankees continue to draw a crowd whose demographic advertisers find desirable. Like Rizzuto, they no longer reside in the neighborhood.

## SOSAMANIA

*The game particularly attracted members of ethnic groups—especially the children of immigrants—because a player's ability or a fan's knowledge marked him as possessing something singularly American.*

—Elliot J. Gorn & Warren Goldstein

*SOSA 62*

—Anonymous yet ubiquitous

The Dominican Americans who live in Washington Heights, like the Cuban Americans across the Hudson, did not need to migrate north to the United States to discover a love for baseball. *El beisbol* is as much the national religion in the Dominican Republic as Catholicism. The Dominican Republic produces more major leaguers per capita than any other country, or, for that matter, any American state. The battleground for the next generation of baseball fans in New York City is Washington Heights, home to many of the Dominicans who have flowed into the city faster than any other group over the past decade. For a century, the upper Manhattan neighborhood, Yankee domicile during their twenty-plus years at Hilltop Park and the Polo Grounds and just across the river from Yankee Stadium, has bred fans of the Bronx Bombers like Idaho's plains produce potatoes.

The events of the summer of 1998 proved that once-reliable loyalties have become fluid. First of all, Manny Ramirez, the Dominican-American kid from the Heights who became a perennial All-Star, played for one of the Yankees' most feared rivals, the Cleveland Indians. His success tugged many Dominican fans away from their original love for the Yankees. For baseball fans in the tri-state area, the Yankees reigned supreme over the summer of '98. However, in baseball-mad Washington Heights, Yankee Fever paled in comparison to Sosa Mania. Cubs caps were more ubiquitous than Yankee headgear. Tributes to Sosa could be spotted all along upper Broadway. Every other car had SOSA 62 traced in soap on its rear window. The autocratic Giuliani responded to these displays by threatening to have the police ticket every Sosanista who decorated his car in this manner because the reduced visibility, according to the mayor, endangered public safety. No similar campaign was initiated against the thousands who drove cars with trademarked stuffed animals stuck to their rear windows. The graffiti Giuliani despised was everywhere as Sosanistas painted tributes to their hero on streets and buildings throughout the northern half of Manhattan. Though it was acceptable for Nike to plaster entire buildings with ads, spontaneous, noncommercial art that celebrated an icon of community pride remained an eyesore at City Hall.

Fortunately, enforcement of the mayor's strict mandate was restrained because Washington Heights is not on continuous display to tourists and commuters. Restaurants in Washington Heights don't get written up in the *Times*, the *Zagat* survey, or the supposedly more inclusive *Voice*. The residents of Washington Heights—listening to their own radio stations, reading their own newspapers, and watching their own television stations, all stuffed full of baseball and Sosa during the summer of '98—might as well be in San Pedro de Macoris as far as the city's English-language media is concerned. Actually, in San Pedro de Macoris, they would get more attention, thanks to the *Times'* Sunday travel section and the sports media's growing recognition of that town as baseball's most productive greenhouse.

For immigrant New Yorkers who did not excel on the field, the mere act of becoming a fan could both reinforce a sense of ethnic pride and facilitate inclusion in a larger civic community. If 1998's Sosanistas suggest the increasing visibility and power of the Dominican community in Washington Heights, then the signal moment of the season for many Hispanic Americans came after the Cubs clinched the wild card in a playoff game on ESPN. In the locker room during the postgame celebration, Sosa was, of course, the first player interviewed. As Sammy incorporated a few of his universal hand signals into his monologue while he ducked the inevitable champagne shower, televisions across the country blared with a background noise unfamiliar to most baseball fans: merengue. Dominican dance music bounced off the walls of the Cub clubhouse and into American living rooms. The following day, at the first Yankee playoff game, I sat in the bleachers among dozens of young Dominican and Puerto Rican Yankee fans who talked only about their team and ESPN's new Latin beat. When the game's action was slow, they would chant in Spanish at Panamanian relievers Rivera and Mendoza. Inevitably, the targeted Yank would wave or smile, temporarily removing the mask of concentration his bullpen mates rarely discarded.

Spanish-speaking athletes are rarely interviewed—and never in Spanish—by reporters on English-language TV. That made Sosa's celebration more amazing: not only were Latinos visible, but they had a soundtrack and a respected voice. What a difference a generation makes. The brilliant right fielder from Puerto Rico, Roberto Clemente, Sosa's precursor afield and in charitable good works, was often punished by white middle-aged sportswriters for errors in his second tongue and his subsequent reserve. Clemente's distance seemed reasonable given how he was treated, but the writers quickly painted him as angry and dangerous. That image changed only after his starring role in the 1971 World Series and untimely death less than three months later when his plane crashed during a mission to bring humanitarian aid to earthquake victims in Nicaragua.

Sosa, who could rediscover his smile seconds after suffering a tough loss or hearing news about the devastation back home caused by Hurricane Georges, evaded the box Clemente had been placed in because he never seemed less than the happiest man on earth. His boundless joy charmed jaded sportswriters tired of reporting on the exploits of multimillionaires who were annoyed by their questions. Sosa aped *Saturday Night Live*'s playful yet racially reductionist mockery of Latino ballplayers of a quarter-century earlier (Garret Morris's recurring rendition of Chico Escuela, Met middle-infielder, featured this oft-repeated line in broken English, "Baseball been berry, berry good to me.") with such generous humor that his impression allowed his audience to laugh without feeling uncomfortable. Any time he was asked about evidence of structural racism suggested by his treatment, Sosa brushed it aside with the repeated refrain, "Come on, man, it's 1998." Sammy allowed the sports media to demonstrate its self-perceived sense of honor and fair play by embracing him. He welcomed the attention, and the media responded in kind by refusing to practice anything that resembled journalism. In the midst of McGwire's andro controversy, the writers following the Cubs around asked Sosa if he took any supplements. When Sammy denied any drug use and managed to joke that the only thing he took was children's vitamins, that was that.

Sosa's starring role made Washington Heights baseball's ground zero. After watching the Bombers destroy another patsy in the Bronx on the final day of the regular season and honor Joe DiMaggio by replacing World Series rings stolen decades ago, I hopped on my bike, zipped across the Macombs Dam Bridge over the Harlem River, pedaled up the long, steep hill that used to overlook the Polo Grounds, and cycled up Broadway over numerous SOSA 62 tributes painted on the street. At the stadium, we'd heard that McGwire had knocked two more out of the park to reach an incomprehensible total of seventy. The news, of course, had spread to the Heights, where the usually busy Coogan's, the neighborhood's most prominent sports bar, was half-empty. No one wanted to see Sammy lose the home-run race; to make matters worse, the Cubs, who'd entered the last Sunday dead even with the Giants in the wild-card race, looked like they were going to lose and miss the playoffs. To watch Sammy fall just short was too much for many to bear. When the Rockies rallied to beat the Giants as the Cubs lost to the Astros, the sense of relief at Coogan's was palpable. Although the Cubs won the playoff against the Giants the next day, Sosa was held without a home run, and the Braves dispatched Chicago easily in the first round of the playoffs.

Mark McGwire, a white son of the suburbs lacking any strong sense of ethnic identity (everyone knew that he was divorced and loved his ten-year-old son, but were the last name, fiery hair, and pale skin proof he was Irish? Was he Catholic?), was honored in his request to disappear for a while after the season ended. The man from nowhere became a Nowhere Man, and no one seemed to mind. People just wanted to watch the big guy hit; only Cardinal fans felt they owned him. Sosa's experience could not have been more different. The man was clearly from somewhere, his people adored him, and he suddenly became ubiquitous.

If the Church's interaction with Sosa demonstrated a continuing respect for the ethnic diversity of its worshippers and a good command of public relations, Giuliani's efforts would not prove nearly as successful. The mayor threw a parade for Sosa but refused to hold the celebration in Washington Heights either along upper Broadway or in Riverbank State Park. Local leaders who had filed the appropriate permits only to be rebuked were unhappy when Giuliani instead planned the party for the opposite end of Broadway along the Canyon of Heroes. One cop explained that the city avoids huge gatherings in upper Manhattan for fear that they won't be able to maintain order. After the mayor's and police's mishandling of the sparsely attended Million Youth March in nearby Harlem, perhaps the cops were right to be worried. Sosa, however, was hardly Malcolm X. If the NYPD cannot keep the peace during a daytime celebration for a universally loved ballplayer, perhaps it's time they asked for a new job description.

Despite the controversy surrounding the location and the absence of a lunchtime downtown office crowd spilling onto the sidewalk, the Saturday parade for Sosa outdrew that for NASA icon John Glenn a month later. Giuliani's involvement proved comically inept. First, his car broke down in the middle of the parade, forcing him to walk the rest of the way. Then the crowd showered him with boos when he presented Sosa with a key to the city at City Hall. Finally, when accepting the key, Sosa assured his fans in Spanish, a language Giuliani doesn't understand, that he would indeed make an appearance in Washington Heights the following day. On Sunday morning, with dozens of police on hand, Sosa kept his promise.

Steinbrenner's performance was even worse than Giuliani's as he went out of his way to make Sosa feel less than welcome. He spent the week leading up to the World Series fighting with major-league officials about who would throw out the first pitch. The ceremonial aspects of the postseason are under the domain of the commissioner's office. Selig wanted Sosa to throw out the first pitch before the game in New York and McGwire, a Southern Californian, to do the same in San Diego to remind casual fans tuning in for the World Series about the brilliant season that had just passed. The superstitious Steinbrenner preferred good-luck charm Joe DiMaggio, and the tabloids backed the Boss by pushing the story that Sosa had no business intruding in the World Series. Failing health forced DiMaggio to stay in Florida to receive medical attention, and the controversy happily disappeared.

\*                    \*                    \*

After the Yankees won the 1998 World Series, General Mills rushed out a special collectible box of Wheaties with Wells, Jeter, and Williams on the front to celebrate the achievement. Based in Minneapolis, General Mills is one of the last corporations you would expect to be multiculturally sensitive, which made the back cover of the special edition box a complete surprise. Aware of baseball's huge appeal to Hispanic Americans and the ballooning Latino presence in New York City, General Mills put together a bilingual design. *Los Yankees estableciendo un nuevo record en la Liga Americana* read the back cover.

Such commitment to Hispanic-American fans is rarely evident in Yankee Land. A visit to the Yankee clubhouse store in Midtown during the 1998 holiday shopping season afforded consumers the chance to buy a lot more than an official World Series program. A fan could nap in Yankee sleepwear, drink from a Yankee mug, and discard trash in a Yankee wastebasket. But missing was any sign of the new bilingualism in the Yankee Nation. Los Yankees maintained English as the sole language in the team store with no merchandise available in Spanish. This is not smart business, which suggests it is motivated by some ideological fervor.

Given how deeply baseball boils in the blood of the newest New Yorkers, the Yankees' failure to dominate the Hispanic-American market is attributable solely to their own neglect. Until they re-renovate the ballyard in the Bronx or move into a new home that works to subtly exclude certain groups, the Yankees will continue to draw fans from outside their favored demographic. With a 1998 roster that included two Puerto Ricans (Posada and Williams), two Panamanians (Rivera and Mendoza), a Cuban (El Duque), a Venezuelan (Sojo), four African Americans (Bush, Davis, Raines, and Strawberry), and a man from Japan (Irabu), the Yankees attracted baseball fans from many of the strands within New York's urban fabric. Add in frequent visits by opponents featuring stars from the Dominican Republic, and heroes for the city's newest communities performed at the stadium nearly every night.

The devotion of bleacherites was spread over every Yankee, but the Hispanic Americans in the cheap seats paid special tribute to Bernie Baseball. Williams has been repeatedly disrespected by Yankee management during his decade in the Bronx. They felt he was holding something back. Graceful big men are frequently accused of loafing in sports. Make the agile giant an egghead and you have a recipe for managerial frustration, the nagging sense that something more can be squeezed out of the big guy. This complaint would fall on deaf ears in the bleachers, where the complaints about Williams could be reduced to mere tribalism. ("How can Bernie even consider playing for another team when we love him so much?") The fans from the surrounding borough, which had evolved from being mostly Irish, Italian, and Jewish a half-century earlier to primarily African- and Hispanic-American, waved huge flags honoring their native Puerto Rico and chanted Boricua ("Puerto Rican" in Spanish) every inning as Williams loosened up.

Yankee outreach to the more than one million Hispanic Americans in New York City, most from baseball-mad Puerto Rico, Cuba, or the Dominican Republic, has been minimal, consisting of little beyond broadcasts in Spanish over the radio and, infrequently, on television. This uninviting approach contrasted directly with that of their crosstown rivals. The Mets aggressively promoted the exploits of their brilliant gloveman, Cuban shortstop Rey Ordonez, and their rising star in the hot corner, Venezuelan Edgardo Alfonzo. Beyond that, the Mets reached out to their fans by hosting International Week toward the end of July during the 1998 season, five consecutive promotions that appealed directly to groups that formed the city's ethnic patchwork. Hispanic Night featured a postgame concert by Tito Nieves and drew over 42,000 fans, one of the biggest crowds of the year. None of the other promos—African-American Day (free Negro League Caps given away), Asian Night (a Japanese pitcher started against a Korean), Jewish Night, and Irish

Night—matched that success, but attendance went up. The Mets neglected one prominent ethnic group in the city, Italian Americans, a recognition that those Italian Americans who loved baseball had been locked up by the Yankee Nation since the days of DiMaggio.

With their efforts, the Mets sent a clear message to baseball fans throughout the city. We respect your culture; we want your business. That embrace was especially clear to Dominicans, Puerto Ricans, and Cubans who witnessed the rise of Omar Minaya, the Mets assistant general manager, the highest ranking Hispanic American in major-league baseball.

## THE PURPOSE OF BASEBALL

*In my first draft of "Shoeless Joe," I kept the J. D. Salinger character as it was in the book. Whereas it worked great in the novel, I thought the movie would benefit more from a fictional character. So I sat down to create a new character, and my first several attempts were just pale substitutes. Boring, weak and uninspired.*

*So, for the first and only time in my life, I said to myself "Just as an exercise, let's think of an actor." I asked myself who would it be fun to see in this role? What is the role? It's a guy Ray Kinsella has to kidnap. Who would it be fun to see being kidnapped? Answer: a big guy. A really big guy. I had just seen "Gardens of Stone," and "Fences" on Broadway, and thought it might be fun to see someone have to kidnap James Earl Jones. Then, like the proverbial lightbulb, I realized how wonderful it would be to have the character be black. (It is, after all, a film about America, and absent this character, it was shaping up to be whiter than me in winter.) At that point, I had a ball inventing a history for him: civil rights pioneer, Pulitzer Prize winning writer, coiner of the phrase "Make love, not war," friend of the Beatles, etc. It was one of those occasions when you just LOVE writing.*

—Phil Alden Robinson

*The one constant through all the years, Ray, has been baseball.*
*America has rolled by like an army of steamrollers. It's been erased*
*like a blackboard, rebuilt, and erased again. But baseball has*
*marked the time. This field, this game, is a part of our past, Ray.*
*It reminds us of all that once was good, and that could be again.*
*Oh people will come, Ray. People will most definitely come.*

—Terrance Mann, *Field of Dreams*

*The real symbiotic alliance is between the white administrators*
*and owners of college and professional teams, and the white-dom-*
*inated media ... Lacking intellectual curiosity, reformist zeal,*
*and the professional aggressiveness that is characteristic of inves-*
*tigative reporters, most people working in the sports media do*
*their part to present the American sports world as a theater of rec-*
*onciliation.*

—John Hoberman

George Steinbrenner frequently proclaims *The Pride of the Yankees* his favorite movie of all time. It is a striking film for many reasons, including its essential whiteness—the various immigrant voices at the start of the film have disappeared by its end as the Irish and Germans become Yankees in every sense of the word. It is little wonder that the jingoistic Steinbrenner, ever sensitive about his German origins, should embrace this tribute to the melting pot theory of America.

This subtext essentially disappears in the middle of the film only to reappear in one of the work's most discordant moments. After Gehrig starts to slump at the plate (the audience knows Gehrig's painful demise will soon follow), the film cuts to a quick sequence of scenes in which common men and women argue over his decline. A white man in a suit gets up after a shoeshine, and the audience sees the first and only black actor in the film. As he dusts off his customer, the shoeshine man echoes popular refusal to give up on the Iron Horse, proclaiming (the actor's line reading is so mannered it calls to mind

Robert Townsend's spoof in *Hollywood Shuffle*), "No sir, he ain't through, I tell you, Mr. Gehrig can't be through." In the five-second scene, Hollywood stamped its seal of approval on blacks in a film designed to promote national unity at the outset of World War II.

Half a century later in the film *Field of Dreams*, the more things change, the more they remain the same. James Earl Jones certainly has a lot more screen time, but his platitudes here are seductive and thus more troubling. Phil Alden Robinson was widely praised, as far as I can tell because he had made that most rare of films, a male tear-jerker that allowed millions of grown men with strained relationships with their fathers to find some release. Kevin Costner's lead character Ray Kinsella, a gullible white boy seeking authenticity, rejects his father after reading *The Boatrocker*, a revolutionary tract by black author Terrance Mann. One wonders if Robinson's kids were playing Public Enemy a little too loud while he penned the script. Robinson's self-confidence that he had invented a progressive character for Jones in Mann, a civil rights pioneer and a pacifist with a mean pen, seems entirely misplaced.

In W. P. Kinsella's novel, *Shoeless Joe*, the embittered writer is the reclusive Salinger. The idea that he is scarred by the world but could be healed by a return to a gentler past and a reconnection to community is a compelling premise, and the novel is intriguing. The ever-litigious Salinger scared the studio out of using him as a character, so Robinson had to invent a new character. The problem with Mann lies in the nature of the field of dreams. It is inhabited by the ghosts of major-league baseball past. In other words, all the ballplayers are white. Baseball is back, color line firmly restored, and there is the booming baritone of James Earl Jones as radical black activist Terrance Mann welcoming the vision of Shoeless Joe Jackson and his ivory-skinned pals with a joy ("It reminds us of what was once good, and what could be again") that is incompatible with his core nature. The sight of a field with Josh and Satchel and Cool Papa Bell and Ray

Dandridge might get his blood stirring, but that would be an entirely different film. Once a symbol of racial pride, Mann now serves only to ratify Kinsella's exclusionary dream. How very sad.

As the quote above suggests, however, Robinson sees himself as another great Hollywood liberal. He is so deluded by his fantasy of racial harmony that he doesn't even recognize his own backlash. Jones, too, somehow escaped this empty fantasy unscarred. Try to imagine Paul Robeson taking such a role.

*           *           *

An article entitled "The World Champions: Yankees a Winning Mix of Cultures" appeared in the special eighty-page section that the *New York Post* ran to celebrate the 1998 World Series triumph on the morning of the Yankee victory parade. The article featured a picture of black *Post* sportswriter George Willis and the first black Yankee Elston Howard. Willis cleared his throat first by acknowledging past injustices:

> Why it took eight years for the Yankees to sign a player of color is something that's not totally documented. But it isn't too difficult to figure out that the ownership of the time wasn't exactly rushing to change the practice of exclusion and discrimination that prevailed in those days.

After a quick glimpse back, Willis churned out a piece that was a perfect example of Hoberman's "theater of reconciliation." Willis described other teams as suffering from racial divides before praising the unified Yankees:

> If any team can truly represent the multi-ethnic makeup of New York, it is these Yankees, who are an international blend of cultures that formed one of the greatest teams in the history of baseball.

. . . Together they worked in harmony to win a World Series that most had given them halfway through the season. There were no egos, no prejudices, no bickering. No jealousy, no fights, no back-stabbing. Just a team that bonded into one proud unit to wear the pinstripes.

. . . Think this is trivial? It isn't. This is the 1990s, where we're all supposed to be politically correct and racially tolerant. But the headlines tell you different. Even our athletic fields are still soiled with racial incidents that we thought would be a thing of the past by now.

. . . But such conflicts were nonexistent on this Yankee team that genuinely liked and supported each other.

. . . The Yankees have always been the world's most famous baseball team, primarily because of the franchise's storied history. But today they represent so much more.

. . . Panama. Japan. Australia. Venezuela. Cuba. Puerto Rico, and from Washington to Texas to Florida. The Yankees aren't just New York or America's team. They are the world's team.

Willis's argument went beyond Hoberman's harmony between black and white (although it was certainly incorporated) and envisioned a utopia in New York where people from around the world came together as one. The page preceding Willis's article contained a full-page promo for Kodak that congratulated the Yankees on their twenty-fourth World Series title. The ad highlighted the very history Willis only glanced at. Team photos from each Yankee championship squad were aligned chronologically in six rows of four shots apiece. The photos were small and grainy. Close examination revealed that in the first four rows of photos, representing the

Yankees' sixteen titles between 1923 and 1953, every single face that appeared was white, an accurate reflection of the team's stalwart defense of the color line. And the fifth row, the four champions of the mid-Mantle era, featured just one black Yankee, Elston Howard. It took the Yankees three decades after Jackie broke in to the game to win a title with a fully integrated roster.

*       *       *

If so many sportswriters seemed naïve about race, one man in pinstripes offered reason for hope. Derek Jeter was raised in a household with an Irish mom and an African-American dad. Growing up, he was called nigger by local whites and criticized for acting white by some blacks. In the face of this abuse, Jeter embraced both sides of his family in an effort to escape the boxes others were placing around him. Asked what his ethnic origins are and he answered simply, "I'm biracial. People ask if I'm black or white. I'm both. I'm not one race." Asked which he would choose and Jeter didn't hesitate. "Both," he answered. "I wouldn't change a thing. I have the best of both worlds."

Jeter is clearly the heir to Gehrig and DiMaggio thanks to his brilliant play afield and easy grace off the diamond. Unafraid to express his mind, Jeter attacked a few of the game's patrons who act one way at the park and another way in the real world. "If I like you, I like you. It doesn't make a difference who you are, where you're from, where you've been. But people are funny," Jeter asserted. "You can cheer for somebody as long as you don't have to deal with them."

The direct words of the future Yankee captain offer glimpses of something rare in Yankee history, a player with a hint of political awareness. Jeter is unlikely to change the world. After all, baseball hasn't even had a practicing Muslim in a major-league uniform yet. And the Yankees are run by an owner who bans facial hair, long hair, and earrings on his employees, even his multimillion-dollar ballplayers. But given his widespread appeal, Jeter's conscious doubling offers the tantalizing possibility that he could become the game's next race man if he so desired.

As he exploded onto the national scene, Tiger Woods became a lightning rod in part because he refused to depoliticize his image. Sure, he was ready to sell that image to Nike and others for tens of millions, but he used his platform to challenge racially exclusionary policies that persisted in country clubs nationwide. Furthermore, he refused to allow himself to be framed by traditional American definitions of race. Instead of letting others tell him his identity, he announced that he was "Caublinasian," a word that honored his Caucasian, Black, Indian, and Asian ancestors at the same time. This definition satisfied neither those African Americans who wanted exclusive dominion over Tiger nor those white conservatives who saw Tiger's invention as PC multicultural mumbo-jumbo. If it wasn't Muhammad Ali conscientiously objecting to the war in Vietnam, it was as close to political consciousness as athletes get in this image-conscious era.

Few elite athletes engage in significant political activism. Those that do have emerged almost entirely from individual sports. Confident in their own self-worth and unrestrained by fears of a management and/or audience backlash, Muhammad Ali, Billie Jean King, and Arthur Ashe stood their ground when their beliefs called for it and pushed for social justice while others merely picked up their paychecks. Baseball has perhaps the most conservative culture in team sports. Although their activities on behalf of the union have required resilience, most ballplayers rarely express a belief in anything other than lower taxes that will allow them to keep more of their huge salaries. With the notable exceptions of Jackie Robinson, Curt Flood, and a few others, baseball's nostalgia has served only to insulate its performers from politics.

*To hell with newspapermen. You can buy them with a steak.*

—George Weiss

*Nobody was ever afraid of me. Nobody who ever ran a ball club, general manager, president, no player. I wasn't going around derogating people, or looking for bugs. If I saw something good I played it. I wasn't looking to run baseball down. I was eager to run baseball up.*

—Dan Daniel

*We recognized the Babe as a guy we could deal with. We covered him twelve months of the year. I don't think he was ever aware of his role as a circulation builder.*

—Marshall Hunt

*Many in the New York sportswriting fraternity knew that Daley often filled his columns with blatantly fabricated quotations attributed to athletes who could not string two coherent clauses together.*

—Richard Kluger

# 4
# STOP THE PRESSES

## HOW BEATIFIC

In the days before ESPN and endless televised replays, baseball beat writers were journalistic stars. Stanley Woodward, the longtime sports editor of the *New York Herald-Tribune*, believed that his section was responsible for a quarter of the paper's sales. The most popular sports during the first half of the century were baseball, football, and boxing. That made the beat writers for the city's three baseball teams arguably the paper's most significant reporters. Their incestuous relationship with the teams they covered troubled Woodward:

Sportswriters were easy prey for promoters and team owners eager to have their heroes spoken of glowingly in print and thereby improve receipts at the gate. Their persuasion took a variety of forms, ranging from salary supplements in the form of cash payments to liberal applications of free food and liquor, complimentary tickets, and travel accommodations on the house. Until after World War II, many newspapers accepted this last practice as a way for major-league baseball clubs to assure ample coverage of their road games. It was no wonder that many sportswriters turned out copy not far removed from pure press-agentry.

The sycophancy reached its apex any time the Babe got into trouble. The simple truth was Ruth's pals refused to rat on him. They didn't think it was part of their job to tear the Babe down. Marshall Hunt, a longtime Yankee beat writer, begged off a story about Ruth fostering an illegitimate child as follows:

> Listen, we've got along fine with the Babe and he's done a lot of things for us. You try to get somebody else to worm this thing out in New York and not through the Babe, because we don't want to try and go on this personal bend that some of the other papers had tried to do.

Beat writers held a surprising amount of power. Access to a huge audience allowed them the opportunity to shape a story, even down to the names of the teams they covered. When New York's entry into the American League started operations at Hilltop Park in Washington Heights in 1903, they called themselves the Highlanders. Two beat writers during that first season, Jim Price and Mark Roth, began calling the team the Yankees in most of their stories. Within ten years, popular use of that nickname caused the franchise to officially change its name. When the Yankees moved into their third New York home on May 22, 1923, the Babe celebrated with a towering home run before an unprecedented crowd of over 60,000 fans. In his game story, sportswriter Fred Lieb referred to Yankee Stadium as "the House That Ruth Built," a phrase that lingers to this day.

Not all the writers' activities were so positive. The late Dick Young was responsible for hounding Tom Seaver, the greatest pitcher in Met history, out of New York in the mid-seventies after the ace demanded that M. Donald Grant renegotiate his contract in light of the rising market. Young pounded Seaver for refusing to honor the contract and then got personal, accusing Seaver's wife Nancy of being jealous of Nolan Ryan's wife. Young had become a reflexive apologist for management, and his son-in-law worked in the Met front office. He made the situation so venomous that the Mets finally decided to trade away their best player.

Young wasn't the first writer to trash a famous New York ballplayer. In the fifties, Jimmy Cannon was probably New York's most influential sportswriter. He would lose his way and his audience during the turbulent sixties, but, at the beginning of the decade, he still had enough juice to take down the man who beat the Babe. During the last two months of the great home-run race of 1961, Roger Maris, reticent but sharp-tongued, was overwhelmed by the media attention he received on a daily basis. It made him physically ill, although his relations with the Yankee beat writers had yet to turn sour. In the offseason, Maris tried to reclaim his privacy. When he showed up for spring training, he wanted to keep it that way. Cannon scheduled an interview with Maris, but the outfielder blew him off. Stung and with a column (or two) to fill, Cannon lit into the home-run champ over the next two days as if Maris were the worst SOB you could ever hope to meet. Cannon's words, along with the abuse heaped on by a few of Cannon's pals, turned the tide for Maris in New York where once-supportive Yankee fans became nasty.

Maris was caught by changing times. A generation earlier, beat writers wrote stories based only on what they saw on the field, but the advent of night games and television suddenly made quotes an essential feature of every game story. Beat writers needed access and cooperation for this part of the job. Newspaper coverage of the game had changed to favor the man who could draw out or manufacture the most interesting quotes. The two best baseball writers in New York in the decade after World War II, the Golden Age of baseball in the five boroughs, were Cannon at the *Post* and Red Smith at the *Herald-Tribune*. Both men wrote brilliantly on other subjects as well, using only their powers of description to comment on the action they had seen or the characters who had performed. They did not need an athlete to describe what he felt when they could see it with their own eyes. While Cannon and Smith attracted the most readers, Arthur Daley, champion of piped quotes in the *Times*, was celebrated by the industry, winning a Pulitzer in 1956 that his rivals mocked as undeserved.

Because they are nowhere near as close to the ballplayers as the beat writers of Woodward's day, today's baseball writers allow the ballplayers space to fool around. Despite their increased distance, baseball reporters see their role as proactive. They will generate heat on a story in order to sell papers or to prove to their editors that they are a step ahead of the other beat writers. And when they're bored or in need of an angle, they'll just make something up. In his book *The Hustler's Handbook*, maverick owner Bill Veeck tells a great story about how Yogi Berra first became a managerial candidate toward the end of his career in the early sixties. Restless at baseball's 1960 winter meetings, three young writers—Stan Isaacs of *Newsday*, Leonard Shecter from the *New York Post*, and Larry Merchant, then in Philadelphia—decided to create a false rumor about a hot new managerial candidate. They put their heads together to come up with the most shocking name possible. The winner was Yogi Berra. Other reporters bought the fabrication and the Yankee catcher indicated his interest in the idea. Yogi was soon featured on the short list of candidates any time a manager's job came open. By the start of the 1964 season, Berra was in charge of the Yankees.

The Yankees' first great manager had arrived in a similarly convoluted fashion. New owners Jacob Ruppert and Tillinghast Huston were looking for a new manager who could turn around a franchise that had been at best mediocre. Huston coveted Uncle Wilbert Robinson. J. G. Taylor Spink, the publisher of *The Sporting News*, recommended to his friend Ruppert that he go after Miller Huggins. When Ruppert was able to convince Huggins to come to the Yankees with Spink's help, the resulting conflict between the two owners was so deeply felt that it was not resolved until Huston sold off his shares in the club after supervising the construction of the colossal new stadium.

\*            \*            \*

Through the years, beat writers have generally run baseball up. Conflicts between team owners and players seemed to create a bind for writers so inclined. In reality, baseball writers have reliably taken one side in such disputes throughout the century, often with hyperbolic ferocity. Whether condemning Joe DiMaggio for a holdout during spring training after his brilliant second season, or ripping Bernie Williams for his disloyalty in exploring free agency after the 1998 season, most baseball writers have been little more than owners' mouthpieces when salary disputes arise. Holding out was DiMaggio's only leverage to get a fair salary under the oppressive reserve clause, and the free-agency route was Williams's best strategy to maximize the amount he secured from Steinbrenner. No matter. The same sportswriters who'd built them up now tore them down for their impudence, greed, and disloyalty.

Forced to choose between players and owners, beat writers will side with management every time for two reasons. First, the writers believe management will outlast the players and therefore make a

pragmatic decision to nurture the relationship that seems more important over the long haul. Second, the front office controls access to the
kind of stories, especially trade rumors, that make a beat writer appear
enterprising to his readers and editors. Count the number of attribu-
tions to "a team source" or "a high-level Yankee official" the next time
you read the sports page. Those quotes almost never come from players. The idea that baseball's front offices need the protection of anonymous sourcing to spread their gossip seems absurd. These guys aren't
exactly protecting state secrets. Nevertheless, baseball writers and
their editors offer owners and general managers exactly that privilege in coverage identical to front-page pieces about the Pentagon and
the State Department in the *New York Times*. Sportswriters, like political journalists, allow management to run their spin through the
papers in exchange for favored access.

Two stories written by Buster Olney, a former Baltimore Oriole
beat writer now covering the Yankees for the *New York Times*, illustrate this symbiosis beautifully. If you ask the average baseball fan to
choose whether Cal Ripken, Jr. or George Steinbrenner is more
admirable, it's safe to assume everyone would choose Ripken, the
ironman who broke Gehrig's consecutive game streak while maintaining an image cleaner than any other American celebrity. Not
Buster. In the course of two long articles (an A1 story about Ripken
toward the end of the 1997 season and a cover story about the Boss
in the Sunday magazine exactly one year later), Olney, a writer whose
biting prose indicates an ambition to be the Maureen Dowd of the
sports page, shredded Ripken while elevating Steinbrenner.

Olney presented Ripken's desire to maintain his consecutive-games
streak as an obsession, the selfish pursuit of an individual goal that was
hurting his team. He attacked Ripken as a poor teammate who was the
beneficiary of special privileges. Cal was benched only subject to his
approval, stayed in his own hotel away from the rest of the team on the
road, kept his own private doctor to treat his ailments, and called pitches

from the shortstop position. Olney even noted that Ripken had "the best parking spot at Camden Yards," as if the ballplayer's long years of service and desire to maintain his privacy despite his fame were unjustified.

Even then, Olney was not through. He accused Ripken of being petulant and vengeful, tossing in an anonymous quote from a "club official": "With Cal, nothing is easy." Perhaps Olney's bludgeoning was a product of an unspoken enmity from his days covering Ripken and the Orioles. Maybe it was a sign that the rivalry between the Orioles and Yankees had heated up to the point where even the Times felt compelled to run the kind of "we're great, they suck" piece usually found in the tabloids. Either way, the piece was a devastating attack on a widely loved player.

With Steinbrenner, it was quite a different story. Olney claimed that "there has been a Steinbrenner evolution." He admitted that Steinbrenner had been one of the most hated men in sports but then proceeded to rehabilitate the Boss:

> A funny thing happened on Steinbrenner's way to infamy. He returned from his last suspension in 1993, and three years later his Yankees won the World Series.
>
> ... Whereas some players despised or feared Steinbrenner in previous years, the '98 Yankees seem to genuinely enjoy his presence, his effect. He, in turn, basks in his players' reflection and adores the attention he is receiving as a result of their play. He loves being loved, and in the Bronx, the 1998 season has so far been a George Steinbrenner lovefest.

Olney presented Steinbrenner as a competitive but lovable old man who had learned from his mistakes. Howard Rubinstein, the Boss' PR flack, could not have scripted it any better. Yet another justifiably reviled owner was being celebrated as if he'd won the Nobel Peace Prize. Like beat writers throughout history, Olney was firmly on the side of the owners.

## SYMPATHY FOR THE DEVIL

*At a time when Steinbrenner is lobbying/threatening hard for a new, taxpayer-subsidized ballpark, people who can hold the most sway over public opinion are accepting Steinbrenner's invitations to spend the postseason as his wined-and-dined guests within one of Steinbrenner's suites at Yankee Stadium. Top executives at all the local papers have accepted.*

*. . . Worse, virtually every local major news entity is in on this friendly little arrangement, so there's little chance that one publication or electronic media entity will blow the whistle on the others.*

*Interesting, too, is that at a time when polls find New Yorkers prepared to reject a proposal to build Steinbrenner a new stadium—should the issue come to a vote—many editorialists see it George's way. Do free tickets and red-carpet treatments at Yankee playoff and World Series games enter the editorial process? . . . these guardians of good should know better than to place themselves in a position where the question needs to be asked.*

—Phil Mushnick, *New York Post*

*He is far nicer than the negative image that was portrayed. So I figured if some of the writers who were writing about him and killing him saw him up close, a truer version of Steinbrenner would emerge. If someone has spoken to a person and he is civil and cordial, you'll get a different attitude going into a story than if the person is never available and thought of in a negative way.*

—Howard Rubinstein

Buster Olney was hardly alone in his sycophancy. Steinbrenner was lionized by fawning articles in all the dailies, a softball half-hour interview on ESPN, and overheated columns in the tabloids begging him not to sell the team because his departure would assure the franchise's decline. Even the liberal-left at *The Nation*, in a piece by longtime Steinbrenner crony and apologist Sidney Zion, joined the chorus. That the Boss owned the team during its longest absence from the postseason and had been seen as the worst scoundrel in the game—twice suspended by major-league baseball, once convicted of election fraud—was no longer interesting. Given enough time, the infinitely renewable pool of American innocence cleanses all. To the sinner (if he is a winner) go not only the spoils, but also a forgotten past, especially if he has thousands of World Series tickets lying around to disperse.

Getting a ticket to see the 1998 World Series at Yankee Stadium was probably more difficult than at any other time in Series history. Just two years earlier when they reached the '96 Series, the Yankees made 16,000 seats per game available to the public. The demand for those scarce tickets created a near-riot at the Stadium. In 1998, the supply was even tighter as less than 5,000 seats were sold for each game. While some of the 11,000 tickets that had disappeared from the market were certainly claimed by new season-ticket holders, thousands had been siphoned off to be distributed by the Yankees, Major League Baseball, the Mayor's Office, and the Fox Network. It was appropriate that the Fox cameras caught a shot of Steinbrenner, Murdoch, and Giuliani together in a field box during the playoffs. Given that the city owned the stadium Steinbrenner played in and Murdoch owned the network that broadcast his games, their presence, if not their seating arrangement, seemed appropriate.

The sudden influx of other members of the New York media elite could not be so easily explained. Howard Rubinstein, Steinbrenner's public relations manager, recognized that the incredible demand for tickets presented an excellent opportunity to curry favor with the city's leading image makers by finding them seats at an event millions wanted to witness. Those lucky enough to receive invitations were entertained with the best view in the house, a free meal, team souvenirs, and the chance to shmooze with the Boss. With

Steinbrenner in the midst of an attempt to dislodge the city coffers of as much as a billion dollars for a new or renovated stadium, invitations went out to the journalists who could affect the stadium story: newspaper and television executives, columnists and reporters who worked in the metro sections at the dailies.

As Phil Mushnick noted in his column in the *New York Post*, those who received invitations seemed to have few ethical concerns about accepting tickets. *Crain's New York Business* was the only other local publication to mention this practice in the fall of 1998. While the article disclosed that the magazine's publisher, Alair Townsend, was among the invitees, it merely described Rubinstein's campaign to soften Steinbrenner's image and glossed over any ethical issues.

In 1996, when the Yankees revisited the World Series for the first time in fifteen years, the invitations had created a small media furor. Mushnick wrote about the unfairness of the arrangements, as did James Ledbetter in his media column at the *Village Voice*. *Editor and Publisher*, the leading trade publication in the newspaper business, explored the ethical quandary in a series of stories. Rubinstein told the industry watchdog that the invitations had nothing to do with influencing the coverage of the Yankee attempt to secure a huge public subsidy for a new ballpark. "It's a harmless episode that gained nothing for the Yankees," Rubinstein claimed while asserting that some of the invitees had been tough on his client. "Some of the worst stories ever published about George Steinbrenner were in their newspapers. We certainly didn't invite them to say 'thank you' for their coverage."

While some reporters apparently rejected the tickets, Joseph Lelyveld, executive editor of the *Times*, saw no conflict of interest at all. "I don't understand the conflict. I do not see it as a good ethical issue of the day. We paid for our tickets," Lelyveld, who sat with Steinbrenner in the owners' box during a playoff game, explained. "I go to as many New York events as I can. I go to an opening night on

Broadway once a season. I am the executive editor of the paper. I move around quite a bit."

## START SPREADING THE NEWS

*The vast majority of citizens have relatively little at stake in sta-dium subsidies, for the annualized cost of even the most heavily subsidized and expensive facilities is only tens of dollars per household. The people with unusually intense interests include team owners, construction interests, diehard sports fans, and sports journalists, all of whom are likely to have atypically favorable views about a new stadium and to advocate a more elaborate facil-ity than most citizens would find ideal.*

—Rodney Fort

Pick a town where a new stadium is being debated, and you will be hard-pressed to find a mainstream media outlet questioning the wis-dom of spending the money. The response by the New York media was no different. The *Post*, the *Daily News*, *Newsday*, and the *Times* each praised the idea of a stadium move from the Bronx to Manhattan on their editorial pages in the aftermath of the expan-sion-joint collapse. Critiques on local TV news could not be found, and local weeklies including *Crain's*, the *New York Observer*, and *New York* magazine each found space to welcome the Yankees to an address nearer their Midtown offices. Convenience surely helped cre-ate this echo chamber, but there was money at stake, too. The owners of the *Times* and the *Daily News* had significant property interests near the proposed site that might rise considerably in value if the Yankees moved into a neighborhood that was underdeveloped by the standards of Midtown Manhattan. The papers had an even greater stake in insuring the Yankees stayed somewhere within the five bor-oughs that they considered their domain. If the Yanks moved to

Jersey, the millions the tabloids gleaned from covering the team might be in jeopardy.

Even the gossip pages evinced an intense interest in the goings-on within Yankee Nation. Days after the conclusion of the 1998 World Series, Page Six of the *Post* reported on a sighting of the Boss at Trump Tower and gushed that "Steinbrenner is working around the clock, and not always getting the respect he deserves." The piece claimed that Steinbrenner was involved in extended negotiations to sell the Yankees to Cablevision CEO Chuck Dolan, a resident in the eponymous apartment building, for $650 million. The article did not mention that Dolan's partner in his cable operations is Rupert Murdoch, the owner of the *Post*. In fact, the piece never mentioned Murdoch's name at all.

While Murdoch lurked in the deep shadows behind this story, the gossip columnists could not resist dropping the name of Randy Levine, New York City's deputy mayor for economic development, who breakfasted at the Regency with Steinbrenner. Levine's conflict of interest was even greater than Murdoch's. He had been an attorney for the Yankees before working for baseball's owners as a labor negotiator. Even as the city attempted to conduct negotiations with two major-league franchises regarding new ballparks, Levine's office maintained a direct phone line to Major League Baseball's Midtown offices. Steinbrenner flack Howard Rubinstein was sensitive enough to the appearance of impropriety to try to dismiss the meeting as insignificant, asserting that "[Steinbrenner and Levine] didn't have time during the season to get together. They just wanted to catch up."

The gossip columnist went even further in asserting that everything was above board:

> The two might have discussed the weather the whole time, because they weren't talking about baseball: Levine's previous job was as a labor negotiator for Major League

Baseball. Levine avoids any conflict of interest by recusing
himself from any baseball business—including the issue of
whether the city should help Steinbrenner build a new stadium in Manhattan—and handing the ball to Giuliani's
counsel, Denny Young.

Levine had been on Steinbrenner's direct payroll before, was still
drawing money as a consultant to major-league baseball, and had
access to inside information at City Hall that would have been interesting to a potential future employer. With all this real news to discuss, the columnist instead covered his eyes and claimed that the two
only talked about the weather.

When the stadium race heated up, even self-proclaimed critics
could not be relied upon. In *The Nation*'s first issue devoted to sports,
an article entitled "Why Baseball Needs New York to Just Say No" by
Mark Rosentraub, a professor of urban planning from Indiana
University, was a perfect example of a critic lining up his bonafides
just before selling out to the opposition. In his piece, Rosentraub,
recent author of *Major League Losers: The Real Cost of Sports and
Who's Paying for It*, used the language of outrage ("Steinbrenner joins
the long line of team owners who have held up their city governments for new facilities"). He was especially concerned about the
destabilizing impact a new stadium would have on other municipalities who wanted teams to compete with the Yankees. After racing
through numbers that proved the Yankees were making money,
Rosentraub unveiled a two-part solution: the Yankees build their own
stadium because they can afford to and the two border states (New
Jersey and New York) cut the Yankees' negotiating power by agreeing to share tax revenue generated by the Yankees no matter where
the franchise locates.

"No one has ever analyzed this before," Rosentraub congratulated
himself, as if the Boss' more critical observers in town (including the

city's Independent Budget Office, the *Daily News'* Mike Lupica, the *Post*'s Phil Mushnick, the *Times'* Bob Herbert, and the *Voice*'s Wayne Barrett) hadn't attacked the idea of public financing for a new or renovated Yankee Stadium as misguided corporate welfare from the outset. Everyone in town understood the problem wasn't the Boss' shallow pockets, but his lack of enthusiasm for dipping into them. Don Imus managed, on air, to shame the Boss into admitting he would contribute something toward the cost of a new stadium. The democratic process had failed New York City in such a way that Giuliani could ramrod through any damn deal he wanted, even though polls showed that nine in ten residents disagreed with him.

Given the longstanding rivalry between New Jersey and New York, including battles over Ellis Island, Liberty Island, and the invention of baseball, Rosentraub's suggestion of cooperation between the two states was, if well-intentioned, nevertheless ridiculous. The idea that Jersey suburbanites should share some of the resources an already underfinanced New York City receives when they keep the Yankees begs the question of whether Jersey will turn over revenues from their sports teams, or, better still, from the dozens of companies they've enticed through tax incentives across the river to Hoboken and Jersey City. Given their competing interests and the tribalist loyalties of the communities they serve, Giuliani and Whitman could never work out a fair deal.

At least Rosentraub's motives were sound: he wanted to slow down the ever-expanding Municipal-Athletic Complex so that smaller cities were treated fairly. Or, at least, so he claimed. But Rosentraub soon produced a twenty-three-page report paid for by Major League Baseball on behalf of the proponents of Proposition C, the 1998 ballot measure in San Diego County that would hand over $275 million in public funds for the construction of a new ballpark. Rosentraub's study was clearly designed to have an impact on the vote. The essential message: stadium critic tells San Diego we're not getting ripped off. The report was released in October three weeks before the election, and Rosentraub went to San Diego to promote his endorsement of Proposition C based on the project's role (alongside yet-to-be-constructed hotels and stores) in revitalizing a deteriorating section of downtown and strengthening the Padres' ability to reform Major League Baseball by restoring competitive balance. "If you don't do something to create a synergy of downtown economic development, then San Diego continues to be a series of suburbs in search of a city," the urban planner told one reporter for the *San Diego Union Tribune*, before explaining to another that "having a lousy team in a new ballpark is a prescription for disaster."

Southern Californians have demonstrated for over a century that they want their own yards and are not interested in merely replicating the urban archetypes of Manhattan, Boston, and Baltimore that emphasize a central business district above all other priorities. A new ballpark in downtown San Diego will hardly cause homeowners in North San Diego County to put their homes on the market and buy up waterfront condos a few blocks from a central business district. Furthermore, Rosentraub admitted that he had not even studied San Diego's fiscal condition, which included a $40 million deficit and $80 million that had to be found for infrastructure maintenance. The man who had written in his book that cities should put schools, libraries, and other traditional civic functions before having quality pro teams had not even examined the state of San Diego's books before urging its voters to spend $275 million. (The report concluded, "If I lived in San Diego, I would vote for Proposition C.") In two months, Rosentraub had transformed from leading stadium critic to key ballpark proponent, although he assured one reporter that his thesis that ballparks per se do not stimulate surrounding economies remained valid.

This time it cost more than George Weiss's steak, but, of course, the opinions of academics are worth more than the scribblings of mere sportswriters. Major-league baseball paid Rosentraub $13,000 plus travel expenses for his efforts, more than half the amount spent by opponents of the measure. In fact, Prop C's supporters (primarily the Padres) spent about $3 million to get the measure passed, outspending their opponents by more than 100 to 1. There was no clearer illustration of the proposition's benefits to the team's owners and a resulting imbalance of power in the "democratic" process, a fact that the old Rosentraub surely would have decried.

In an interview, Rosentraub asserted that he supported Prop C because San Diego was unique. He had met with the Padre owner and trusted him to do the right thing (i.e., spend money to win ball games). This reasoning sounded a lot like the Connecticut state legislator who said he wanted to give Patriot owner Robert Kraft the state treasury because he was moved by the sight of Kraft kissing his son. San Diego is not a special case. They are just another team trying to keep up with the sport's wealthy elite. Of course, a small-market team would try to emulate the playbook established by the upwardly mobile Oriole and Indian franchises. With an incredible spending advantage, the best Padre team in fifteen years, and a bit of late-inning relief from a once reliable critic of public financing for stadia, Prop C passed by a comfortable margin.

## CUBA LIBRE

*In Cuba, baseball is the only sport. There's a saying in Cuba that you're born with a bat in your right hand and a glove in your left.*

—Joe Cubas

*Fidel Castro was turned down by the Senators because a scouting report said that he didn't have a major league fastball. An aspiring pitching ace spurned can be a dangerous man with a long memory.*

—Eugene McCarthy

*I'd get me a buncha bats and balls and learn them kids behind the Iron Curtain how to play baseball instead of totin' rifles and swallerin' lies. And if Joe Stallion ever learnt how much dough there was in the concessions at a ball park, he'd quit commanism and get into a honest business.*

—Dizzy Dean

*The magazine Smena, under the title "Beizbol," explained to its readers today that baseball, the American national sport was a "beastly battle, a bloody fight with mayhem and murder" and furthermore nothing but a Yankee perversion of an ancient Russian village sport called "lapta." Smena presented a vivid description of the American national sport for its readers, declaring that far from being "amusing," "noble" or "safe" beizbol was actually a dangerous game in which both players and spectators frequently suffered terrible wounds or even death.*

—*New York Times* (1952)

Narratives are shaped by the boundaries of acceptable discourse. El Duque's flight from Cuba was not on a raft as widely reported but rather on a twenty-foot sailboat with seven compatriots. After they failed to encounter the speedboat scheduled to pick them up, it took the refugees roughly ten hours at sea to sail forty miles and reach an unpopulated island in the Bahamas. The inflated story of a harrowing journey on a raft through shark-infested waters—the waters that surround the continental United States are similarly shark-infested—quickly evolved into a useful explanation for El Duque's ability to pitch under pressure. As his agent pursued a sale of the movie rights to El Duque's story, the myth grew and the boat shrank.

El Duque had suffered while his party waited for days to be found and rescued, but that only spurred on broadcasters, coaches, and teammates who asserted Raft Man would be fearless on the mound because he'd faced far greater danger at sea. Hernandez pitched brilliantly during the postseason, but there was no reason to assume that someone who faced a life-threatening crisis with dignity would be similarly at ease on a playing field under a national spotlight. After all, if Steinbrenner believed this hokum, spring training for the Yankees would quickly be transformed from baseball camp into a simulation of *Lord of the Flies*.

The journey from the Bahamas to the Yankees disappeared from El Duque's story because it reveals the less-than-complete freedom granted to the most talented practitioners of the national pastime. A U.S. Coast Guard helicopter spotted and rescued El Duque and his friends. Hernandez was immediately offered a humanitarian visa and the opportunity to go to Miami to reunite with his half-brother, but instead he asked to be transported to the nearest safe haven as instructed by his agent, Joe Cubas. He boarded a Lear jet chartered by Cubas and flew to Costa Rica, where he began to train for his big-league audition.

El Duque's reluctance to accept America's welcoming embrace was caused by an anomaly in baseball's collective bargaining agreement. Under that deal, baseball players in the United States are subject to an entry draft that assigns players' rights to one team for an extended period of years. Unlike almost all other Americans, ballplayers that want to make a living cannot negotiate with a number of different employers seeking a good fit, the best financial package, or a desired location. By keeping his distance, El Duque retained his ability to choose among interested teams. Free-agent status in hand, Hernandez became a Yankee when Steinbrenner offered the most money.

Once a Yankee, El Duque emigrated from Costa Rica to the United States easily, suggesting an American acceptance of immigrants unsupported by popular opinion or law. The earliest long feature about Hernandez appeared in *ESPN The Magazine* (Disney's recent shot across the bow at Time-Warner institution *Sports*

*Illustrated*) and remains unmatched for its conscious appeal to stereotype: an America offering unlimited freedom, openness, warmth, and
wealth alongside a Cuba rife with corruption, poverty, fear, and injus-
tice. It concluded with an image of a statue in the parking lot outside
the café where Livan and Orlando finally reunited, a smaller rendition of Liberty herself atop the following Spanish-language inscrip-
tion: "Light the path of our Cuban brothers so they are safe and
sound in the land of liberty." Powerful stuff, but ask the Haitian
refugees fleeing Duvalier about our open-door policy. Our on-again,
off-again embrace of Cuban immigrants ends the day Castro dies.
The Cubans will suddenly see the "No Vacancy" sign posted for their
Latin American brothers and sisters.

The final piece of El Duque's unexamined story concerns his
tremendous physical conditioning. During spring training, the
Yankees were pleasantly surprised to find that by any measure
Hernandez was the fittest athlete on the team. The press took notice
because El Duque hadn't pitched for two years, and the news was
incorporated into a story of good things to come for the Yankees'
Cuban investment. Left unexamined however was how an athlete
trained in the miserable conditions of poor Cuba could be in better
shape than dozens of ballplayers with access to every advantage—
personal trainers, medical research, expensive equipment, and "nutri-
tional supplements"—American sports could offer. Hernandez'
superiority did not generate even a scintilla of interest in such a question, an illustration of America's true perception of Cuba's impotence.

## TALE OF TWO YANKEES

*It's Cone's option to accept $5.5 million for 1999 or become a free
agent if no extension is agreed upon. That's the way the contract
was written, and Cone would be a fool not to take advantage of
that option. So the Yankees are left with one chore before the clock
strikes midnight: Sign him!*

*... Much is made of the power of the New York press. Little is made of Cone's power over the New York media. ... He does such a deft job of filling notebooks that the one question if asked the right way at the right locker on the right day could result in a pair of teammates blasting each other with all of New York as an audience often goes unasked.*

—Tom Keegan, *New York Post*

*What do you suppose the average fan of my baseball team thinks when he hears Bernie's agent say he's embarrassed that we offered him $7.5 million a year? I have deep affection for Bernie Williams. But somebody should point out to him that if his character hasn't changed, the perception of his character has by the tactics his agent has taken with Bob Watson. And if this is coming from the player, as a lot of people seem to think, then maybe he isn't the sweet homespun kid from up the block that we've always thought he is.*

—George Steinbrenner

*There is no more honored piece of real estate than center field in Yankee Stadium, and if allowed to negotiate, the Yankees in all probability would pay Williams between $8 million to $9 million a year—their top dollar—to keep playing there.*

— Bill Madden, *New York Daily News*

After the 1998 season, the contracts of a number of Yankee players expired. Right away, the Yankees picked up the $3.4 million option for Joe Girardi, a weak-hitting catcher who was a part-timer. Two of the veteran starters preferred pitching to Girardi than throwing to rising young star Jorge Posada. Furthermore, Torre relied on the aging catcher as a clubhouse leader. Instead of buying Girardi out of his contract and re-signing him at a discount, the Yanks signed the journeyman to preclude the negligible risk he might find a better offer. The deal was proof that money was not an issue for the richest team in baseball. They could bring back any of their players at any price. If they did not re-sign a player from the championship team, that was either by design or the result of a foul-up in the negotiating process.

The best two players who the Yankee front office had to deal with in the 1998 offseason were David Cone and Bernie Williams. Cone had had a variety of ailments over the previous few years, but when he was able to pitch, he had been among the top ten starters in the league. He held an option that allowed him to explore the open market if he so desired after he pitched 200 innings in 1998. Williams, although younger than Cone, was also plagued by injuries that would cause him to miss a few dozen games every year. When healthy, Williams was the most complete player on the best team in baseball: batting champion as a switch-hitter with good power off both sides as well as an excellent eye, speed around the basepaths, and tremendous range in center field. As good as Cone was, the Yankees had six quality starters, perhaps the only team in the league to have an excess of pitching talent, but they had nobody to replace Williams in the middle of both the offense and defense.

Given that reality, it was logical to assume that the Yankees would hardball Cone and accommodate Williams. In fact, the opposite occurred. The front office made it clear to Cone and the media that a deal would be done as soon as the two sides worked out the numbers. The Boss had decided Williams wasn't worth what the market would bear. Or perhaps he didn't want him on the Yanks any more. Maybe he was willing to bluff until the last minute. Whatever the reason, the Yankees' front office badmouthed Williams, and the papers that had praised him all season long now turned on him with a vengeance even as they backed up Cone. Keegan's article in the *Post* entitled "Gotta Keep Cone" begged Steinbrenner to sign the player, something he'd already decided to do.

"Why is Bernie Williams being painted as just another greedy (How dare he not want to continue patrolling the hallowed ground at the Stadium) ballplayer looking to pocket some major free agent booty, while David Cone gets a free pass from media and fans alike?" wrote Bob Raissman in the *Daily News*. "Cone has the media here wrapped around his pinkie. The guy has filled up so many notebooks and videotape machines his willing media servants are cutting him major slack while Williams and his agent Scott Boras take the heat."

When Cone was re-signed, the writers and the public shrugged their shoulders. Everyone knew it was a done deal. A few weeks later, when Williams and Steinbrenner came to terms on an agreement worth $84 million over seven years, the writers, having been fed stories about a half-dozen Williams replacements, were stunned. Veteran *Daily News'* columnist Mike Lupica described that credulous faith in Steinbrenner's leaks perfectly:

> Bernie Williams was suddenly a terrible guy after being with the Yankees since the age of 17, giving them his whole baseball life, because he was looking to make all the money in the world. He was leaving the Yankees, that is what you heard all over the place. Except Williams never said he was leaving. So people were just guessing. As usual, speculation immediately became fact. That is the game now in New York.
>
> . . . In a year, Steinbrenner went from offering Williams five years and $37 million to giving him a deal for seven years, $84 million. Even a week ago, the last best offer from the Yankees was supposed to be $60 million for five years.

Steinbrenner paid Williams tens of millions more than he would have had to if he'd made a reasonable offer in the spring before the season. With Williams safely in the fold, beat writers scrambled to get back in the outfielder's good graces while trying to voice the populist resentment of their readers toward such a big deal.

## STRAWBERRY SURPRISE

*Two weeks ago, when Steinbrenner wanted Darryl Strawberry at
the head of the Yankee parade, he couldn't even wait to get back to
New York to get an answer from Strawberry. Now he makes
Strawberry wait, and worry about money, at a time when that is
the last thing he should be doing.*

*. . . When Eric Davis was undergoing chemotherapy in '97
after his colon cancer—and before he came back in the summer of
'98 and had a 30-game hitting streak and became the kind of star
he had been in his baseball youth—Orioles owner Peter Angelos
didn't wait one minute. He announced that he was picking up
Davis' contract for '98 right now, there you go, no questions asked.*

*. . . This was in great contrast to the way Davis was treated by
Marge Schott once. Davis ruptured a kidney in the '90 World
Series and spent a month in the hospital after that. Schott wouldn't
even buy Davis a plane trip home from Oakland.*

*. . . Angelos or Marge Schott? Steinbrenner can go either way.
. . . If Strawberry doesn't have a contract to play for the Yankees
next season, then it is fair for him to think—for all of us to
think—that his last significant role for the team was as a prop.*

— **Mike Lupica,** *New York Daily News*


Writers who cover the Yankees have tremendous influence because
the Boss is sensitive to criticism and obsessed by what is written
about him. Mike Lupica, perhaps the leading sports columnist in
town, does not much respect George Steinbrenner, and the Boss—a
moniker coined by Lupica—clearly does not like that fact. The article above, clearly designed to shame Steinbrenner into doing the
right thing, provoked his wildest reaction of the year.

With a chance to look like a hero (in the end, he was going to pay
Strawberry the money in question, $2.5 million), the Boss managed
to come out smelling like a sewer. His PR man Rubinstein could have

been instructed to tell everyone that the deal would be done by a certain date and gloss over any other details. Instead, Steinbrenner chose to unload a vicious story on a player about to undergo his first chemotherapy treatment. Through Rubinstein, Steinbrenner told the tabloids that there were two reasons for the delay in signing a deal with Strawberry. First, the Boss did not want to have Strawberry's salary credited against the salary cap if he could not play. It would cost Steinbrenner an extra $800,000 or so that would go into the pool for the small-market teams. That part of the story just made Steinbrenner look cheap, searching for any way to weasel out of the income redistribution needed to keep the game healthy. The second part of the story was that Steinbrenner wanted to make sure the money, or at least some of it, got back to Strawberry. According to Steinbrenner, the outfielder owed the IRS millions and might have other serious debts as well. On the eve of chemotherapy, the last thing Strawberry needed was his financial condition in the papers. At the same time, he could hardly attack Steinbrenner because he needed the Yankee owner to pick up his option.

Charisse Strawberry told a reporter her husband did not want to comment.

"Darryl does not want to say anything to antagonize George or anything," she said. "I believe Steinbrenner at this point. We'll see what happens on the deadline. I believe George will try and work with us."

With the Yankees a new broadcast partner of Murdoch's Channel 5, the *Post* was now in bed with Steinbrenner. The *Post*'s Yankee writer Joel Sherman performed the unenviable task of trying to make the Boss look good in a couple of articles. In his first, a news story, Sherman gave Steinbrenner the floor unfiltered:

> Steinbrenner wants to clarify exactly how much Strawberry owes for back taxes, alimony and child support. He particularly wants to put Strawberry on a schedule to reimburse the

government and said he might even pay more than $2.5 million if it eliminates Strawberry's financial nightmare.

... "I am trying to determine what this kid owes," Steinbrenner said. "His agent, his wife, Darryl himself, all give me different numbers. Some say $2 million, some say more, some say less.

... "It's crazy. This kid does not even know how much he owes. And I mean kid because when it comes to business he is a kid. When it comes to being an athlete, he is a man."

As sad as it was for Sherman to let Steinbrenner take cheap shots at a person he claimed to care about, it was to be expected. Anything Steinbrenner tells the tabloids, no matter how scurrilous, either on the record or on background, will get printed because they fear that they will get beaten on the story by their rival. The navel-gazing that goes on at the news side of a paper in the midst of a story with tabloid elements (like the Lewinsky story) about what should and should not be reported simply never happens in the sports pages. In a column, however, Sherman went beyond reporting and offered a rationalization for the source who happens to be a partner of his paper's owner:

George Steinbrenner gets into his worst trouble when he's defending himself. That's when the deceptions and meanness almost always are worst. His initial handling of the Darryl Strawberry matter is no exception—but rather illustrative of the rule.

... there are times we must look beyond the easy-to-criticize Steinbrenner caricature to see the harder-to-embrace character. In this case, actions speak louder than words. Even if they are misguided and, ultimately, mean-spirited words.

. . . It is easy in that light to paint Steinbrenner as the villain, since that has become the knee-jerk sport of choice in this city the past quarter century. And here you can paint recovering cancer patient vs. bullying ogre.

> . . . I know everyone talks big, but no one out there except George Steinbrenner will help.

Rubinstein had shopped this same story at the *Daily News*. His first call was to Lupica, who saw the Boss' response to his column as even worse than his prior inactivity:

> . . . Yesterday afternoon, Steinbrenner—who does not have the guts to make this sort of phone call himself—has his flack, whispering Howard Rubenstein, call this newspaper.
>
> "I've some information on the Steinbrenner-Strawberry relationship," Rubenstein said.
>
> . . . The purpose of the phone call, the tip he wanted to hand the *Daily News*, was about Strawberry's finances. So this was Howard Rubenstein's job late yesterday afternoon: leak private financial information about a cancer patient. Why not? The patient isn't his client.
>
> . . . Rubenstein did this because George Steinbrenner told him to do it. There weren't two weasels anywhere in town who could touch either one of them yesterday. You would tell both of them they should be ashamed of themselves, but the whole notion of shame on this one would just confuse them.

Lupica went on to attack Steinbrenner's paternalism in a highly critical piece, but failed to discuss the ethical issues raised by his paper's decision to run the story. The editors at the *News* knew Strawberry was about to undergo chemotherapy, too. If they had chosen not to run with Steinbrenner and Rubinstein's leak, they could have saved the Strawberrys a lot of angst at a difficult time.

Worried about getting beat by the *Post*, they never hesitated in airing the dirty laundry.

## HOLY COW

*The Babe hits it clear into the centerfield bleachers for a home run. For a home run! Did you hear what I said? Where is that fellow who told me not to talk about Ruth any more? Send him up here. Oh, what a shot. Directly over second. The boys are all over him over there. One of the boys is riding on Ruth's back. Oh, what a shot. Directly over second base, and almost on a line, and then that dumbbell, where is he, who told me not to talk about Ruth? Oh, boy. Not that I love Ruth but, oh, how I love to see a shot like that. Wow! That's a World Series' record, three home runs in one World Series' game. And what a home run. That was probably the longest hit ever made in Sportsman's Park. They tell me this is the first ball ever hit in the centerfield stands. That is a mile and a half from here.*

— Graham McNamee

The excerpt above comes from the first ballgame broadcast nationally over the radio, game four of the 1926 World Series. Within a decade, radio would become as important to the game as the print media. Its era of dominance is long past, but any serious baseball fan still listens to games on the radio. The radio was the first outlet for teams to sell their own product and that of their advertisers. This made a popular radio man a valuable commodity, as worthwhile to his team as the baseball beat writer was to his paper.

From the late forties until his mysterious release in the mid-sixties, broadcaster Mel Allen was consistently among the Yankees' ten highest paid employees, better paid than most of the Yankee regulars. While the Dodgers, apparently believing a good chunk of their audience consisted of connoisseurs, always selected guys with wonderful narrative ability and a sense of objectivity like Red Barber and Vin Scully, the Yankees preferred melodramatic boosters like Mel Allen, Phil Rizzuto, and John Sterling. If the Bronx Bombers and their fans seemed to represent the city's upper crust, the wild emotion of their loyalist announcers created a wider appeal.

Radio remains a place where teams endlessly move product. Rarely does a pitch go by without Sterling or his sidekick Michael Kay pushing a sponsor. Sometimes they push politicians, too, over the airwaves at WABC. During game six of the hard-fought series with Cleveland, Mayor Giuliani found his way into the broadcast booth in the bottom of the second inning. The Yankee season was in as much jeopardy as it faced all year; the mayor, however, was interested in other matters. First he pumped up the new stadium idea, then he plugged Matt Fong, Republican candidate for senator in California, before discussing the difficulty of protecting President Clinton when he visited New York City.

While Giuliani dissembled, the WABC radio audience wondered what the hell was happening on the field beneath. The *Daily News'* Bob Raissman assessed the situation perfectly: "With George Steinbrenner looking to get a new Stadium and MSG owner Charles (Man From Monopoly) Dolan looking to either buy the Yankees or raise the cost for fans to see every local team — Yankees, Mets, Knicks, Nets, Rangers, Islanders and Devils — on TV, it can't hurt to have Giuliani's support. And what better way than to let him take over the radio booth anytime he wants. This ain't about baseball anymore. It's about business and it stinks."

## MR. MURDOCH, I PRESUME

*Mr. Murdoch not only controls the national media contract, but he controls twenty-two to twenty-four of the thirty local television contracts for the thirty baseball teams. So these teams are now beholden to Rupert Murdoch and he has much more leverage and much more control than anybody has ever had before.*

*Fox has put together a package on Direct TV where you can get out of market games, so that if you happen to be a Los Angeles Dodgers' fan living in New York, you can buy this package. But Fox has required anybody who wants to see the Dodgers to buy a package of all major league teams and they charge $140 for it for the year. That's an antitrust violation, and it stems from the kind of control that Fox has garnered over the industry.*

—Andrew Zimbalist

*How can it be baseball when one man sits in a dark room and stares at a glowing screen? Baseball isn't solitude. It is a game that should occur with a multitude sitting around it.*

—Jimmy Cannon

*In truth, the corporate ownerships have really been more responsible than many of the individual ownerships. Now, I understand all the sort of intrinsic conflicts of interest it sets up, OK? But so far, those things haven't come to pass, and I'm grateful for that.*

—Bud Selig

*With the Dodgers, Murdoch gets a three-hour show 162 times a year. And it's not just seen in Southern California. The Dodgers are by far the most popular team in Japan and around the Pacific Rim. For what Murdoch wants—worldwide programming—it makes perfect sense to pay what seems to other people to be an outrageous amount of money.*

—Dennis Wilson

Rupert Murdoch owns Dodger Stadium, a large share of Madison Square Garden, and a piece of the new Staples Center in downtown Los Angeles that will host three pro teams every winter. His Fox network owns broadcast rights for Major League Baseball and the National Football League. He also owns a publishing house, magazines, and newspapers that profit from their coverage of sports. With the exception of longtime rival Ted Turner, the owner of the Atlanta Braves, the baseball owners welcomed the Australian media monopolist with open arms. Given their great dependence on his rights fees, they would have been hard-pressed to turn Murdoch down. Michael Knisley, a columnist for *The Sporting News*, tracked the long reach of the media king:

> You may not have noticed just how far and wide Fox Sports Net ranges because the brilliance of the concept is that it concentrates its coverage on regional levels. You watch Fox Sports New England in Boston, or Fox Sports Rocky Mountain in Denver, or Fox Sports South in Atlanta, or Fox Sports Fill-in-the-blank in 19 other major metropolitan areas. Each bears the same Fox Sports logo and each carries the same SportsCenter-like national wrap-up show, but each also gives its viewers the regular coverage of their local pro and college teams that ESPN doesn't.
>
> ... There are 76 U.S.-based teams, combined, in the NBA, the NHL and Major League Baseball. Fox Sports Net owns the local cable rights to 71.

New Dodger manager Davey Johnson expressed his boss' philosophy perfectly on his first day of work: "Parity is not the American way. The American way is to dominate somebody else."

Murdoch's plans to dominate the American media market depend upon owning as much programming content as possible. From the

Dodgers to Manchester United, Murdoch is placing a stranglehold on the elite teams in pro sports. His partner at Cablevision, Charles Dolan, is clearly trying to acquire the Yankees. A staggering conflict of interest will be created if Murdoch, the majority owner of the Dodgers, becomes a significant minority owner of the Yanks. It will, of course, be in his best interest to see his Dodgers and Yankees win. Nothing will stop him from reducing his payments on local rights contracts to other teams. Given Murdoch's near complete domination of the cable sports market, rival franchises have few other suitors for their television rights.

Baseball's other owners got their first taste of a Brave New World during the 1998 Winter Meetings. The only remaining high-priced free agent on the table was Kevin Brown. Murdoch's people wanted him and were willing to outbid all comers. They made Brown, perhaps the best pitcher in baseball, the first $100 million man in the history of the game. The owners who had welcomed Murdoch and his bottomless bank account were now wondering about the wisdom of doing so. The gap between the haves and have-nots, already wide, had become unbridgeable.

## LET'S NOT MAKE A DEAL

*Privately held translates into we could get a whole lot more money, but I'm a control freak. He starts talking about moving the team, and he's got every politician in New York in a lather. That's amazing power. He's not going to give that up. Who's going to give a rat's ass what George Steinbrenner does if he's not the owner of the Yankees?*

—Stephen Berglas

*Steinbrenner did so much talking this week, had so much misinformation leaked to newspapers, that his deal with Cablevision falls apart at least for now. Charles Dolan got tired of reading* *how Steinbrenner was outsmarting him and told him to see if he could get $500 million for the Yankees somewhere else.*

—Mike Lupica, *New York Daily News*

*The people who want to follow baseball are going to have to do the bulk of it by watching it on television 100 times a year. And if you're a media conglomerate that is both in the television business and in the baseball business, you don't mind that at all. You don't mind if you're increasing your television audience while you're decreasing your live audience.*

—Leonard Koppett

*The most significant event of the 1964 baseball season was the news on August 13 that the Columbia Broadcasting company had bought control (80 percent) of the New York Yankees for the sum of $11,200,000. . . . Television now exerts the most intense pressure on all aspects of baseball. Since the war, its total exposure of major-league games has destroyed most of the minor leagues. The widely varying amounts of TV revenue enjoyed by the big-league clubs have made the rich teams richer and do much to explain why so many poorer clubs want to shift franchises. . . . To drop CBS into the middle of this rich, untidy gumbo as the owner of baseball's No. 1 attraction may look like an engraved invitation for Congressional antitrust investigations, but it is an entirely appropriate symbol of television's enormous interest in the game.*

—Roger Angell

Angell's fears about CBS proved to be unfounded. The game's greatest writer was prescient, but he was a generation early. Cable TV is the medium that allows a few powerful men to corner the market and diminish competition even as they sell us a simulation of the thing itself. Charles Dolan, as owner of the Knicks, Rangers, and Madison Square Garden, as well as every available cable TV package in town, has a tight grip on the New York sports market.

Despite his holdings worth $1.7 billion, Dolan is just one of Murdoch's many partners. Through his 40 percent stake in Dolan's operations, Murdoch adds a piece of the Garden's inhabitants to his ownership of the Los Angeles Dodgers and his options to buy sizable interests in the Lakers and Kings. As soon as Dolan buys the Yankees or Murdoch exercises his option on the Kings and Lakers, the still inchoate conflict of interest haunting professional sports will become reality. With a piece of both sides in competitive games, as well as a role as the broadcast partner, nothing will be in place to restrain Murdoch from attempting to dictate outcomes.

Unlike his partners Murdoch and Steinbrenner (Yankee cable games are broadcast on Dolan-owned MSG), Dolan seems uninterested in gaining media attention for himself or his empire. In an era of self-aggrandizing media titans, the man who owns Radio City Music Hall and set up the first cable system in a major city while founding Home Box Office to provide programming for his system, should be a legend. Dolan's company is publicly traded, but his persona is well protected.

That mystery will end if Dolan purchases the Yankees. The deal is likely to go through because both parties benefit from the arrangement. Steinbrenner's likely heirs don't seem interested in running the ballclub, and the estate taxes to pass the club along would be hundreds of millions. Dolan's current television-rights deal with Steinbrenner expires at the end of the 1999 season. Although there are few visible competitors to Dolan, any mogul with a lot of cash could snatch up the Yankee contract. Just as Murdoch used his NFL deal to accelerate the growth of his national network, a cable programmer could use the Yankees as the first step in crashing the New York market. Dolan, who has overpaid for television-rights contracts in the past as he strengthened his local monopoly, understands this risk. Buying the team allows him to own the television rights in perpetuity, like Murdoch and the Dodgers and Turner and the Braves. As the next television package might cost as much as the team itself, it is no surprise that Dolan is eager to find a way to take the team off Steinbrenner's hands.

Dolan backed away from the negotiations in the face of leaks by Steinbrenner about his continuing control of a Cablevision-owned franchise. The Boss even spread a rumor that he would have some role at MSG running the Knicks and the Rangers and that he would receive a huge price valuing the Yanks near $1 billion. Those rumors caused Cablevision's stock price to drop by over 10 percent in just two days. An agitated Dolan chose to let Steinbrenner wait. Perhaps he will use his control over the television audience to squeeze the Boss into making a better deal. In 1988, Cablevision tossed the MSG network off its Long Island cable system in the middle of a price dispute with MSG's then-owner, Paramount. Deprived of programming, Knicks and Rangers fans went ballistic but Dolan held his ground. Within a few years, he gained control of MSG.

It is hard to believe that Dolan might muscle the Yankees this way during the 1999 season, especially if he anticipates ending up in some form of partnership with Steinbrenner. However, Mets fans should not be so sanguine if Dolan takes over the Yankees. There are many nights when the Dolan sports empire has more programming to televise than channels to show it on. While some games are moved to open channels, others are blacked out. During the hockey season, the Dolan-owned Rangers are reliably available while the Islanders and Devils are sometimes invisible, frustrating their loyal fans and triggering rumors about forthcoming pay-per-view packages. Dolan represents the same danger to major sports in New York City that Murdoch poses to baseball nationally, our reward for decades of neglect of the antitrust laws.

*It takes one hundred thousand dollars of government money to create a single stadium-related job. If you were to take one hundred thousand in twenty-dollar bills and dump it over Manhattan, you'd create seven or eight jobs.*

—Allan Sanderson

*If taxpayers want to spend millions making rich people richer, fine. What is objectionable is that stadiums are routinely sold to the public as sources of economic development. They are not.*

*Moreover, it is not impossible for teams to finance their own stadiums. And it is a little ironic that as sports revenues reach record heights, owners cry poverty. Note that until the 1960s, when the sports business was much more modest, owners almost always built their own ballparks. Curious, that.*

—*Fortune*

# 5

# THE HOUSE THAT RUDY BUILT

## EDIFICE COMPLEX

In an era of increasing skepticism about the role of government in fostering social justice, what cities are supposed to do for their citizens has become an open question. It seems incongruous that municipalities in financial trouble across the country should be lining up to spend hundreds of millions of dollars on sports complexes, but that is exactly what they are doing. John Rowland, the governor of Connecticut, decided to launch a renaissance in Hartford, the impoverished capital city with a public school system that had been taken over by the state. His plan was to steal the NFL's Patriots from the Boston suburbs by offering Robert Kraft, the team's owner, a free stadium and nearly all the revenue generated as well as ticket guarantees. The package, the most generous in American sports history, was going to cost Connecticut taxpayers anywhere from a quarter of a billion to three times that amount. When Rowland encountered significant public opposition, he defended the project as unique because it would draw young people back to the city. He also asserted that the tiny bit of the revenue stream not going to Kraft would enable the government to get something back for the dollars they put in, something he claimed never happens with dollars put in education.

The American economy today favors Robert Reich's famed "symbol manipulators," who require an excellent education to be able to obtain their specialized, high-paying jobs. Those young people with children or plans to raise them who heard Rowland's urban theory could hardly have been impressed by the idea that ten Sundays of football was more important than Junior's education. Rowland seemed to have the same voices echoing inside his head that haunt Ray Kinsella in the movie *Field of Dreams*, urgently whispering to the governor, "If you build it, they will come."

Rowland was also trying to find a way to change his image, his state's image, and Hartford's image. He wanted to do something to capture the national stage. If it was the country's attention he wanted, then the governor must have been thrilled to see NBC, PBS, the *Boston Globe*, and the *New York Times* at his doorstep. But his pleasure didn't last long. The national media were unanimous in their belief that the state and its taxpayers were getting ripped off and that Rowland was a dupe for arranging the deal. When that criticism came from Boston, it was seen as little more than sour grapes from the city that had just lost its team, but other critics were not so easily dismissed.

They came from all over the spectrum. In Connecticut, a group named Stop the Stadium formed to halt the project. It included the leaders of the Green, Libertarian, and Reform parties, third parties who rarely agreed on anything. A month before Rowland announced the deal with the Patriots, Ronald Utt, a fellow at the conservative Heritage Foundation, published a study that analyzed the issue by comparing two states, Maryland and Virginia, that had taken different approaches to the stadium wars. With its stadium authority and two huge new complexes for baseball and football near the Baltimore waterfront, Maryland had decided that attracting entertainment dollars would spur an economic revival. Although several owners coveted the wealthy D.C. suburbs as a potential market, Virginia had chosen not to play, instead investing more in education and other programs. The results were enormously one-sided, with Virginia growing rapidly as Maryland declined, data so stunning that anybody reading the study had to have doubts and wonder what other factors were at work. Nevertheless, it seemed that Maryland's ambitious pursuit of the entertainment dollar had not spurred an economic revival.

A study by the Maryland General Assembly's Office of Policy Analysis concluded that the new football stadium would create only 889 jobs, amounting to a cost of $200,000 per job. Robert Baade's research for the Brookings Institution supported these numbers, concluding that new sports facilities have a negligible, possibly negative effect on overall economic activity and employment. Baade concluded:

> Upon some reflection, sport's slow growth pattern should not be surprising. The slower growth reflects the kind of economic activity that investments in professional sports spawn. Sports diverts economic development toward labor-intensive, relatively unskilled (low-wage), part-time jobs. Other cities in the region that invest in economic activity

that promotes full-time, non-seasonal, and high wage jobs
can be expected to capture a greater share of the regional
economic pie.

In New York, the majority of taxpayers did not want their money
to be used for a business owner's construction costs. However,
Mayor Giuliani had his eye on higher office, anywhere from the
Senate to the national ticket in 2000, and remained fixated on spending hundreds of millions on a gaggle of new sports stadiums. This
was not about saving the Yankees for New York City. Giuliani's
desire to create a monument that would outlast his eight years in
office, as well as a series of public works projects that his favorite
developers could profit from, became apparent after the Jets
emerged as the city's winter darlings during a comeback season.
The mayor proposed a football stadium for the Jets, currently playing across the Hudson in Jersey, on the West Side site he had previously offered to the Yankees.

A few months after the end of the 1998 baseball season, the *New
York Times* ran a three-part series of long cover stories about the
abysmal state of high-school athletics in New York City. It was not
about abusive coaches or violent fans, although both existed, but
rather about the lack of facilities for most of the city's public school
athletes. It revealed how empty the public school budgets had
become. The response from City Hall was to encourage privatiza-
tion, urging high schools to go out and tap wealthy alums for funds.
Sixteen-year-old high-school kids without fields to practice or play
their games on were supposed to go out and hustle up money while
the owner of the Yankees was invited to pillage the city treasury.
Only in New York.

## THREE MILLION FAN MARCH

*I feel bad for my team. They've got the best record in baseball and they're playing to huge crowds on the road, but when they come home the crowds aren't there. Why should we be sixth in the American League in attendance? If I didn't put a good product on the field, then I'd take the blame. The fact is we have a $72 million payroll, we paid another $8 million in revenue sharing and we spent $24.5 million in scouting and player development this year. If it's not the Bronx, what is it?*

— George Steinbrenner

*Look at how the Rangers and the Knicks draw. They're sold out every game. Location, location, location ... I'm trying to compete with Cleveland for an American League Championship and I was competing with Baltimore for the division. How do I compete when they draw 15,000 to 20,000 more fans a game? The perception, right or wrong, is that people don't want to come to the Bronx at night. ... Does Fernando Ferrer want to guarantee we'll get 3 million? Tell them to put their money where their mouth is. If he can guarantee we'll get three million, then I'll sit down and talk about the Bronx.*

—George Steinbrenner

Steinbrenner's repeated complaints rest on a false premise. When the Yankees field a great team, the Boss believes, they are entitled to lead the league in attendance. Because the Yankees, located in the nation's largest city, have been baseball's most successful team on the field, many mistakenly assume that the franchise has also ruled at the box office. The last year the Yankees topped the majors in attendance was 1952. Over the next forty-five years, the Yankees claimed sixteen American League pennants, nine World Series, and zero box-office crowns. While the last half-century of Yankee baseball includes two long absences from the postseason (from 1965–75 when CBS' detached ownership tolerated a slow decline, and 1982–94 when Steinbrenner's many errors turned the Mattingly era into a period of longing and regret), those sorry decades do not explain the gap between performance afield and at the gate during the other twenty-five years in question.

New York City's reputation as baseball-mad is deserved. During this century, teams based in New York City have led the majors in attendance twenty-nine times. Only Los Angeles, with twenty-one attendance crowns thanks to O'Malley's Dodgers, can boast a comparable record. In fact, New York City has at least one attendance crown to show for each decade of this century, save the present one.

Table 5.1 reveals the attendance champs of the expansion era in baseball are the Los Angeles Dodgers. Since they moved into Dodger Stadium in 1962, the Dodgers have drawn more than 97 million fans to the ballpark. This staggering figure beats the Yankees over that period by 30 million fans. The Dodger average attendance per season in Chavez Ravine is higher than the Yankees' 1988 attendance of 2.63 million, the franchise record prior to the 1998 campaign. The Dodgers have a similar-sized market in Southern California and a rival in Anaheim that siphons off potential fans like the Mets do in New York. Are fans in Los Angeles actually more loyal than New Yorkers? No. Two other factors fully explain the Dodgers' box-office dominance: lower ticket prices and restricted access to home games away from the ballpark.

Unlike the Yankees, who sold as many games, home or away, to television as possible, the Dodgers kept the supply of home games on broadcast TV to a bare minimum and relied on Vin Scully (in English) and Jaime Jarrin (in Spanish) to deliver the games over the radio. If you wanted to see the Dodgers play at Dodger Stadium, the O'Malleys made sure you had to go to their ballpark. In combination with this part of the strategy, they kept their prices as low as

## Table 5.1

Annual Major League Attendance Leaders

| YEAR(S) | TEAM | YEAR(S) | TEAM |
|---------|------|---------|------|
| 1903 | New York Giants | 1938 | YANKEES |
| 1904 | Boston (AL) | 1939 | Cincinnati |
| 1905 | Chicago (AL) | 1940 | Detroit |
| 1906 | Chicago (NL) | 1941–43 | Brooklyn |
| 1907 | Chicago (AL) | 1944–45 | Detroit |
| 1908–09 | New York Giants | 1946–47 | YANKEES |
| 1910 | Philadelphia (AL) | 1948 | Cleveland |
| 1911–12 | New York Giants | 1949–52 | YANKEES |
| 1913 | Chicago (AL) | 1953–58 | Milwaukee (NL) |
| 1914–15 | Boston (AL) | 1959–66 | Los Angeles |
| 1916–17 | Chicago (AL) | 1967 | St. Louis |
| 1918 | Chicago (NL) | 1968 | Detroit |
| 1919 | New York Giants | 1969–72 | New York Mets |
| 1920–24 | YANKEES | 1973–75 | Los Angeles |
| 1925 | Philadelphia (AL) | 1976 | Cincinnati |
| 1926–27 | YANKEES | 1977–86 | Los Angeles |
| 1928–32 | Chicago (NL) | 1987 | St. Louis |
| 1933 | YANKEES | 1988 | New York Mets |
| 1934–35 | Detroit | 1989–92 | Toronto |
| 1936 | YANKEES | 1993–98 | Denver |
| 1937 | Detroit | | |

Source: *Total Baseball*

possible. In *Lords of the Realm*, John Helyar notes that O'Malley "drew station wagons full of families by keeping ticket prices low (box seats stayed $3.50 for eighteen straight years) and starting games early. ... cash registers rang steadily at the concession stands as [spectators] filled up on Dodger Dogs. 'We once figured out,' said former team general manager Buzzie Bavasi, 'that if we let everybody in for nothing we'd still make a profit.'"

In this way, the O'Malleys drew huge crowds that enabled them to forego reliance on revenue from local broadcast media. I lived in Los Angeles for five years and, as a baseball fan (but most certainly not a Dodger fan), went in for a one-third share of two season tickets in the second deck near first base during the 1992 season (I still have my tickets to the games that were canceled in late April when Los Angeles was burning). Those seats cost eight bucks a game and still do while a comparable seat at Yankee Stadium costs twenty dollars a game during the 1998 season.

During the Yankees' incomparable 1998 season, the Dodgers ushered in the Rupert Murdoch era with a poorly played, turmoil-filled season that included the trade of Mike Piazza, the franchise's only great player. Even during a season certain to anger most loyalists, the Dodgers outdrew the Yankees. With Dodger home games much more available on local TV now, price differential alone remained the key factor. In Table 5.2 below, I have used the section names familiar to those who attend games at Yankee Stadium. Dodger Stadium has a slightly different configuration and the ticket office assigns different names to seat locations, however, the seats are comparable.

### Table 5.2

1998 Dodger and Yankee Ticket Prices by Seat Location

| LOCATION | DODGER PRICE | YANKEE PRICE |
| --- | --- | --- |
| Field Box | $14 | $45 |
| Loge Box | $12 | $45 |
| Main Box | $12 | $35 |
| Outfield Box | $12 | $23 |
| Tier Box | $8 | $20 |
| Tier Reserved | $6 | $12 |
| Bleachers | $6 | $7 |

As the price structure shows, there is a simple reason the Yankees have never drawn 3 million fans: their prices are too high. Only the Boston Red Sox (with over 20,000 fewer seats to sell in Fenway) charge more per ticket than the Yankees. These high prices reflect a trend after the 1994 labor dispute that did what world wars and depressions could not, causing the World Series to be cancelled for the first time. When the owners saw most of their core audience return, they recognized the power of fan loyalty and the subsequent inelasticity of demand. Attendance and ratings were down but not dangerously low; the owners had a delayed invitation to jack up their prices. None has been bolder in this regard than Steinbrenner. The field boxes that cost $45 (just $14 at Dodger Stadium) during the 1998 season were only $17.50 three years earlier.

Steinbrenner clearly does not want to maximize the number of people at the games, and he has no right to complain when raw attendance data shows he's losing to his competitors. Those numbers mean nothing out of context. Given a ticket price more than twice as high, Steinbrenner drained much more money out of the pockets of Yankee fans than Rupert Murdoch sucked from Dodger faithful during 1998. In his race against Disney, Nike, and Adidas for planetary control of pro sports, Murdoch responded to the Dodgers' mediocre season by keeping most ticket prices steady for 1999 and raising the field boxes two dollars for a top price of sixteen dollars. At Yankee Stadium in 1999, sixteen dollars will buy you a seat in the upper deck and a cup of coffee. Steinbrenner celebrated the team's twenty-fourth title and record attendance by raising prices roughly 15 percent across the board.

If other teams are generating more stadium revenue (available 1998 data suggests that the Yankees were among the league leaders), they deserve to do better. Few ballparks are as poorly run as Yankee Stadium. The miserable state of concessions and lavatories should not be blamed on the city; contracts with concessionaires and the hiring of service personnel are Steinbrenner's responsibilities. When the

Boss took over, he terminated a contract with the union that still provides much better service at Shea Stadium; their employees unreasonably wanted to earn a living wage. Looking to save a buck at every turn, Steinbrenner hired the cheapest labor force he could find.

When people talk about Steinbrenner's willingness to spend freely to put out a good product, they are only referring to the men in pinstripes with numbers on their backs. Off the field, Yankee fans get exactly the level of service Steinbrenner pays for. The bathrooms stink of piss, floors slick with who knows what and the toilets regularly out of service a few innings into the game. The food is truly abysmal. Soggy pretzels, stale peanuts, bland hot dogs, flat soda, lousy beer. A pleasure palace this isn't. Nevertheless, Yankee fans produce some of the highest PCAPs (per capita spending on concessions) in all of sports. During game six of the 1996 World Series, the average Yankee fan spent almost $31 on concessions for a record total of $1.7 million. Given the greater attention to behind-the-scenes detail at Cablevision-owned properties like Madison Square Garden and Radio City Music Hall, expect service to improve if Dolan and company close the deal and take over day-to-day operations of the club. Until then, the only places to find decent service at the Stadium will remain the players' clubhouse, the press box, and the owner's box.

### Table 5.3

Yankees Average 1998 Attendance by Day of Week and Month

| DAY | ATTENDANCE | MONTH | ATTENDANCE |
|-----|-----------|-------|-----------|
| SUN | 48,864 | APR | 31,018 |
| SAT | 44,279 | MAY | 36,559 |
| FRI | 38,004 | JUN | 34,922 |
| WED | 32,415 | JUL | 42,412 |
| THU | 31,348 | AUG | 40,344 |
| TUE | 30,953 | SEP | 34,197 |
| MON | 29,960 | | |

Table 5.3 demonstrates the effects of work and weather upon spectators. When fans have leisure time to fill on Friday nights and Saturday and Sunday afternoons, Yankee attendance rises almost 50 percent. The peaks in the summer reflect the larger audience that can go to the park when the kids are out of school, as well as the relative absence of damp, cold nights that keep fans home. Given the natural advantage of weekend and mid-summer games, a rational entrepreneur, someone who wanted to host 3 million fans a year, would put most of his energy into promoting midweek, early season and late season games. Not George Steinbrenner. His main marketing effort to move less desirable product involved discounting his worst seats at the top of the third deck tier. These seats, relatively empty at less popular games and absurdly priced at twelve dollars a pop, were cut by three dollars on Tuesdays all year and by six bucks on weeknights the first five weeks of the season. The discount created little extra demand because the Yankees didn't promote it aggressively.

Even more misdirected is the Yankees' schedule of thirty-two promotional giveaways. When the Yanks provided goodies during the week, they reaped significant rewards. On Wednesdays, the Yankees drew an average of 27,309 to seven games without freebies. The five Wednesday games that involved promotions attracted 39,471 apiece to the Stadium, an increase of over 12,000 fans per game. Nevertheless, the Yankees offered gifts before only eight midweek contests, choosing instead to hand out trinkets before all twenty-four weekend games. The team apparently wished to attract fans to contests they already had decided to attend. If Steinbrenner scheduled his promos with a rational strategy, he'd easily draw an extra couple hundred thousand fans a year.

If he wanted to draw more fans, Steinbrenner could lower prices, improve concessions, spend more to hire better stadium employees, or schedule his promos during the week. He did none of this and instead attacked his customers. Early in the 1998 season, the Yankees drew 16,606 fans for a Tuesday night game against the Royals. The low turnout was caused by several factors: bad weather, a lousy opponent, fans' responsibilities at work and school the following morning, and the lack of any giveaway. From his home in Tampa, Steinbrenner, who missed the game, complained to the local media, "This team has had an absolutely tremendous start and certainly deserves better support. I am very disappointed. We have great fans, but we come home in the midst of one of the best starts in club history to the smallest crowd of the season. Something is wrong. It's hard to come to any conclusion other than the fact that we have an outmoded stadium in a location that people don't want to go see a game. The fans just don't come out on weeknights like they do in other cities."

Build me a palace in Manhattan, implied Steinbrenner, and they will come. Exactly six weeks later, facing a quality opponent, Ted Turner's Braves, the Yankees drew over 54,000 fans to the Bronx on a beautiful Tuesday evening. Steinbrenner doesn't have to make the games so easily available. By selling all of his home games to television and radio (and reaping tens of millions in extra revenue annually), the Boss invites his fans to stay home on nights when the weather's bad and they have to get up early the next day.

Furthermore, Steinbrenner's complaints about the success of the Knicks and Rangers, as well as the competitive advantage of rivals in Baltimore and Cleveland, are misplaced. The Knicks and the Rangers sell out their games because their schedules are half as long and Madison Square Garden holds one-third as many fans as the Stadium. While the Yankees try to move over 4.5 million seats over the course of a season, the Garden's primary tenants each have under 800,000 tickets available all year. If Yankee tickets were so scarce, the Yanks would sell out all their games and charge even more than the absurd prices asked by the Knicks and the Rangers.

In fact, the Yankees finished the 1998 season third behind Baltimore and Cleveland in the league in attendance, with a team-record 2,955,193 paying customers. As Table 5.3 illustrates, crowds picked up as the weather improved and the historic nature of the Yankees' performance became apparent. While the Bombers trailed the Orioles by 8,500 fans a night and the Indians by 6,000 a game, revenue generated at the Stadium may have been equal to that of the franchise's two rivals, thanks to higher ticket prices. And even if the Boss trailed by a few million at the ballpark, he made it up and more with tens of millions in revenue coming from broadcast media and various advertising packages.

Despite their supposedly obsolete digs, the Yankees outdrew three American League rivals playing in new parks during the 1998 season. The Rangers won baseball's only marginally interesting division race during 1998 in their Camden Yards clone in the Dallas suburbs, yet trailed the Yankees by about 25,000 fans at season's end. The Blue Jays had a surprisingly good year in the Skydome, hanging around the outskirts of the wild-card race well into September, but the former gate kings could not stay within a half-million fans of the Yankees. The disappointing White Sox drew fewer than 18,000 fans a night to their new eyesore on the Southside, less than half the numbers at the Bronx each night. The Yankees do not need a new park or 3 million fans at Yankee Stadium to compete with the Orioles or the Indians. Their record over the past four years—two titles and four playoff appearances—proves they are doing just fine, thank you.

## SLOUCHING TOWARD CAMDEN YARDS

*Maryland, historically one of the more prosperous states, has pursued economic revitalization aggressively by investing in costly tourist and entertainment-related infrastructure projects. It has built or subsidized three stadiums and a variety of tourist facilities, including convention centers, over the past two decades and is contemplating several other major projects such as a racetrack. In*

*the 1980s, the state and the city of Baltimore assisted in the devel-*
*opment of a world-renowned downtown retail, museum, and*
*restaurant complex on Inner Harbor. Although its attractions are*
*impressive and heavily used, they appear to have had no signifi-*
*cant impact on the city's or the state's economic well being.*
*Baltimore continues to lose residents, jobs, and businesses, and*
*today houses its smallest population since about 1915.*

— Ronald Utt

Every analyst spilling reams of words about the Yankee Stadium controversy glossed over the effect of a new venue on spectators. In 1998, the Stadium opened its gates to the fan paying $16,000 a year for one cushioned front-row seat at field level with waiter service available, as well as the fan paying seven dollars a night for an unreserved seat atop the metal stands in the outfield bleachers. A new or renovated stadium is not likely to be equally accessible to those fans in the cheap seats.

Camden Yards, built near the Baltimore waterfront in 1992, has become the star to follow for those who would build a new stadium. In the team's first six years in their new ballpark, attendance jumped by almost 1.5 million fans per season. In the first season alone, Oriole profits surged by $20 million, a reflection of the wealthier fans who doubled their per-capita spending on concessions. This remarkable growth occurred despite a smaller seating capacity, a much greater distance from the field for the average fan, and a huge rise in ticket prices. Rival owners drooled with envy over similar success at the gate for teams playing in Camden Yards clones in Atlanta, Cleveland, Denver, and Arlington, Texas.

When George Will, the game's favorite conservative scribe and a board member of the Baltimore Orioles and the San Diego Padres, trumpeted the resurgence of baseball in the summer of 1998, he praised Camden Yards as one of the three most important events in baseball since World War II, alongside free agency and Jackie Robinson. At the time, Will's Padres were in the midst of a tough battle over a local referendum on public funds for a ballpark. The man who saw no conflict between his public role as columnist and private role preparing Ronald Reagan to debate his electoral opponents rediscovered his hypocrisy, presenting himself as a disinterested observer who understood the central role of new stadia in successful urban renewal. It's worth noting that San Diego is in the midst of an economic boom despite the lack of a new ballpark, while Camden Yards has brought little prosperity to those beyond its gates in Baltimore.

I spent roughly half my childhood in the D.C. suburbs as an Oriole fan and went to a couple dozen games in Memorial Stadium, the former Oriole home located in North Baltimore. The site was inconvenient, miles from the nearest highway and thousands of parking spaces short at the stadium. In contrast, Camden Yards offers ease of access: walking distance from the white-collar offices and tourist attractions shadowing the Baltimore waterfront, commuter trains from downtown Washington to the front door, immense parking lots, and, a few blocks away, a ramp to I-95, the key highway south to D.C.

With its asymmetrical dimensions amidst an urban neighborhood, Camden Yards openly evokes an earlier era when ballparks had an organic relationship to their surroundings. The design even incorporates an esplanade behind left field where fans walk between the field and the old brick warehouse that houses the team's offices. Moving crowds along the walkway can purchase food, drink, and souvenirs while catching a glimpse of the action below. Once in their seats, Oriole faithful can look out at downtown and view an ancient clocktower that helps to unify the pastoral experience of watching men playing a boys' game on a green by contrasting it with the less leisurely urban reality a stone's throw away.

Oriole Park at Camden Yards pretends to be open in its effort to evoke a gentler era. The demise of Union Grounds in Brooklyn during the nineteenth century did not end the era when fans watched the best ballplayers from beyond the friendly confines. Photos of important games at the Polo Grounds show hundreds of spectators lining the edge of Coogan's Bluff so they can watch the action from above. The esplanade at Camden Yards was created to reproduce the sense of those informal, passionate gatherings, but it is an illusory public space, controlled as closely as any other destination in Tourist America. The esplanade can be traversed only by ticket-holders. Save for vantage points high in the prohibitively expensive office towers a half-dozen blocks away, there is no point where one can peek at the game without paying for it.

The renovation of the original Yankee Stadium in the early seventies included construction of a high wall behind the outfield seats that served to close off the ballpark from its surroundings. Before this disruption, those in the reserved seats could see out into the Bronx neighborhood. Even better, fans could stand on the elevated platform for the #4 subway line and get a free thrill by looking in on the game. A good 200 yards away from home plate, it may not have been the best seat in the house, but it certainly was the cheapest.

You can still sneak a peek across town at Shea Stadium. Shea's design includes openings behind left and right field. The failure to enclose has damaged the underrated park's reputation; the view of a yawning chasm of underused urban space is an eyesore. However, someone looking back from the top of the stairs to the subway entrance nearest the Stadium can gaze across the parking lot and through right field to take advantage of one of the few remaining free glimpses of major-league baseball.

Having moved out to the West Coast a few years earlier, I used the excuse of journalistic interest to come home to witness the first game at Oriole Park at Camden Yards. Looking at the stands when I entered the stadium that day I was immediately struck by the uniform whiteness of the crowd. While crowds at Memorial Stadium had been predominantly white, with a taste for country music along-side their crabcakes and beer, the gathering was far from racially exclusive. Furthermore, the neighborhood of little brick houses that bordered Memorial Stadium was primarily African American. For games at the old yard, fans parked their cars a half-mile or more from the stadium. The walk to the park required Oriole rooters to interact with the residents who sat out on the porches of their homes to watch the crowd. Those encounters forced suburbanites and residents of more gentrified urban communities to notice this neighborhood. And the economic benefits to locals who sold peanuts, soda, and parking at below stadium prices were real.

The experience at Camden Yards involves far less interaction with the surrounding environs. Park the car, walk through the lot to an entrance, and go inside. If Memorial Stadium crowds gave off a vibe that reflected Baltimore's blend of tough working-class pride and Southern hospitality (half-Pittsburgh, half-Charleston), then Camden Yards lacks any such sense of place. This is unsurprising since less than half the fans at the new park come from Baltimore.

The move across town left more than a neighborhood behind. Memorial Stadium had cheap bleacher seats. The clean new design had no room for the ratty feel of bleachers and their loyalists. The closest thing to bleachers at Camden Yards is the much more expensive and much more distant upper deck in the outfield.

Why does the crowd of well-educated, friendly, and casually but expensively dressed white people come to worship at the new temples in such staggering numbers? While the distances from the field are greater than in the more intimate old parks, the sightlines are often better. The accessories—from huge, clean restrooms to a wide variety of upscale food and beverage to polite stadium employees—are much more consumer-friendly. The new parks are not only safe, they feel safe. The illusion is more important. Statistics show Yankee Stadium to be the safest place in New York City during a night game, yet the perception of danger, reinforced by Steinbrenner's incessant babbling about the Bronx, has chased away fans.

Most significantly, public financing of the Orioles' new stadium added tens of millions in revenue and over a hundred million in value to the franchise instantly. That increase in wealth was used to buy a consistent contender that keeps fans satisfied. Camden Yards' urban setting belies its function as an upscale baseball mall, equivalent to the new Vegas or Disney at the diamond: attracting young singles out for a few thrills and a chance to hook up alongside families in search of a night of safe entertainment. For an adult, going to a game at Camden Yards produces water-cooler material for the following morning. That Camden Yards demographic is the one Giuliani brought to Times Square. When the mayor attended his first game at Camden Yards early in 1998 to help raise funds for some local Republican candidates, his behind-the-scenes tour of baseball's crown jewel left him dazzled and ever more determined to present Steinbrenner with his own palace.

The House That Rudy Builds will likely eliminate the bleachers, too. When the Yankees sold out a game at the Stadium in 1998, they generated roughly a million dollars in revenue from the gate alone. Of that million, bleacher sales represented well under a hundred thousand. Not only is the added revenue generated by the bleachers insignificant, but making the new stadium smaller creates greater scarcity. A decrease in supply accompanied by an increase in demand will trigger higher ticket prices and, in all likelihood, higher profit margins and increasing franchise value. Downsizing Yankee Stadium puts even more millions in Steinbrenner's pockets. For the Boss, those bleacher creatures are more valuable if they stay home and watch the game on television.

## GREAT EXPECTATIONS

For two decades now, Steinbrenner has threatened to move the Yankees out of the Bronx at the slightest provocation. The Boss was all set to leave for Jersey four years ago, or so we were told. And now he's going to sell the team before he even reaches the end of the lease with the city. Some of this uncertainty no doubt mirrors Steinbrenner's temperament, but a lot of it reflects the uneven bargaining power caused by the city's self-inflicted weakness. In fact, the Boss is in no hurry to strike a deal. The current lease expires in 2002, but the team owns two five-year options to extend it. Time pressure is entirely on the city, as the Boss stretches out the endlessly recursive negotiations for some new deal.

If Steinbrenner strikes a deal with the city (and the odds are high that Charles Dolan will make any decisions about a stadium), it will only be when he is offered terms so favorable that they would make a defense contractor blush. Steinbrenner's expectations are shaped by the deal Tampa made with him a few years ago. The city gave the Boss a $31 million complex, including three stadiums to house his major-league team during spring training and his rookie club during the summer, for free. The primary stadium was a scaled-down version of the House That Ruth Built capable of holding 10,000 spectators, and featuring the first luxury suites in the history of exhibition baseball. The boxes held up to two dozen with plenty of room for corporate parties. The new ballpark ensured that the Yankees would win the stadium revenue battle in March every year, but Tampa wasn't through giving to their local hero. They built the Boss a state-of-the-art office complex on the grounds, too.

I suspect there was a moment after that expansion joint fell through a box seat that Steinbrenner imagined he might be handed a new stadium costing anywhere from $600 million to over a billion dollars free of charge just so he wouldn't leave town. But even

Giuliani has thus far declined to match Tampa's ridiculous terms. And so Steinbrenner waits. Perhaps he will sell his club. Perhaps he will receive a better offer. He has no need to hurry.

Born with a silver spoon in his mouth and handed a gold-plated deal by his second hometown, Steinbrenner will show a restraint that many claim he is incapable of as he waits for New York City to bid against itself. No one else is at the table. For municipalities, the stadium race is akin to an arms race. Claims of danger everywhere—leaked by a Pentagon desperate to maintain its bloated operating budget after the Cold War—are mimicked by sports moguls and their lackeys in municipal government.

In a time when cities have diminished revenues and lowered expectations, the idea that all the bleeding can be stopped if a pro team comes to town has proven quite seductive. However, the increasingly generous deals offered by seemingly captive cities divert much needed dollars from decaying schools and infrastructure while destroying municipal credit ratings. By choosing not to join forces to battle against owners working in concert, most large cities have signed deals in the last decade that are more generous than any in the history of sports. In the aftermath of each deal, the owners make more money and so do the players, but the cities they represent do not fare nearly as well.

## WORST DEAL EVER

*Extra! Extra! Read All About It! I want New York to pay my rent and utility bills. If the city doesn't fork over the money, I'll haul my ass to New Jersey.*

— Posted on a *New York Times* online forum

*By a margin of 81 to 7 percent, New York City voters want to keep the Yankees in their current stadium in the Bronx. Among*

*Yankee fans, support for staying in the House That Ruth Built is
91 to 6 percent.*

—Quinnipiac College poll

*I understand the awe around Yankee Stadium. It's part of base-
ball's tradition, but baseball's life has changed dramatically. And
you certainly can't fault a club for trying to stay competitive. It's a
fair statement to say that the Yankees in terms of doing proper
long range planning are going to need a new ballpark with new
revenue streams.*

—Bud Selig

What Giuliani and Steinbrenner are up to is anything but novel. A
hundred years ago, John McGraw's Giants were the toast of the town
and the team's owner used his considerable clout with corrupt
Tammany bosses to keep all competitors out of Manhattan.
American League president Ban Johnson, who was perceived to be a
moralist, needed a team in New York to make his league a Major
League. After a few years of frustration, Johnson struck a deal with
two men well connected to Tammany Hall—Frank Farrell and
William Devery, a former police commissioner and the racketeer who
owned him—to get around the Giants.

Two decades later, when the Giants decided to send their tenant
packing, the search process for a site for the new stadium involved at
least as many feints and dekes as Steinbrenner has used in the last
few years. Ruppert and Huston first looked hard at a few sites in
Queens, including one not too far from where Shea Stadium is
presently situated. The duo then announced an agreement to develop a site in Washington Heights at 163rd and Amsterdam just blocks
from their existing address in the Polo Grounds. The direct threat
to the Giants was just a fake, and Ruppert and Huston exercised an
option on a property owned by the Astors in the Bronx firm in the

belief that the Grand Concourse would emerge as the next great area of the city. CBS also claimed an interest in New Jersey in the early seventies that scared New York City into buying the Stadium and then renovating it, all of which benefited new owner Steinbrenner. The Boss has been more than willing to float offers, no matter how nebulous, from New Jersey, Manhattan, and the Bronx in the media to pressure whoever he's trying to make a deal with.

What he has not done is produce much tax revenue for the city. According to reports compiled by the New York City Parks Department, New York paid $1.7 million to the Yankees under the terms of the lease over the ten-year period beginning in 1986. In 1995, for example, they cost the city $300,000. The city has consistently undercalculated the amount of taxable revenue generated by the team. The Yankees are supposed to pay the city 10 percent of cable TV revenues for broadcasts of home games. This clause should generate several million dollars a year for the city, but it never has. Some years, the Yankees have paid over half a million under this clause. Other years, nothing at all. Multiple freedom of information act requests and repeated interviews with the appropriate individuals at the Parks Department left the impression that no one there understood the meaning of a key clause in the contract. And when Jim Dwyer of the *Daily News* mentioned the lost money in passing in an article about corruption around the Stadium in the fall of 1998, phone calls stopped getting returned. Giuliani and his predecessors have allowed Steinbrenner to withhold millions in back taxes owed to the city. No wonder the Boss expects the city to build him a new stadium.

*         *         *

Ruppert's partner, Tillinghast Huston, was the man responsible for the design of Yankee Stadium. It was the first ballpark of its kind, with enormous dimensions more suited to college football, which made it difficult to integrate into the surrounding neighborhood. Its field was sunk below ground level and its upper deck towered over nearby buildings. The Yankees expected their audience to arrive on foot and by train, so few accommodations for automobiles could be found at the original site. A massive crowd on Opening Day endured the first of thousands of traffic jams at the Stadium over the last seventy-five years. Any time the Boss moans about the Bronx, those traffic jams are near the top of his list of complaints.

Steinbrenner—a billionaire who grew up and inherited his fortune in Cleveland, resides in Tampa, and occasionally visits New York—has spent a quarter-century as Yankee owner opting in and out of a sense of community as it serves his purposes. As the Yanks neared the three-million mark, Steinbrenner rediscovered a long-lost fondness for his Bronx neighborhood and asserted that he would meet with Bronx Borough President Fernando Ferrer to discuss keeping the Yankees in the Bronx if they reached that magic number. Ferrer offered to spend a million dollars to buy up the necessary tickets to get the Yankee owner to seriously consider staying in the Bronx, a much cheaper option than building Steinbrenner a park along the Hudson.

The mayor, demonstrating a weak understanding of freshman economics, intervened before the Bronx borough president and Steinbrenner began to find common ground. Giuliani asserted that he was ethically opposed to handouts for private businesses and would not allow any public agency to buy up the tickets. This principled stand came from a mayor who responded to every threat by a big institution to move out of the city with an open-wallet policy. A billion here for a new ballpark, 900 million there for a new stock exchange downtown, 50 million over there to expand the Midtown museum.

When the mayor released absurdly optimistic projections about the revenue a Midtown stadium would generate for the city, the city's Independent Budget Office responded with a detailed, balanced study that suggested Giuliani should be a much tougher negotiator. The

IBO came to seven key conclusions. First, new stadiums do not produce economic growth in cities. Nevertheless, a stadium's location within a region does affect local patterns of economic activity. Third, both franchises—the Mets and the Yanks—will make more money if new stadiums go up. Fourth, most recent stadium projects involved significant subsidies, but there is an emerging trend back to private financing. Fifth, the baseball monopoly's restriction on the number of franchises increases the owners' bargaining power, however, the New York media market insures the two teams will stay put. Sixth, New York City is uniquely situated to challenge an owner's expectation of subsidy. Finally, a large subsidy would raise equity concerns because a number of wealthy fans from the suburbs would reap the benefit while the burden rests on city dwellers.

Faced with an independent analysis that challenged his numbers, overwhelming public sentiment against his proposal, and a ballot referendum designed to stop his shenanigans, the mayor could have graciously accepted defeat. But instead he formed a charter commission whose sole purpose was to come up with a ballot issue, any issue that would knock the stadium off the ballot. An angry city council sued, and the city's corporation counsel defended the mayor's position, losing before a district court judge in the Bronx before finding more sympathetic judges on appeal. No vote was taken, and Giuliani remained free to open the city treasury to his pal Steinbrenner.

It remains unclear whether a new stadium will even draw more fans in the long run. Comiskey Park in Chicago appears obsolete after less than a decade of service, and Toronto's Skydome, baseball's most popular palace a decade ago, may not be far behind. Build a new park for the Yankees in Midtown Manhattan and nothing will stop them from doubling their already high ticket prices. They will point to the ticket prices of their neighbors, the Broadway theaters up the street. With a cast that includes Derek Jeter, Bernie Williams, Roger Clemens, and any other elite veterans the Bombers can poach from weaker teams, they will certainly be putting on the most expensive production in midtown. It's far less certain whether the initial attendance gains—every new ballpark triggers at least some rise over its first few years—will remain a decade later.

The Yankees are already the wealthiest, strongest franchise in baseball, if not all of American sports. The idea that they need a greater amount of stadium income to remain competitive is absurd. They could play all their home games in an empty Yankee Stadium and remain among baseball's elite based on their media revenues alone.

*I see sports at its finest as the glue that holds society together. It's the commonality of a CEO being able to talk to a janitor in the elevator about the relief pitcher the night before.*

*I think we have some dangerous times ahead in that [respect]. There has been an introduction of classism in sports. Everything that rolls through the tips of people's mouths is "suites," "VIP this" and "restricted entrance that" and "private parking."*

*There is an anthropology to sports, and that anthropology is very simple: We come together to share an experience that is an emotional one. But now we're taking what [former baseball commissioner] Bart Giammati called our modern-day cathedrals—our ballparks—and asking people to come together, but then separating them again into rich and poor.*

— Doug Logan, commissioner, Major League Soccer

*Green Bay has been to the Super Bowl twice in the last three seasons. Green Bay not only doesn't have a major-league baseball team, they couldn't support a minor-league team.*

— Sandy Alderson, executive vice president of operations
  for Major League Baseball

*With the single exception of Green Bay, no community has gone beyond lip service when it comes to taking ownership or trying to take ownership of a major league sports team. A number of cities have shown a willingness to fork over tens of millions of dollars to build and renovate stadiums, to improve access roads and parking, and to provide direct financial incentives to owners. But none has launched a serious effort to actually own a team, nor has any city worked with local businesses and citizens to help them purchase a franchise.*

— E. G. Nadeau and David J. Thompson

# 6
# FIELDS OF DREAMS

## AMERICA'S TEAM

Despite playing in the smallest city to host a major pro sports franchise in North America, the Green Bay Packers are often seen as America's team. Polls always place the Packers in the top three favorite teams. This is not a reflection of a national infatuation with Wisconsin or a lingering love of Lombardi's dynasty of the sixties. The Packers are beloved because they are seen as so closely tied to their community. "There's a charm with the Packers," explains team spokesman Jeff Blumb. "We have players jumping into the stands, and there's no owner who's visible at games. Not everybody lives in New York. Let's face it, there are a lot of people in small-town America out there, and this team associates with a lot of those people."

The ties that bind are created by the ownership structure of the club, a community-based model that gives each of the shareholders voting rights without equity (and no special right to impossible-to-find tickets to games) and directs that if the club is ever sold the profits will go into the local American Legion. That structure insures that the Packers will never leave Green Bay. It means that money will be plowed back into acquiring talent and maintaining the team's infrastructure because it has no other place to go. The other element in the NFL that keeps the Packers viable is revenue sharing in the media contracts. As long as the NFL continues to divide the tremendous national TV contracts equally, a team in a city of a hundred thousand like the Packers can compete with a team from a city a hundred times larger like the Bears.

Seventy-five years ago, the Packers were unsure if they were going to survive financially, so they decided to sell 1,500 shares of five-dollar stock certificates to raise the cash to stay alive. The structure of the company has not changed much, except for a recent sale of hundreds of thousands more shares to raise cash for the stadium and practice facilities. Given the size of its local market, the team has been immensely successful over the years. More importantly, it has fostered an enormous sense of civic pride in Green Bay and the surrounding area, an example from the progressive state that the nation would be well served to follow.

However, both the NFL and the major leagues have essentially banned community ownership. Joan Kroc inherited the San Diego Padres from her husband Ray, who founded McDonald's. Late in life, she wanted to insure that the Padres remained in San Diego. In 1987, she tried to donate the club to the city. The other major-league owners blocked the transaction at least in part because they were in the midst of collusion, their illegal refusal to abide by the collective bargaining agreement, and didn't want any public closely examining their books. The owners did not specifically pass a rule against community ownership but the message was clear.

Two small-market teams, the Pittsburgh Pirates and the Montreal Expos, took public funds during recent sales; however, in neither case was the city given any equity or a voice in team decision making. E.G. Nadeau and David J. Thompson, co-authors of the book *Cooperation Works!* (which included a chapter about the Green Bay Packer model of community ownership), believe that it would be possible through public pressure, legal challenges in the courts, and congressional changes in antitrust rules to erode some of the monopolistic power that restricts community ownership. They warn that there is another problem besides the power of the owners—the unwillingness of communities to pursue strategies for local control. The pair argues that the public's will, if expressed strongly enough, often prevails:

> . . . One might argue that the owners would never approve such a sale because their charter prohibits this type of broad-based ownership structure. As a former representative on the NFL owners council put it, the owners make the rules and they can change the rules. If there were a broad sentiment among sports fans that the sale be approved, the owners may acquiesce to the pressure and let the sale go through. Then, there are always the courts. Recent court cases involving the sale or relocation of professional sports teams have tended to favor the rights of the individual owner over the rights of the league. For example, the courts upheld Al Davis, right to move the Raiders from Oakland to Los Angeles over the objections of the NFL owners association.

... To a large extent then, community ownership boils down to will and commitment. If the business, political and sports leadership of a community really want to assure themselves of having a local franchise, they can do it. They can secure ownership of an established team or an expansion team, or they can enter into a long-term agreement with a team owner.

One clear benefit of community ownership is a more reasonable pricing structure. While the Yankees charge some of the highest ticket prices in the majors, the Packers have always offered among the cheapest tickets in the National Football League. That difference is not a function of a lack of demand. The Packers have sold out hundreds of consecutive games. They choose to sell their tickets at a below-market price so that they don't restrict access to games only to the wealthy. They want to be good citizens of their town.

## YOUR NEW YORK YANKEES

*Why shouldn't Vinnie from Queens own a piece of the Yankees? Why shouldn't Ron Weiss, a Yankee fanatic from East 82d St.?*

—Wayne Coffey

*I always regarded baseball as our national game that belongs to 150 million men, women and children, not to sixteen special people who happen to own big league teams.*

—Former Commissioner Happy Chandler

*It's certainly better than spending one billion on a stadium. We need to step up to the plate and do this. We need to end the corporate blackmail.*

—Assemblyman Scott Stringer, proposing New York City buy the Yankees

*Scott Stringer's proposal is a concept that could conceivably work in two places: Communist China and Cuba. They would be among the few governments left on Earth that would approve government ownership of a baseball team.*

—Colleen Roche, a mayoral spokeswoman

Community ownership would allow us to avoid bittersweet scenes like the one that occurred at the newly opened Yogi Berra Museum in Montclair, New Jersey, after the Yankees' 1998 title run. Fourteen years earlier, George Steinbrenner had promised his manager Yogi Berra that a bad start to the 1985 season would not be a firing offense. When the Yanks started 6-10, the Boss changed his mind and sent a subordinate, general manager Clyde King, to tell Berra he was no longer needed. Being dismissed irked Berra, but Steinbrenner's decision to delegate the bad news to another messenger struck the Hall-of-Fame catcher as so lacking in class that he decided to take a principled stand against the Boss' abuse. No matter that Berra was one of the greatest players in Yankee history and lived just across the Hudson River, he would never enter Yankee Stadium again as long as Steinbrenner owned the team.

Steinbrenner had been able to bury the hatchet with almost all of his famous antagonists. This frequently required that Steinbrenner open his wallet, but he always seemed willing to buy the affection of his past and present employees. The Boss tried everything he could think of to get Berra back to the Stadium, but nothing worked. He even held a day to retire the number 8 worn by Berra and another great Yankee catcher, Bill Dickey, but the catcher refused to show up.

The new museum gave Steinbrenner a place where he could meet with Berra on Yogi's terms. Suzyn Waldman, an ambitious broadcaster who is tremendously protective of Steinbrenner, orchestrated a surprise meeting and organized a subsequent radio show around a reconciliation. Berra, after a lot of coaxing from his family, generously agreed to meet with Steinbrenner and accept his apology. One glance at the museum made it clear that Berra had no need of Steinbrenner's approval or blessing, however, he sensed that his stand created a burden for his family, especially his grandchildren, who wanted to go back with him to his old stomping grounds.

During the radio broadcast that followed their private meeting, Steinbrenner made it clear who owned the Yankees, even the team's history. Asked about the meaning of the reconciliation, Steinbrenner said, "It means a lot to New York and to Yankee fans and to the Yankees to have Yogi and Carm (Yogi's wife) back in the family." Steinbrenner kept marveling at how wonderful it was for Yogi to come back to be a part of the Yankees. In the Boss' mind, Berra wasn't a Yankee unless Steinbrenner said so.

Later in the show, Joe Garagiola, a lifelong friend of Berra and Steinbrenner's close pal as well, joined the festivities by phone. "What do you feel when you think that maybe now Yogi is back in the Yankee family and this is finally over?" asked Waldman. When Waldman unconsciously used Steinbrenner's language, Berra's oldest buddy recoiled, even in the midst of the reconciliation.

"Well, I don't think Yogi was ever out of the Yankee family," replied Garagiola. "He's always been a Yankee."

*             *             *

There is only one way to cure all this nonsense. It's time for voters to apply the same kind of force to the owners that the owners have been using to extort cities for fifty years. Unwilling to do anything for three-quarters of a century, Congress is unlikely to take the initiative, although they already have an excellent piece of legislation before them. U.S. Rep. Earl Blumenauer of Oregon is the sponsor of the H.R. 590 "Give the Fans a Chance Act." That bill would eliminate all league rules against community ownership. The legislation would also require teams to notify their communities before making relocation decisions and give communities an opportunity to purchase their teams. It also ties the leagues' broadcast antitrust exemption to the requirements in the bill.

Along the same lines, in early December, State Assemblyman Scott Stringer (D-Manhattan) proposed that New York City purchase the team from George Steinbrenner for $600 million. If the City owned the Yankees, Stringer said, it would be impossible for the team to threaten to leave. The mayor's assertion that public ownership would violate the rules of Major League Baseball was countered by Stringer, who pointed out that a vote of 75 percent of the owners could change those rules—exactly the same proportion that would have been needed to approve the anticipated purchase of the Yankees by Cablevision. Stringer suggested the city establish a public authority to run the Yanks. "It would be the greatest show in town," he said. In response, the mayor's office offered only sarcasm. "Imagine the City Council trying to decide on Bernie Williams' salary," one source said.

Franchise owners claim they can't afford to build stadiums themselves given current team revenues. But if the city is to build the yard, why not invest in the team as well? Community-based ownership will prevent teams from moving. Those concerned about community control over finances and strategic decisions should ask Packer fans if they're satisfied with their team's appearances in two of the past three Super Bowls. If Steinbrenner, Murdoch, Eisner, and Turner are allowed to buy and sell teams, why shouldn't the community be able to own the New York Yankees as part of a municipal nonprofit?

*                    *                    *

Daniel Kraker and David Morris of the Institute for Local Self-Reliance have proposed an interesting way to circumvent the rules in the major leagues that forbid community ownership. With professional leagues insensitive to fan interests, courts unwilling to dissect baseball's antitrust exemptions, and legislatures too timid to take any real action, they suggest small-scale community ownership in New York City. Recent polls show that New Yorkers support fan ownership. In an October 1998 poll by the Working Families Party, 66 percent felt the city should buy the Yankees and renovate Yankee Stadium rather than build a new taxpayer-funded stadium in Manhattan. Two-thirds of those felt "very strongly" that New York should purchase the Yankees. Surprisingly, more than two in five said they would be at least "somewhat likely" to purchase a share in the Yankees if they were community-owned.

Mayor Giuliani and City Council President Peter Vallone have refused to take up Assemblyman Stringer's proposal, focusing only on the issue of a stadium subsidy. They disagree over spending $1 billion on a new Yankees ballpark in Manhattan, but they see eye-to-eye on committing $40 million in city dollars to two minor-league stadiums, one in Brooklyn's Coney Island and the other in Staten Island. While welcoming the potential return of baseball to Brooklyn, Borough President Howard Golden wants more than a Rookie League team because he believes that Brooklyn, with a population of 2.3 million, is a major-league town. Brooklyn has more residents than Milwaukee, Kansas City, and Cincinnati, all homes to major-league baseball.

For the kind of money the city and state have committed to stadiums, New York could create its own independent minor league. By establishing its own minor league, New York City could host the number of teams that its citizens are able to support without ripping teams away from other supportive communities. Minor-league baseball can be brought to the city without permission from George Steinbrenner, who has no power over the independent minor-league teams that are free of the constraints of the Professional Baseball Agreement.

## BABE IN THE WOODS

*I believe in the church of baseball. I've tried all the major religions and most of the minor ones. I've worshipped Buddha, Allah, Brahma, Vishnu, Siva, trees, mushrooms, and Isadora Duncan. I know things. For instance, there's 108 beads in a Catholic rosary and there's 108 stitches in a baseball. When I learned that, I gave Jesus a chance. But it just didn't work out between us. The Lord laid too much guilt on me. I prefer metaphysics to theology. You see, there's no guilt in baseball, and it's never boring. Which makes it like sex. The only church that feeds the soul, day in, day out, is the church of baseball.*

— Annie Savoy, from *Bull Durham*

Thirty miles north of the city, a world apart in the wooded, rolling hills of Westchester, lies the Gate of Heaven cemetery, burial ground for the New York Catholic Church and home to the remains of actor James Cagney, New York City mayor Jimmy Walker, and former Yankee manager Billy Martin. Just down the hill from Martin lie the bodies of George Herman Ruth and his second wife Claire. On the massive headstone, an adult Jesus reaches out with his left hand to the boy Ruth, adorned in a baseball uniform. The area around the site is well maintained yet the grass before the stone shows the wear that proves the procession to pay respects to the game's greatest player never ends.

When Ruth died on August 16, 1948, his remains were initially brought to Yankee Stadium to rest in state, like a national dignitary in the Capitol Rotunda. Tens of thousands lined up and waited for hours to look into the open coffin and get one last glimpse of the Babe. A boy placed a baseball in one of the Babe's huge paws, with the hopes that the great Yankee would play ball again at his final destination. A few days later, services were held at St. Patrick's Cathedral. An ex-teammate serving as a pallbearer was straining with Ruth's weight and the oppressive heat. He told his buddies he wished he had a beer right now, and Waite Hoyt, perhaps Ruth's best friend on the Yankees, quickly replied, "So does the Babe."

Five decades later, on the golden anniversary of the Babe's death, 50,000 fans are screaming their lungs out in the Bronx as the Rangers and Yankees duel at the Stadium. In White Plains, a few miles down the road from the cemetery, a baseball memorabilia show comes to a close as Yogi Berra cranks out yet another autograph for money. The scene at Gate of Heaven is much quieter. The immense sloping fields are lined with thousands of headstones yet empty of people save the baseball fans who have come to pay tribute to the slugger's childlike nature and his boundless appetites. Never mind the game's lords and their pompous utterances, those who remember are baseball's true owners.

Every few minutes, another car parks near the gravesite. Middle-aged men, fathers with their sons, whole families, even a few elderly couples find their way to the Babe. Some just gaze with awe, while others leave an offering on the stone. The man who loved attention and crowds as much as any ballplayer who ever lived still enjoys their embrace.

At the grave, an American flag rises from the grass in front. Lying against the stone are a pair of wooden bats and, above the bats, a couple of well-worn gloves; the stone's base serves as a home to old newspaper and magazine articles about the Bambino, pictures, too, and flowers, dozens of them; on the right side, three beer bottles stand alongside a half-eaten hot dog; and stuck under a loose rock atop the right side of the stone is a Mark McGwire rookie card, a direct link between past and present. Memories intact, the game continues. Thirty miles south, Bernie Williams wins one at the Stadium with a Ruthian shot in the bottom of the ninth. The afternoon passes, and when the rain comes, the McGwire card begins to ooze, bleeding into the stone below.

# AN EVEN MORE PERFECT SEASON

Was the 1999 baseball season an illusion? As in 1998, the Yankees had the best record in the American League, the Braves the top mark in the National League, and the Indians, Rangers, and Astros repeated as division winners. Even the Red Sox returned as wild-card winners, which enabled the American League to reenact the 1998 first-round playoff matchups, a duplication which before the season started had 1 chance in 480 of occurring. McGwire and Sosa surpassed Ruth and Maris once more, and the Yankees claimed another World Series. The 1999 season mirrored the "perfect season" universally praised as baseball's comeback year.

Any differences between the two campaigns favored 1999. The duel between Sosa and McGwire for home-run champ was more competitive than the year before. The 1999 playoffs featured the first postseason encounter between the rival Red Sox and Yankees, as well as an incredible series between the Braves and the Mets. In the World Series, the Yankees faced a much tougher foe than the Padre team they so clearly overmatched the prior year. And the Yankees, coming off a season for the ages on and off the field, generated even stronger feelings in a year marked by the deaths of legends DiMaggio and Hunter, as well as the passing of the fathers of three current players, and the illness of Torre. The Yankee season also featured Cone's perfect game, Yogi's return, and the continued rise of Jeter, Rivera, and Hernandez.

The team's first aggressive ad campaign in years encouraged fans to witness history being made and combined with the season-long emotional roller coaster to draw spectators to the Bronx like never before. Steinbrenner's long-standing complaints about the inaccessibility of the site and undesirability of the neighborhood were disproved by the nearly 3.3 million fans who visited Yankee Stadium in 1999. The Yanks trailed only the Orioles, Rockies, and Indians in attendance and were less than 200,000 fans short of being the top draw in the game.

Yankee success notwithstanding, fans and analysts alike reacted to the 1999 season as if they were distinctly underwhelmed. McGwire and Sosa's near-repetition of their historic 1998 numbers only cheapened their original effort. After all, only one player topped even 50 home runs in the fifteen years after Maris hit 61. In 1998, Sosa and McGwire finished first and second in the NL MVP voting. In 1999, McGwire led the league in home runs, runs batted in, and slugging percentage while drawing more walks and scoring more runs than Chipper Jones. Sosa, too, had more homers, runs batted in, and total bases than Jones. Nevertheless, Jones won the NL MVP award in a near-unanimous vote. Neither McGwire, who finished fifth, nor Sosa, who finished ninth, received even one first-place vote, and two voters left McGwire off their ballots entirely.

For the first time since the cancellation of the 1994 World Series, attendance dropped. Significant declines occurred in places Major League Baseball could hardly have expected. In their second seasons, the Diamondbacks and Devil Rays demonstrated how fast baseball could wear out its welcome. The expansion teams lost a combined total of 1.34 million. While Arizona still drew 3 million despite a 16 percent drop, Tampa Bay's league-leading 30 percent decline in attendance left the team drawing just 1.75 million fans. 1999 was 1998 redux, but nobody seemed happy about it.

*                    *                    *

The key cause of dissatisfaction during the 1999 season was the growing realization that fair competition no longer existed. Fans in small markets know their team has no chance at the beginning of the season. When the average salary of a Yankee player is higher than the salary of their team's best player and only teams among the top ten spenders make the playoffs, it's hard to keep hope alive.

What makes watching sports enjoyable is the idea of competition. No one would pay money to watch a fight between a 21-year-old Tyson and a 55-year-old Ali suffering from Parkinson's. A race for a playoff spot between the Yankees and the Devil Rays, Twins or Royals resembles that mismatch, which explains why attendance is dropping off so precipitously in certain cities. Since the 1994 strike, eight American League teams—the Blue Jays, Devil Rays, White Sox,

Twins, Royals, Tigers, Athletics, Angels—have not even gotten a whiff of the playoffs.

In 1998, all eight playoff teams had been among the top twelve in payroll; in 1999, all eight resided among the top ten in payroll. The top ten teams spent almost $75 million apiece in payroll to produce an average record of 94-68. Meanwhile, the bottom ten spent a mere $24 million each and finished on average twenty-two games behind the big spenders. All ten teams that have reached the World Series since 1994 have been in the top ten in payroll; in fact, six have been among the top three.

In the face of prolific evidence that the only way to win the World Series was by outspending your opponents, some of the media continued to insist that any team could win. According to the wise guys, the poor performances of the Orioles and Dodgers, both big spenders, offered proof that you couldn't just buy a pennant, while the success of the Reds and Athletics meant that small-market teams still had a chance. These exceptions proved the rule.

Despite the hype, the two biggest success stories of the 1999 season were not the Reds and the Athletics, teams that missed the playoffs, but instead the Diamondbacks and Mets, the two new entrants to the playoffs. The Mets ranked second in the National League in payroll, and their postseason loss to the top spenders from Atlanta reflected that status perfectly. Meanwhile, the Arizona Diamondbacks increased their payroll by a record $37 million and won 35 more games, rising from the National League West cellar to a runaway division title. Even the underdog Reds increased their payroll by $17 million, which was one of the largest increases in the game.

As for the Athletics, no other team caught so much lightning in a bottle during the 1999 season. The kids at shortstop and third base and out in right field had solid seasons, unheralded sluggers John Jaha, Matt Stairs, and Jason Giambi smacked over 100 homers, and young ace Tim Hudson was the best rookie pitcher the American League had seen in a decade. Even their midseason trades worked out beautifully as Kevin Appier, Omar Olivares, Jason Isringhausen, and Randy Velarde played well down the stretch. In a season in which nearly everything went right, the Athletics won 87 games yet still finished seven games short of the wild card and eight games behind the division champs from Texas. Oakland's miracle summer had only insured that the cost of keeping the club together would soar immediately, and, considering that the playoff run drew only 200,000 extra fans, it was hard to imagine where the revenue to support those expenditures would come from.

During what both teams would admit were miserable seasons, the big spenders from Baltimore and Los Angeles finished about as close to the Athletics as Oakland did to the playoffs. With some players hurt and others struggling in clubhouses rife with tension, the Orioles and Dodgers still managed to outperform a dozen of the low-revenue teams. The 1999 season proved that a wealthy team could have a disastrous season and still beat more than half of the poorer franchises.

The revenue gap between baseball's whales and minnows now exceeds $150 million. Nine teams spent over $70 million on major-league payroll alone—seven made the playoffs—while an equal number of teams did not even pull in that much in gross revenue. In the face of this depressing reality, Kevin Kietzman, a sports talk-show host and sports director at KCTE, a radio station in Kansas City, recognized the discontent of local baseball fans who had lost their reason to believe. Kietzman organized a protest that drew attention to competitive imbalance and urged owners to split their revenue more equitably.

In anticipation of the first game of the 1999 season in Kansas City between the Royals and the Yankees, the station gave away more than three thousand T-shirts that read "Share The Wealth." Kietzman explained to his audience that the Yankees would receive nearly half a million dollars more in media-rights fees from one contest than the Royals. Thousands of fans sat together in the left-field bleachers, chanted "share the wealth," threw dollar bills at the Yankees when they were in the field, and turned their backs when the Yankees were batting. The protesters exited during the third inning, leaving skeletons on their seats with signs reading, "Small Markets Are Dying." That protest attracted national attention, and the ratings for KCTE nearly doubled.

The Yankees did not win three of the last four World Series because they are the best-run organization. They won because they outspent everyone else at the table. In 1999, the Yankees spent $11 million more than the team with the second highest payroll in the majors. That allowed the Yankees to get away with making all kinds of mistakes. The Yankees' young catcher Jorge Posada had a half-season slump where he couldn't hit .200, second baseman Chuck Knoblauch failed to make simple plays for much of the year, third baseman Scott Brosius returned to offensive mediocrity, neither kid in left field played well enough to claim the job, and veterans Tino Martinez and Paul O'Neill began to show their age as their numbers tapered off.

The Yankees traded David Wells, their best starting pitcher, Graeme Lloyd, a quality left-handed setup man, and Homer Bush, a reserve infielder with speed and a good bat, for future Hall-of-Famer Roger Clemens. In his new uniform, Clemens flopped, allowing nearly two more runs per game than the prior season while taking home $8 million in salary. Veteran ace David Cone proved that he is no longer durable. After pitching a perfect game and winning nine games with an ERA under three during the first half of the season, Cone was reduced to a once-a-week, five-innings-per-game pitcher who won just three games during the second half of the season. And what team can afford to keep someone as inconsistent as Strawberry?

Steinbrenner paid Darryl $2.5 million to do what he has done each of the past eight seasons: not play.

On any other team, those performances would be catastrophic. For the Yankees, such failures only mean that they rule over the regular season by a smaller margin. Remember how much went right for the Athletics, yet the Yanks still won eleven more games. The Yankees' 1999 postseason performance perfectly illustrates why the money matters. The Yankees outspent the Red Sox by $20 million and the Braves by $13 million. In the American League Championship Series, this disparity showed up in the Yanks having a deeper pitching rotation and bench than the Red Sox. In the World Series, the extra money shelled out by the Yankees was visible in the more well-rounded skills shown by the Yankee regulars, as well as the greater depth of the bench and bullpen.

The mercurial Strawberry resurfaced after the Yankees' only postseason loss, the massacre of Clemens at Fenway. Early in Game 4, Strawberry lined a homer off the foul pole in right field to give the Yankees a lead and turn the direction of the series for good. After being babied the last two months of the season, Cone delivered masterful performances against Boston and Atlanta that helped him secure a $12 million deal for the 2000 season despite repeated late-season collapses. El Duque, who had come to the Yankees as an international free agent when they offered the most money, pitched even better than Cone during the postseason. In the World Series, Chad Curtis, a reserve outfielder who would have been starting for at least a dozen weaker teams, demonstrated the value of veteran talent. First, Curtis made a brilliant reflex play on the basepaths that kept a critical rally alive in Game 1, and then, in Game 3, he delivered two homers, including a game-ending homer in extra innings that put the Series away. After Curtis' heroics, even the much-maligned Clemens got into the act, delivering a solid start to beat John Smoltz and end the season.

In 1999, the Yankees outspent the average major-league team by about $40 million. To level the playing field would mean replacing Clemens, O'Neill, Pettitte, Brosius, Chili Davis, Girardi, Irabu, and Curtis with minor leaguers. Take those eight players away, which still leaves the franchise's most productive per dollar players on the roster, and there is no way the Yankees repeat as world champs; it's likely that Jeter, Williams, Rivera and the rest would fail to make the postseason. The disparity seems only to be getting worse. Davis, Girardi, Irabu, and Curtis are gone and may all be replaced by minor leaguers, but remaining veterans like Jeter, Cone, Pettitte, Rivera, Mendoza, and Posada received huge raises that will push the Yankee payroll over the $100 million mark for the 2000 campaign.

In his *Historical Baseball Abstract*, Bill James wrote about the rebirth of baseball attendance in the 1970s: "I honestly cannot visualize the return of baseball's popularity as occurring in the face of continued Yankee domination." In 1999, Yankee domination was so complete that *The Sporting News* headlined its World Series coverage: "Yankees dynasty is alarming." The replacement of honest competition with dishonest noncompetition was so obvious that even mainstream observers (from George Will to *The Sporting News* to baseball commissioner Bud Selig) realized something needed to be done. Selig formed a blue-ribbon panel to study the issue. "Disparity among the teams is the biggest problem facing the clubs. It [competitive imbalance] is the number one item on my agenda," said Selig.

Even most of those running large-market franchises understood their game was diseased. "You look at the bottom tier of teams, and those guys aren't making any more money than they did four or five years ago," said Astros owner Drayton McLane. "And that's what caused anarchy in Europe 200, 300 years ago. A few people had all the money." "I'd prefer we were all operating on the same plane financially," asserted Dodger GM Kevin Malone, "I would like to see all 30 clubs on a level playing field. That would be good for the fans, it would create more competition."

The Yankee Boss, of course, was unrepentant. "Go back to baseball since it began. I think you'll find the Yankees were always one of the teams that spent more than others. There were a lot of years when we spent a ton of money and didn't win. There's disparity in the world and in this country. There's disparity between General Motors and some little company. You can't say, 'Well, let's all share everything equal,' or else we should be over in Russia. And it didn't work over there," Steinbrenner proclaimed.

With nearly everyone else recognizing that a problem existed, the key issue became the nature of a solution. An industry cartel like OPEC or the NFL is only as healthy as its weakest member. The way to aid the poorer partners is to increase revenue sharing. By recognizing that simple reality—communal greed is more powerful than individual selfishness—those who own NFL teams have seen a growth in franchise values that dwarfs all other sports. Baseball's owners, however, have been trapped by their blind self-interest, with strong teams showing little concern for the health of their partners. Every time the owners have had a problem amongst themselves during the past quarter-century, instead of addressing the issue, they have looked to stick it to someone else: the players, the umpires, the fans, their broadcast partners, and the municipalities and their taxpayers.

When Major League Baseball refused to allow the sales of the Athletics and Royals to go through during the offseason, the cartel revealed its true interests. The powers that be wanted to give the blue-ribbon panel on competitive balance a chance to look at small-market viability issues. Rumors were floated that the big-market teams did not want to subsidize these teams anymore, and that the teams might even be disbanded and the players redistributed in a dispersal draft. Among the concerns of the big-market owners was that if MLB franchises sold for around $100 million (more for the A's, less for the Royals), the value of their franchises (and the next expansion franchises) would be damaged at a time when their fellow owners in the NFL were seeing values routinely above half a billion dollars. The contemporaneous Reds sale was approved because the Reds played the municipality extortion game and secured a publicly financed stadium, thereby increasing their franchise value to an acceptable level.

Selig did not need outside experts like George Mitchell and Paul Volcker to study the issue. He needed to find a way to get Steinbrenner to understand the difficult concept that his team would be worth more if he shared more money (in the same way that franchise values rose in conjunction with and even faster than the phenomenal and much-maligned growth of player salaries over the last two decades). But the commissioner is a slow consensus-builder. His panel recommended that the owners expand his power to take the necessary action to insure an appropriate level of long-term competitive balance. The owners did just that, giving Selig the ability to redirect revenue from Major League Baseball's central fund, along with total control of revenue generated by baseball over the Internet, while granting him the authority to deal harshly with teams who refuse to comply.

Any move by Selig to increase revenue sharing comes under the terms of the collective bargaining agreement and, therefore, requires the agreement of the Major League Baseball Players' Association (MLBPA), arguably the world's strongest union. The agreement expires at the end of the 2000 season, but the union holds an option for the 2001 season that it is certain to exercise. Paradoxically, the biggest danger for the players is their success in labor wars. As their wages rise to 50–100 times that of the average American, athletes no longer want to be represented by trade unionists who get them what they deserve but instead by labor lawyers who protect what they have. The result, according to the pioneering Marvin Miller, is that ballplayers today are less educated than ever before about the struggle that made them millionaires.

The players' union not only sat out the recent dispute between NBA owners and players that was resolved with the players agreeing to the imposition of a hard salary cap, but the MLBPA also stayed in the dugout during Major League Baseball's beheading of the umpires' union. Those two events will give the baseball owners a renewed sense of their own authority. Don't be surprised if Selig uses the advice of his blue-ribbon panel to lock out the players next year rather than create the revenue-sharing system so desperately needed.

Gene Orza, second-in-command at the players' union, worries about the owners' rhetoric. "'Revenue sharing' and 'competitive balance' have been code words in this industry for not letting markets determine salaries," says Orza. "When you hear those words, alarm bells should go off."

Given the commissioner's absurd, unsupported claims that only a quarter of major-league teams turns a profit each year, it's easy to understand why the union distrusts the owners and their hired hand. And when the guy who runs a team that reached the World Series complains that he has no chance to compete just six months later (which is what Padre boss John Moores claimed in a bizarre editorial in the *Wall Street Journal* at the beginning of the 1999 season), then one can see why claims about a lack of competition may be seen as little more than preparation for an attempt to contract salaries.

The reality, however, is that baseball players and owners are a bilateral monopoly. You will never hear anyone from the union express their concern about higher ticket prices or cable bills for fans because much of that increased revenue goes right into members' pockets. Not once has a player stood up to stop an old stadium from being torn down or complained about the extortion of municipalities by owners threatening to relocate. Instead of outrage, what you hear is self-interested silence.

The union's concerns over possible salary caps, as well as the warm feeling that more generous owners engender even in players they treat like dirt, may lead to a dangerous alliance with the Yankees against any serious revenue-sharing plan proposed by the commissioner. The players' union should realize that large-market clubs survive labor disputes in much stronger condition than their small-market partners. While every small-market team in the majors that remained in the same ballpark drew more fans in the four years before the 1994 strike than the four years after, teams like the Yankees and Dodgers saw their attendance grow after the dispute, further solidifying the tremendous revenue advantage produced by their media contracts. Wealthier teams like the Yankees and Dodgers will have the strongest backbones in any attempt by the owners to break the union after the current agreement expires.

The most publicized judicial decision of 1999 was Judge Thomas Penfield Jackson's finding of fact illustrating Microsoft's predatory, anticompetitive behavior. Judge Jackson ruled that the company controlled the market to the point where "Microsoft could charge a price substantially above that which could be charged in a competitive market" and also detailed Microsoft's efforts to restrict entry into the marketplace. With Yankee and Met ticket prices more than doubling since the 1994 strike and the New York City market still limited by the baseball cartel to just two major-league teams, the sport's bosses are behaving no differently than Bill Gates. But unlike their fellow monopolists in the NBA and NFL, they have been unable to deliver a consistently competitive product.

\*         \*         \*

During the last season of the century, there were moments of incompetence and toadying in the print media that rivaled the worst work of writers generations earlier. George King, the *Post*'s Yankee beat writer, stunned his colleagues and the baseball world by leaving Boston Red Sox ace Pedro Martinez, who had one of the greatest pitching seasons ever, entirely off his MVP ballot. This inexplicable action cost the brilliant pitcher a legitimate chance at the award he so richly deserved. Justifying his decision, King claimed that pitchers didn't deserve to be considered because they don't play every day. The rules on the ballot require voters to consider all players, and, furthermore, King had listed two pitchers on his MVP ballot after the 1998 season.

While King's errors were obvious, some sins of omission were not so apparent. For the fourth straight year, the scramble to get Yankee playoff tickets left most of the public unhappy while thousands of insiders secured special invitations. In 1999, no one in the media even noticed a corrupt process that entitled powerful media players who had not been to the Bronx since the prior year's World Series to reclaim their seats at the start of the fall classic as if they'd been faithful fans all season long.

If journalism involves reporting something that would not be released by either the PR staff of a team or a player (and his agent), then little "sports reporting" can be accurately called journalism. Of course, this is the reason that the few moments when investigation or analysis occurs create such a stir. After a baseball season where no one remembered what happened on the field, what lingers in the memory are two interviews.

Jim Gray's tough (and needlessly repetitive) questioning of Pete Rose minutes after he received the loudest applause of any member of the All-Century team created a firestorm of controversy that was more a result of populist sentiment about Rose's exclusion from the

Hall of Fame than anything Gray or Rose said during the sixty-second encounter. By contrast, the toughest thing *Sports Illustrated*'s Jeff Pearlman did to John Rocker was turn on his tape recorder in the redneck reliever's presence. While Gray's work could be seen as self-promoting and therefore easily attacked, Pearlman's own sense of ethics—he refused to even promote the piece on CNNSI, the cable network owned by the company that owns his magazine—should have made him relatively invulnerable.

Nevertheless, few of his peers celebrated the accuracy of Pearlman's work or the exposure of an out-of-control bigot. Some writers, worried that the athletes who fed them stories might be spooked by what happened to Rocker, attacked the piece as a case of gotcha journalism. Peter Gammons and ESPN used Rocker's first televised interview after the brouhaha to attempt to rehabilitate the fallen star. Rebuilding Rocker's image required that some excuses be offered; Rocker claimed that his words had been taken out of context and blamed fan violence in New York.

Pearlman told me that "What ESPN did made me sick. When Rocker bragged about having black people in his house, why didn't Gammons question that?" Pearlman challenged Rocker's claims that he had been joking and said that the Braves' reliever apparently thought what he was saying was OK "because we were just two white guys talking." While some of Rocker's teammates stepped up to challenge his excuses, the baseball establishment and much of the media was more forgiving.

Another individual who received an easy passage from the media was George Steinbrenner. Shortly after the World Series, the *Post*'s mean-spirited Steve Dunleavy praised the Boss with a string of self-serving quotes from old Steinbrenner crony Bill Fugazy about the owner's private, charitable side, which were "reluctantly" confirmed by PR maven Howard Rubinstein. What hypocritical nonsense. If

Steinbrenner doesn't want his donations public, he can tell his PR man to keep quiet. Even the Boss' distaste for publicity is a pose, swallowed by so-called journalists.

Worse than Dunleavy, the *Times'* Bob Herbert succumbed to the Boss' charms in an editorial after the World Series. Steinbrenner had neither agreed to stay in the Bronx nor apologized for his campaign-finance crimes on behalf of Richard Nixon. Nevertheless, the Yankee victories, along with assurances from the Boss' handlers that the team would not move, prompted Herbert to praise a wealthy businessman trying to loot the city treasury as if it were his own. If people around the country are wondering why buffoons like Donald Trump think they should be president, the explanation is they read their own clippings in the celebrity-worshipping New York press.

The negative implications of the increasing concentration of media power into a few hands were apparent everywhere. Two incidents in the aftermath of Jim Gray's interview of Pete Rose are instructive. Gray's initial response to the backlash against him for being too negative was to defend his behavior as proper journalism and apologize to no one. However, when the populist outrage overwhelmed the World Series and MasterCard's promotional tie-in, the sponsor demanded an apology from the network. As a direct result of corporate pressure, NBC opened the telecast of the next World Series game with Gray offering an apology to the millions watching at home.

That night's game ended with Chad Curtis' game-winning home run. In the immediate aftermath of the home run, Gray tried to interview the outfielder, but Curtis brushed off the broadcaster because of the Rose interview. Later that night, NBC exec Dick Ebersol confronted Steinbrenner and demanded that his players cooperate with the network that had paid millions to broadcast the World Series. Sure enough, the next night, during the World Series victory celebration, the Yankee players kept their displeasure to themselves and acceded to each of Gray's interview requests.

Monopoly power allowed Major League Baseball to sue its national cable TV partner over a technicality without fear of reprisal. In fact, on the day the trial was to begin, ESPN blinked and signed a deal that essentially quadrupled the rights' fee while extending the contract by just three years. The message was clear. Even the highest-earning arm of the Disney octopus caved in order to avoid offending a key corporate partner that could seek redress in a future bidding process. That cooperation freed ESPN to broadcast Mets playoff games in Arizona to the East Coast at two in the morning.

These media battles are exactly what drove George Steinbrenner to make an otherwise unlikely alliance with the lowly New Jersey Nets. Not only did the new partnership put hundreds of millions in cash in the Boss' pocket, the YankeeNets (perhaps soon to be the YankeeNetDevils) gave Steinbrenner much greater leverage in critical negotiations for his new TV rights package. Given local cable mogul Charles Dolan's continuing pursuit of the Mets and demonstrated willingness to favor Dolan-owned properties in making schedules for Dolan-owned cable companies, Steinbrenner needed that increased might. He could attempt to secure part-ownership of any cable channel that wanted to broadcast Yankee games, or, if necessary, put together his own cable network, complete with year-round programming of local pro sports.

One of the first individuals named to the board of directors of the YankeeNets was James Murdoch, heir to Rupert Murdoch's fortune, which includes 40 percent of Dolan's Cablevision, as well as the local Fox affiliate, both of which broadcast Yankee games. By putting a key Dolan partner on his board, Steinbrenner may have blunted Dolan's desire to play hardball with the schedule or during the next contract negotiations. But if Dolan goes to war to protect his control of the

New York City cable market, Steinbrenner could not have secured a stronger partner than Murdoch. In the end, whichever way the deals fall, the likely result is much higher cable bills for the consumer.

*       *       *

During a season when five general manager positions opened up and every minority candidate was passed over, leaving the front offices of baseball all white for yet another season, the national pastime repeatedly failed to escape its reactionary past. Two lists designed to celebrate the century's greatest players opened old wounds by reinforcing past exclusionary policies. A sport that could find room for an open bigot like John Rocker was not so sure about whether it wanted to include the openly homosexual Billy Bean.

Both the Society of American Baseball Researchers (SABR) and Major League Baseball, as part of a media campaign by MasterCard, unveiled their lists of the best players of the twentieth century. The baseball junkies at SABR excluded Negro Leaguers from their ballots for the Top 100 because they felt the statistical record was insufficient to allow meaningful comparison with major leaguers. Kept off the fields for sixty years, black ballplayers were now banished from historical comparison with their contemporaries by the sport's most dedicated historians.

SABR has an interest in maintaining the sanctity of the statistics compiled over the entire history of the major leagues because much of their work involves comparisons within that database. If a challenge to the database—are the numbers before 1950 as valid as the numbers after 1950?—were taken seriously, the whole enterprise might collapse. SABR's decision allows the system to behave as if Ruth's accomplishments can be compared to McGwire's. They can't.

SABR's bias is racist in effect even if its members intend no harm. SABR's defense is that they don't know enough about Negro League players to put them in their proper context. But if that is true, then how can SABR possibly know enough about the Caucasian Leaguers who were their contemporaries? The vast majority of the best players in the world now play in the majors. There is no way you can make that same statement about the majors before Jackie. Comparing the inflated stats of the 1930s to the numbers of today may be the same as comparing a hitter who plays in Denver with one in San Diego. Take 20 percent out of those numbers to account for the diminished competition and you knock all but the great stars down to a very average level. Make that adjustment 40 percent and everybody but Ruth starts looking ordinary. Nobody will ever tower over the game like Ruth because no one will face such diminished competition again. Take Sosa and Griffey out of the home-run race last year, put them in the Negro Leagues, and then see how much larger McGwire's accomplishments would appear.

MasterCard managed to offend baseball fans because its voting process, which allowed the public to participate, only selected a handful of players. Cultural icons like Roberto Clemente, Juan Marichal, Josh Gibson, and Satchel Paige were excluded, and the African-American and Hispanic-American baseball fans who loved those players seemed nearly as outraged as the Pete Rose fans who wanted to decapitate Jim Gray.

While these slights involved issues of race and culture, the constricting relationship between team sport and male sexuality reemerged, too. Baseball's tolerance for an open homosexual has yet to be proven. The masculine notion of baseball involves a central myth about fathers and sons. Homosexuality breaks down that patriarchal myth by suggesting another means of creating a powerful emotional bond between men.

Billy Bean, a reserve outfielder who played for the Tigers, Dodgers, and Padres during the early '90s, revealed his sexual orientation to

Lydia Martin, a reporter for the *Miami Herald*, who related the story of the closeted ballplayer who quit the game to be with the man he loved. Martin's piece was picked up by the national media within a few weeks. Brad Ausmus, Bean's ex-teammate and closest friend in the game, understood why his teammate had been so private. "If he had been openly gay, it would have been very difficult for him to play," explained Ausmus. "He hasn't played baseball in four years and he's getting more attention now than during all the time he played. I think if a major league player is going to come out, it's going to have to be a superstar, somebody who can answer his critics with play in the field, who can have the focus be his abilities and not his sexual preference."

Yankee players were not as supportive as Bean's ex-teammates and questioned whether an openly gay player would cause problems within the clubhouse. "If you polled every player in this room," Chad Curtis told Buster Olney of the *New York Times*, "they would tell you they wouldn't want to even have the thought another guy on the team might be checking them out. You have a lot of guys in this room who are fairly uncomfortable with the idea of women in the media coming in hereeven just the notion they're being looked at." Andy Pettitte echoed Curtis' sentiments: "There would be a question of being comfortable."

Asked about the Billy Bean controversy, Derek Jeter, the Yankees' rising star, expressed his belief in tolerance in an answer one reporter saw as politically astute if possibly disingenuous. On the subject of John Rocker, however, the future Yankee captain was unambiguous, telling the *New York Post* that "I wouldn't sit in the same room with him. I wouldn't sit with someone who is a racist. He says he's not a racist but he makes racist comments. I look at everything he said, starting with New Yorkers, and what he said about races and nationalities. That's the good thing about New York—the best thing, I thinkthe fact that there are people of different races and nationalities and religions."

If only Jeter's multicultural awareness extended to the Yankee front office. After the 1999 season, first-base coach Jose Cardenal asked for a $30,000 raise to his $120,000 salary. As the organization's only Spanish-speaking coach, Cardenal served as an intermediary between the manager, the front office, and Spanish-speaking players. Cardenal played a large role in the success of Orlando Hernandez, serving as the Cuban's translator and sounding board. His desire to seek an increase in pay roughly equivalent to the amount paid to Hideki Irabu's translator seemed reasonable given his responsibilities. However, in a decision by Steinbrenner to save a few thousand dollars while spending over a hundred million on players, the Yankees cut Cardenal loose. While the coach immediately secured a job with the Devil Rays, the Yankees replaced him with Lee Mazzilli, which left the team without any on-field management fluent in Spanish. On a roster filled with players from Latin America, that decision seems as misguided as it is insensitive.

*               *               *

After Leon Hess, owner of the Jets, passed away last year, a fan group organized on the Internet to put together a serious bid for community ownership of the team, a natural defense strategy in an era of unprecedented franchise mobility in the NFL. The NFL commissioner's office and the local media saw the efforts by these fans as little more than a curiosity. Why is public ownership of sports franchises immediately dismissed by so many observers as a foolish idea?

The left is comfortable with government playing a central role in managing education, health care, and mass transportation while the right has confidence in the government's ability to provide law and order and maintain national defense. These areas of faith in the public sector involve key issues for each group, yet ideologues at both ends of the political spectrum believe that letting a city own a major-league team is dangerous. Of course, municipal ownership is a threat to sports moguls because if their books were open to public scrutiny, everyone would realize what poor citizens ball clubs have been over the past quarter-century while engaging in extortion.

Some politicians try to lure teams with promises of new stadiums and endless revenue streams even before management hints at any displeasure. Thwarted in his efforts to give the Yankees hundreds of millions from the city treasury, Mayor Giuliani renewed his efforts to build a stadium five blocks west of Madison Square Garden. "The West Side stadium proposal is very much alive," the mayor told the press early in 2000 about a project that could cost more than $1 billion. "I think bringing the Jets back to New York City would be terrific."

Apparently concerned about the lack of any great public works to his name at the end of two terms in office, Giuliani worked feverishly to build a new ballpark in every borough, starting, of course, with the most Republican, Staten Island. The public money authorized to build a 6,500-seat waterfront stadium, including a luxury box controlled by the mayor's office, for the Staten Island Yankees, a team in the low minors with a short season, will be the most ever spent, $74.5 million, for a minor-league park. "I've talked with hundreds of young people in Staten Island. They've told me of their need for after-school programs and computers," said Ken Fisher, councilman from Brooklyn and chairman of the Youth Services Committee. "Spending millions to create a short-season, limited-purpose entertainment venue shortchanges those young people."

Unfortunately, the city charter gives the council no power to make changes in lease agreements connected to land use. City Hall and Staten Island borough president Guy Molinari handled the process as if they owned it. The lack of open discussion along the land use review route meant that no one ever asked why the city of Camden, New Jersey could build a waterfront park at the same time with 6,000 seats for a mere $17.5 million. Although the stadium is essentially a gift from city taxpayers, the lease favors the team. If they draw less than 125,000 fans in a 38-game season, they don't have to pay any rent. If they draw under 75,000 for three straight years, then the team can break the lease without repercussions.

While Giuliani was satisfying his edifice complex, Steinbrenner's merger with the Nets brought the Yankee boss hundreds of millions while enabling him to maintain private control of his team and delay any decisions on the stadium. If Steinbrenner had not yet been able to drain hundreds of millions out of the taxpayers' pockets, he was quite effective at securing a lot more money from Yankee fans. Without rent control for spectators at city-owned Yankee Stadium, ticket prices escalated faster than any real estate in the city. Every seat in the house, except for those at the top of the upper deck and out in the bleachers, costs more in 2000 than the best seat cost just four years ago.

While the Boss' marketers successfully sold Yankee baseball through an appeal to nostalgia, 1999 witnessed the death of four stadia, most prominently Tiger Stadium in Detroit, a beautiful old ballpark that drew tears even from those complicit in the killing. Nothing is more sickening than the process by which billionaire owners and their media pals spin the murder of a wondrous stadium into a revenue-boosting last round of remembrances.

When the expansion-joint beam fell at Yankee Stadium during the 1998 season, it seemed to foreshadow another "death by natural causes." However, Buildings Commissioner Gaston Silva told concerned fans that the stadium was actually in good shape: "From a structural perspective, there's no reason why Yankee Stadium can't be around for another 75 years if it's maintained properly." Those honest words triggered an immediate response from City Hall. More interested in propaganda than facts, Giuliani's aides told Silva that he should not repeat his statement publicly because the mayor believed that building a new stadium in Manhattan was in the city's best interest.

Giuliani's efforts were rewarded with the continued loyalty of the Yankee boss, best illustrated by the circuitous route of two charitable donations made by the New York Yankee Foundation after calamitous disasters in Latin America. After a hurricane shredded the Dominican Republic, the Yankees decided to send $100,000 there to aid victims. Instead of sending it directly through an experienced organization, the Yankees gave the money to New York City Public-Private Initiatives Inc. (PPI), a nonprofit run out of the Mayor's Office of Operations that doles out money to Giuliani's favorite causes. How anyone could believe that more money would get into the hands of the needy after being funneled through City Hall is hard to imagine, but the exchange created a great photo-op that confirmed Steinbrenner's image as a soft touch, and linked Giuliani to good works and the Yankees in one fell swoop.

While Steinbrenner's involvement with the nebulous PPI was troubling, his hiring of Randy Levine was scandalous. During Levine's time as deputy mayor for economic development, he remained a consultant to Major League Baseball, and anyone who called baseball's headquarters in search of Levine would have their call forwarded to a phone on his desk at City Hall. Levine's ties to Giuliani and Steinbrenner go way back. He worked as a prosecutor under Giuliani in the 1980s and negotiated Steinbrenner's return to baseball from an indefinite suspension in 1993. In fact, while Levine was serving as the city's chief labor negotiator in 1995, he was described by mayoral spokeswoman Christyne Lategano as a back channel for stadium negotiations between Giuliani and Steinbrenner.

After moving back and forth between the public and private sector twice more, Levine was barred from any dealings with the Mets or Yankees as deputy mayor, but met publicly with Steinbrenner at least once during his tenure. On stepping down as deputy mayor, Levine took a job in the new YankeeNets hierarchy that involved labor negotiations and relations with the commissioner, while he maintained his ties to Giuliani as an informal adviser to the Senate campaign. Levine is supposed to recuse himself from any stadium negotiations between the Yankees and City Hall for a year after retirement, yet city rules allow him to discuss these matters with people from the state. When looking at ways to generate huge sources of new revenue, Steinbrenner has only two avenues: the next media contract and a new stadium. Considering that Levine has little expertise in the world of big media, it would be ridiculous to expect that Steinbrenner will pay the former deputy mayor, a man who dished out corporate welfare at record speed, to sit on the sidelines as the Boss tries to drain the city's coffers.

Levine's tenure included extreme acts of municipal generosity—CBS received $10 million to stay in New York City and the New York Stock Exchange secured $600 million—as well as demonstrations of brute force. Levine allegedly threatened to cut off funds to any institutions that offered public support to the Brooklyn Museum of Art during the squall surrounding the *Sensation* exhibit and also squashed the Miramax launch party for Tina Brown's new magazine because it featured Hillary Clinton on the cover.

Hard as it may be to believe, Yankee baseball could play a central role in the most anticipated Senate race in years. The First Lady's sad attempt to come out as a Yankee fan only confirmed her status as a carpetbagger in the minds of many voters. Every time Rudy wraps himself in Yankee pinstripes it further illustrates the sexism that still drives electoral politics in New York, a state where a woman has yet to win an important statewide race. If the Yankees win yet another World Series in the fall of 2000, Mayor Giuliani, in his role at the Yankee victory parade, will have free access to all local media

for hours just days before the election. Giuliani's last opponent, Ruth
Messenger, saw her campaign kickoff announcement buried in the
media by the interest in the mayor's City Hall welcome for new
Yankee pitcher Hideki Irabu.

Right-wing talk-radio ranters on WABC, the on-air home for the
Yankees and the mayor, routinely attack the First Lady for her perceived inability to name the Yankees' starting lineup. That expertise,
of course, has nothing to do with what is required of a serving senator. In all likelihood, the retiring Senator Moynihan could not name
the current Yankee nine. In a year when two competitive candidates
for president offer up the parts of their resume that read "NBA player" and "Major League Baseball owner" with more pride than their
years of public service, the jock culture appears to be inescapable.

Nevertheless, the nexus between Levine and Giuliani is so troubling that one wonders whether it might not be best to root for the
mayor to win the Senate race. If he loses, he and Levine, who will
then be a year out of office, will work openly to create a monument to
Rudy. A "new and improved" Yankee Stadium costing taxpayers hundreds of millions of dollars would hardly disturb a mayor who had
been rejected by the voters and could not seek reelection. That sce-
nario may be even more frightening than the idea of Giuliani arriv-
ing on Capitol Hill.

# BIBLIOGRAPHY

Abrams, Roger I. (1998). *Legal Bases: Baseball and the Law* (Philadephia: Temple University Press).

Allen, Maury (1975). *Where Have You Gone, Joe DiMaggio?* (New York: E.P. Dutton).

Anderson, Benedict (1983). *Imagined Communities* (London: Verso).

Angell, Roger (1972). *The Summer Game* (New York: Popular Library).

_____ (1977). *Five Seasons—A Baseball Companion* (New York: Popular Library).

_____ (1982). *Late Innings* (New York: Ballantine).

_____ (1988). *Season Ticket* (Boston: Houghton-Mifflin).

_____ (1991). *Once More Around the Park: A Baseball Reader* (New York: Ballantine).

Aronowitz, Stanley (1994). *Dead Artists, Live Theories, and Other Cultural Problems* (New York: Routledge).

Ashe, Arthur R., Jr., et al. (1993). *A Hard Road to Glory: Baseball, the African-American Athlete in Baseball* (New York: Amistad).

Baade, Robert A. (1994). "Stadiums, Professional Sports, and Economic Development: Assessing the Reality," A Heartland Policy Study, No. 62, April 4, 1994.

Baker, Aaron, and Todd Boyd, eds. (1997). *Out of Bounds: Sports, Media, and the Politics of Identity* (Bloomington: Indiana University Press).

Barrett, Wayne (1998). "Moguls 4, N.Y. 0," *Village Voice*, May 19, p. 25.

_____ (1998). "Moonlighting for Baseball: Giuliani Deputy Gets Big Bucks from Wilpon and Steinbrenner," *Village Voice*, August 11, p. 41.

Barthes, Roland (1972). *Mythologies*, trans. by Annette Lavers (New York: Hill and Wang).

Berra, Yogi, and Tom Horton (1989). *Yogi—It Ain't Over* (New York: Harper Paperbacks).

Billet, Bret L., and Lance J. Formwalt (1995). *America's National Pastime: A Study of Race and Merit ir Professional Baseball* (Westport, Conn.: Praeger).

Bissinger, Buzz (1998). "Drive-Through Cities," *New York Times*, November 8, p. A15.

Bogen, Elizabeth (1987). *Immigration in New York* (New York: Praeger).

Bondy, Filip (1998). "Stadium Too Tough for Tribe," *New York Daily News*, October 13.

_____ (1998). "Creatures Climb Family Tree," *New York Daily News*, October 14.

_____ (1998). "Jeepers, Creatures," *New York Daily News*, October 24.

Boswell, Thomas (1984). *Why Time Begins on Opening Day* (Garden City, N.Y.: Doubleday).

Botte, Peter (1998). "Yankees Open Straw Books," *New York Daily News*, November 5.

Bouton, Jim, and Leonard Schecter (1970). *Ball Four* (New York: Dell).

_____ (1971). *I'm Glad You Didn't Take It Personally* (New York: Dell).

Bouton, Michael (1998). "For Bouton, Let Bygones Be Bygones," *New York Times*, June 21, p. C11.

Bratton, William, and Peter Knobler (1998). *Turnaround: How America's Top Cop Reversed the Crime Epidemic* (New York: Random House).

Breslin, Jimmy (1963). *Can't Anybody Here Play This Game?* (New York: Avon).

Brosnan, Jim (1962). *Pennant Race* (New York: Dell).

Brown, Bill (1991). "The Meaning of Baseball in 1992 (With Notes on the Post-American)," *Public Culture* 4:1, Fall 1991, pp. 43–72..

Burk, Robert F. (1994). *Never Just a Game: Players, Owners, and American Baseball to 1920* (Chapel Hill: University of North Carolina Press).

Cagan, Joanna, and Neil deMause (1998). *Field of Schemes: How the Great Stadium Swindle Turns Public Money into Private Profit* (Monroe, Maine: Common Courage Press).

_____ (1998). "Field of Schemes," *Village Voice*, April 28, p. 29.

Coffey, Wayne (1997). "Yankees 'R Us," *New York Daily News*, August 3.

Connable, Alfred, and Edward Silberfarb (1967). *Tigers of Tammany: Nine Men Who Ran New York* (New York: Holt, Rinehart and Winston).

Coover, Robert (1987). *The Universal Baseball Association, Inc.: J. Henry Waugh, Prop.* (New York: New American Library).

Creamer, Robert W. (1974). *Babe—The Legend Comes to Life* (New York: Simon & Schuster).

_____ (1984). *Stengel—His Life and Times* (New York: Simon & Schuster).

Crouch, Stanley (1998). "Why Americans Love Sports," *New York Daily News*, October 25.

Cuomo, Mario (1998). "Don't Drive Yanks to New Jersey," *New York Daily News*, May 26, p. 31.

Danielson, Michael (1997). *Home Team: Professional Sports and the American Metropolis* (Princeton, N.J.: Princeton University Press).

Dickson, Paul, ed. (1991). *Baseball's Greatest Quotations* (New York: Edward Burlingame Books).

Dolan, Jay P. (1992). *The American Catholic Experience: A History from Colonial Times to the Present* (Notre Dame: University of Notre Dame Press).

Douglas, Ann (1995). *Terrible Honesty: Mongrel Manhattan in the 1920s* (New York: Farrar, Straus and Giroux).

Dwyer, Jim (1998). "It's a Foul Ball All the Way Down the Line," *New York Daily News*, October 1, p. 12.

Ellsberg, Robert J. (1990). "Interview with Phil Alden Robinson," *www.wga.org/craft/interviews/robinson.html*.

Falkner, David (1995). *The Last Hero: The Life of Mickey Mantle* (New York: Simon & Schuster).

Finley, Michael (1994). "I Don't Want to Hear About Joe DiMaggio," at *www.mfinley.com/articles/newyork.html*, August 28.

Fleming, G. H. (1985). *Murderer's Row—The 1927 New York Yankees* (New York: Morrow).

Forker, Dom (1989). *The Men of Autumn* (Dallas: Taylor Publishing).

_____ (1990). *Sweet Seasons: Recollections of the 1955–64 N.Y. Yankees* (Dallas: Taylor Publishing).

Fox, Stephen (1994). *Big Leagues: Professional Baseball, Football, and Basketball in National Memory* (New York: Morrow).

Frommer, Harvey (1985). *New York City Baseball: The Last Golden Age, 1947–1957* (New York: Atheneum).

Gallagher, Mark (1982). *The Yankee Encyclopedia* (Champaign, Ill.: Leisure Press).

Gershman, Michael (1993). *Diamonds: The Evolution of the Ballpark* (Boston: Houghton-Mifflin).

Giamatti, A. Bartlett (1989). *Take Time for Paradise* (New York: Summit).

Gmelch, George, and J. J. Weiner (1998). *In the Ballpark: The Working Lives of Baseball People* (Washington, D.C.: Smithsonian Institution Press).

Goldman, William, and Mike Lupica (1988). *Wait Till Next Year: The Story of a Season When What Should've Happened Didn't and What Could've Gone Wrong Did* (New York: Bantam).

Golway, Terry, with Nick Paumgarten (1998). "The Last Superhero: Pride of the Yanks Is a Guy Named Joe," *New York Observer* 12:40, October 26, p. 1.

Golenbock, Peter (1975). *Dynasty: The New York Yankees, 1949–1964* (Englewood Cliffs, N.J.: Prentice-Hall).

Gorn, Elliott, and Warren Goldstein (1993). *A Brief History of American Sports* (New York: Hill and Wang).

Gould, Stephen Jay (1991). *Bully for Brontosaurus* (New York: W.W. Norton).

Graham, Frank (1942). *Lou Gehrig: A Quiet Hero* (New York: G. P. Putnam's Sons).

_____ (1943). *The New York Yankees: An Informal History* (New York: G. P. Putnam's Sons).

Gruneau, Richard (1983). *Class, Sports, and Social Development* (Amherst: University of Massachusetts Press).

_____, and David Whitson (1993). *Hockey Night in Canada* (Toronto: Garamond Press).

Guttman, Allen (1978). *From Ritual to Record: The Nature of Modern Sports* (New York: Columbia University Press).

Halberstam, David (1994). *October 1964* (New York: Villard).

Hall, Alvin, ed. (1989). *Cooperstown Symposium on Baseball and the American Culture* (Westport, Conn.: Meckler)

Helyar, John (1994). *Lords of the Realm: The Real History of Baseball* (New York: Villard).

Herbert, Bob (1998). "Going, Going, Gone," *New York Times,* April 16, p. A23.

Hoberman, John (1997). *Darwin's Athletes: How Sport Has Damaged Black America and Preserved the Myth of Race* (Boston: Houghton-Mifflin).

Holtzman, Jerome (1974). *No Cheering in the Press Box* (New York: Holt, Rinehart and Winston).

_____ (1998). *The Commissioners: Baseball's Midlife Crisis* (New York: Total Sports).

Independent Budget Office, the City of New York (1998). "Double Play: The Economics and Financing of Stadiums for the Yankees and Mets."

James, Bill (1982–87). *The Bill James Baseball Abstract* (New York: Ballantine).

_____ (1988). *The Bill James Historical Baseball Abstract* (New York: Villard).

_____ (1990). *The Baseball Book 1990* (New York: Villard).

_____ (1991). *The Baseball Book 1991* (New York: Villard).

_____ (1992). *The Baseball Book 1992* (New York: Villard).

_____ (1994). *The Politics of Glory: How Baseball's Hall of Fame Really Works* (New York: Macmillan).

_____ (1997). *The Bill James Guide to Baseball Managers from 1870 to Today* (New York: Scribner).

Jennings, Kenneth M. (1990). *Balls and Strikes: The Money Game in Professional Baseball* (New York: Praeger).

_____ (1997). *Swings and Misses: Moribund Labor Relations in Professional Baseball* (Westport, Conn.: Praeger).

Johnson, Richard (1998). "George in Trump Tower Powwow," *New York Post*, October 27, p. 8.

Jonnes, Jill (1986). *We're Still Here: The Rise, Fall, and Resurrection of the South Bronx* (Boston: Atlantic Monthly Press).

Kahn, Roger (1971). *The Boys of Summer* (New York: New American Library).

_____ (1997). *Memories of Summer* (New York: Hyperion).

Kinsella, W. P. (1996). *Shoeless Joe* (New York: Ballantine).

Klein, Alan M. (1991). *Sugarball: The American Game, the Dominican Dream* (New Haven: Yale University Press).

Kluger, Richard (1986). *The Paper: The Life and Death of the New York Herald Tribune* (New York: Alfred A. Knopf).

Kraker, Daniel, and David Morris (1998). "Don't Bribe 'Em, Buy 'Em," *The New Rules Project*, November (Minneapolis: Institute for Local Self-Reliance).

Krich, John (1989). *El Beisbol: Travels Through the Pan-American Pastime* (Englewood Cliffs, N.J.: Prentice-Hall).

Kubek, Tony, and Terry Pluto (1987). *Sixty-One: The Team, the Record, the Men* (New York: Macmillan).

Lally, Dick (1985). *Pinstriped Summers* (New York: Arbor House).

Lankevich, George J. (1998). *American Metropolis: A History of New York City* (New York: New York University Press).

LeBatard, Dan (1998). "Brothers in Arms," *ESPN The Magazine* 1:2.

Lehmann-Haupt, Christopher (1986). *Me and DiMaggio: A Baseball Fan Goes in Search of His Gods* (New York: Simon & Schuster).

Lentz, Phillip (1998). "Yankees, City Head for Payoffs," *Crain's New York Business*, July 20, p. 1.

_____ (1998). "Smooth Pitching Helps George's Image," *Crain's New York Business*, September 28, p. 50.

Leonard, Devin, and Nick Paumgarten (1998). "Steinbrenner and Wilpon Play Rudy Ball," *New York Observer* 12:16, April 27, p. 1.

Levine, Peter (1985). *A. G. Spalding and the Rise of Baseball: The Promise of American Sport* (New York: Oxford University Press).

_____ (1992). *Ellis Island to Ebbets Field: Sport and the American Jewish Experience* (New York: Oxford University Press).

Litke, Jim (1998). "No Money? Cancel Spring Training," Associated Press, December 3.

Lowenfish, Lee (1991). *The Imperfect Diamond* (New York: Da Capo).

Lowry, Philip J. (1993). *Green Cathedrals: The Ultimate Celebration of All 27 Major League, Negro League Ballparks Past and Present* (New York: Addison-Wesley).

Lupica, Mike (1998). "Straw-Stuck," *New York Daily News*, November 4.

_____ (1998). "Boss Plays Sleazy Game," *New York Daily News*, November 5.

Lyle, Sparky, and Peter Golenbock (1979). *The Bronx Zoo* (New York: Crown).

Madden, Bill, and Moss Klein (1990). *Damned Yankees* (New York: Warner Books).

Malcolm, Don, Brock J. Hanke, Ken Adams, and G. Jay Walker (1998). *The Big Bad Baseball Annual* (Indianapolis: Masters Press).

Mano, Keith D. (1994). "Yankee Imperialism," *New York*, July 25, pp. 30–35.

Mantle, Mickey, with Mickey Herskowitz (1994). *All My Octobers* (New York: HarperCollins).

Markham, Jesse W., and Paul V. Teplitz (1981). *Baseball Economics and Public Policy* (Lexington, Mass.: D.C. Heath and Company).

Marqusee, Mike (1994). *Anyone But England: Cricket and the National Malaise* (New York: Verso).

Martin, Billy, and Peter Golenbock (1980). *Number One* (New York: Delacorte).

Mathewson, Christy (1994). *Pitching in a Pinch* (Lincoln: University of Nebraska Press).

McAvoy, Kim (1998). "Cable's Batting Average Keeps Climbing," *Broadcasting & Cable*, March 30, pp. 25–30.

Messner, Michael, and Donald F. Sabo (1994). *Sex, Violence and Power in Sports* (Freedom, Calif.: Crossing Press).

Miller, James Edward. (1990) *The Baseball Business: Pursuing Pennants and Profits in Baltimore.* (Chapel Hill: University of North Carolina Press).

Miller, Marvin (1991). *A Whole Different Ballgame* (New York: Birch Lane Press).

Moglen, Eben (1998). "Antitrust and American Democracy," *The Nation*, November 30.

Morris, Charles R. (1997). *American Catholic: The Saints and Sinners Who Built America's Most Powerful Church* (New York: Random House).

Mushnick, Phil (1998). "Suite Deal For Media," *New York Post*, October 1.

_____ (1998). "Series-Ly, Folks—Yanks Price Gouging," *New York Post*, August 16.

Nadeau, E. G., and David J. Thompson (1996). *Cooperation Works!* (Rochester: Minn.: Oak Lane Press).

Neft, David, and Richard Cohen (1997). *The Sports Encyclopedia: Baseball, Seventeenth Edition* (New York: St. Martin's Press).

Nettles, Graig, and Peter Golenbock (1984). *Balls* (New York: G.P. Putnam's Sons).

*New York Yankees Partnership and Adidas America. Inc., v. Major League Baseball Enterprises, Inc. et al.*, a complaint filed in the United States

District Court for the Middle District of Florida, Tampa Division, May 6, 1997.

Neyer, Rob (1999). "Baseball," *espn.go.com/mlb/features/01054034.html*, January 19.

Noll, Roger, and Andrew Zimbalist, eds. (1997). *Sports, Jobs, and Taxes: The Economic Impact of Sports Teams and Stadiums* (Washington, D.C.: Brookings Institute).

O'Connor, John Cardinal (1998). "Play Ball! But Not on Good Friday," *Catholic New York*, April 16.

Office of Bronx Borough President Fernando Ferrer (1996). *The Perfect Pitch: The Bombers in The Bronx.*

Okrent, Daniel (1985). *Nine Innings* (New York: McGraw-Hill).

Olney, Buster (1998). "How the Boss Changed his Stripes," *New York Times Magazine*, September 27, p. 69.

*Paul Priore v. New York Yankees, River Operating Co., Inc., Brian Cashman, Thomas May, Bob Wickman, Jeff Nelson and Mariano Rivera*, complaint filed in Supreme Court of the State of New York, County of Bronx, July 29, 1998.

Paumgarten, Nick (1998). "A Real Demotion for Steinbrenner, From Boss to Dolan's Hired Man," *New York Observer* 12:45, November 30, p. 1.

Peterson, Robert W. (1970). *Only the Ball Was White* (Englewood Cliffs, N.J.: Prentice-Hall).

Pettavino, Paula J., and Geralyn Pye (1994). *Sport in Cuba: The Diamond in the Rough* (Pittsburgh: University of Pittsburgh Press).

"Pistols on the Ballfield," *Red Bank Register*, September 21, 1887.

Polner, Murray (1982). *Branch Rickey* (New York: Atheneum).

Quirk, James, and Rodney Fort (1997). *Pay Dirt: The Business of Professional Team Sports.* (Princeton, N.J.: Princeton University Press).

Rader, Benjamin G. (1984). *In Its Own Image: How Television Has Transformed Sports* (New York: Free Press).

_____ (1992). *Baseball: A History of America's Game* (Urbana and Chicago: University of Illinois Press).

Raissman, Bob (1998). "Seeing Not Always Believing," *New York Daily News*, November 8.

Ralph, John (1997). "April 15, 1947," *Yankees Magazine* 18:4, July, p. 42.

Rampersad, Arnold (1997). *Jackie Robinson* (New York: Knopf).

Regalado, Samuel O. (1998). *Viva Baseball! Latin Major Leaguers and Their Special Hunger* (Urbana and Chicago: University of Illinois Press).

Reisler, Jim (1994). *Black Writers/Black Baseball* (Jefferson, N.C.: McFarland and Company).

*Report of the Mayor's Committee on Baseball to Mayor F. H. La Guardia* (October 31, 1945).

Richmond, Peter (1993). *Ballpark: Camden Yards and the Building of an American Dream* (New York: Simon & Schuster).

Riess, Steven A. (1984). *The American Sporting Experience* (Champaign, Ill.: Leisure Press).

Ritter, Lawrence S. (1966).. *The Glory of Their Times: The Story of the Early Days of Baseball Told by the Men Who Played It* (New York: Macmillan).

_____ (1992). *Lost Ballparks: A Celebration of Baseball's Legendary Fields* (New York: Viking Penguin).

Rizzutto, Phil, with Tom Horton (1994). *The October Twelve* (New York: Forge).

Robinson, Ray, and Christopher Jennison (1998). *Yankee Stadium: 75 Years of Drama, Glamor, and Glory* (New York: Penguin Studio).

Rogosin, Donn (1995). *Invisible Men: Life in Baseball's Negro Leagues* (New York: Kodansha International).

Rosentraub, Mark (1997). *Major League Losers: The Real Costs of Sports and Who's Paying for It* (New York: Basic Books).

_____ (1998). "Why Baseball Needs New York to Just Say No," *The Nation* 267:5, August 10/17, pp. 20–25.

Rosenwaike, Ira (1972). *Population History of New York City* (Syracuse, N.Y.: Syracuse University Press).

Ruth, Babe, and Bob Considine (1948) *The Babe Ruth Story* (New York: Dutton).

Said, Edward (1993). *Culture and Imperialism* (New York: Alfred A. Knopf).

Salant, Nathan (1979). *This Date in New York Yankees History* (New York: Stein & Day).

Schaap, Dick (1982). *Steinbrenner!* (New York: G.P. Putnam's Sons).

Scheinin, Richard (1994). *Field of Screams: The Dark Underside of America's National Pastime* (New York: W.W. Norton).

Sherman, Joel (1998). "George's Good Deeds Belie the Bluster," *New York Post*, November 5.

_____ "The Boss: I'll Stand by Straw," *New York Post*, November 5.

Senzel, Howard (1977). *Baseball and the Cold War: Being a Soliloquy on the Necessity of Baseball* (New York: Harcourt Brace Jovanovich).

Seymour, Harold (1960). *Baseball: The Early Years* (New York: Oxford University Press).

_____ (1971) *Baseball: The Golden Age* (New York: Oxford University Press).

_____ (1990) *Baseball: The People's Game* (New York: Oxford University Press).

Smelser, Marshall (1975). *The Life That Ruth Built* (New York: Quadrangle).

Smith, Curt (1987). *Voices of the Game* (South Bend, Ind.: Diamond Communications).

Smith, Red (1982). *The Red Smith Reader* (New York: Random House).

Sowell, Mike (1991). *The Pitch That Killed* (New York: Macmillan).

Spalding, A. G. (1911). *America's National Game* (New York: American Sports Publishing).

Sullivan, Neil J. (1990). *The Minors: The Struggles and the Triumph of Baseball's Poor Relation from 1876 to the Present* (New York: St. Martin's Press).

Thorn, John, and Pete Palmer (1984). *The Hidden Game of Baseball* (New York: Doubleday).

_____, eds. (1997). *Total Baseball, 5th Edition* (New York: Viking).

Toropov, Brendan (1997). *101 Reasons to Hate George Steinbrenner* (New York: Citadel Press).

Torre, Joe, with Tom Verducci (1997). *Chasing the Dream: My Lifelong Journey to the World Series* (New York: Bantam).

Torrez, Danielle Gagnon, and Ken Lizotte (1983). *High Inside* (New York: G.P. Putnam's Sons).

Trebay, Guy (1998). "A Bronx Tale," *Village Voice*, April 28, p. 38.

Tullius, John (1986). *I'd Rather Be a Yankee* (New York: Jove).

Tygiel, Jules (1997). *Baseball's Great Experiment: Jackie Robinson and His Legacy* (New York: Oxford University Press).

Ultan, Lloyd (1979). *The Beautiful Bronx* (New York: Harmony Books).

Veeck, Bill, with Ed Linn (1965). *The Hustler's Handbook* (New York: G.P. Putnam's Sons).

Waggoner, Glen, ed. (1984). *Rotisserie League Baseball* (New York: Bantam).

_____, with Kathleen Maloney and Hugh Howard (1987). *Baseball by the Rules—Pine Tar, Spitballs, and Midgets* (Dallas: Taylor Publishing).

Weinberger, Miro, and Dan Riley, eds. (1991). *The Yankees Reader* (Boston: Houghton-Mifflin).

White, G. Edward (1997). *Creating the National Pastime: Baseball Transforms Itself, 1903–1953* (Princeton, N.J.: Princeton University Press).

"Who Says Baseball Is Like Ballet?" *Forbes*, April 1, 1971.

Will, George F. (1990). *Men at Work: The Craft of Baseball* (New York: Harper Perennial).

_____ (1998). *Bunts: Curt Flood, Camden Yards, Pete Rose and Other Reflections on Baseball* (New York: Scribner).

Willis, George (1998). "The World Champions," *New York Post*, October 23, p. 72.

Winfield, Dave, with Tom Parker (1988). *Winfield: A Player's Life* (New York: W.W. Norton).

Wolper, Allan (1996). "Ticket Shortage? Not for Newspapers," *Editor and Publisher*, October 5.

_____ (1996). "Editors Enjoy Ticket Windfall," *Editor and Publisher*, October 26.

Woodward, Stanley (1949). *Sports Page* (New York: Simon & Schuster).

Wright, Craig R., and Tom House (1989). *The Diamond Appraised* (New York: Simon & Schuster).

"Yankees Deep in Debt to Big Apple, says Brooklyn City Councilman," *Associated Press*, October 30, 1995.

"Yankee Doodle Dandies," *Wall Street Journal*, October 23, p. W13.

Zimbalist, Andrew (1992). *Baseball and Billions* (New York: Basic Books).

_____ (1998). "A Miami Fish Story," *New York Times Magazine*, October 18, p. 26.

Zion, Sidney (1997). "The Boss a Racist? No Way, Jose," *New York Daily News*, October 23.

_____ (1998)."What about the Fans? Fuhgeddaboudit," *The Nation* 267:5, August 10/17, pp. 31–35.

Zoss, Joel, and John Bowman (1989). *Diamonds in the Rough: The Untold History of Baseball* (New York: Macmillan).

# INDEX

## A

Aaron, Henry (Hank), 100, 105, 151, 157

Abrams, Roger, 107

Adidas, 53–54, 91–92, 93, 219

Alderson, Sandy, 236

Alfonzo, Edgardo, 166

Ali, Muhammad, 173

Allen, Dick, 154

Allen, Mel, 201, 202

Almeida, Rafael, 134

Alomar brothers, 152

Alou, Moises, 118, 120, 121, 122

American Broadcasting Company (ABC), 9

American League, 2, 3, 58, 63, 69, 76, 83, 88, 100, 102, 104, 105, 116, 118, 146, 149, 150, 154, 176, 215, 223, 231

American League Championship Series, 43

American League West, 118

Anaheim Angels, 8, 36, 122